ACROSS THE BARBED WIRE

A Novel About the Cold War

by

James Pocock

authorHOUSE™

1663 LIBERTY DRIVE, SUITE 200
BLOOMINGTON, INDIANA 47403
(800) 839-8640
WWW.AUTHORHOUSE.COM

First published by AuthorHouse 05/23/05

ISBN: 1-4208-1451-6 (sc)

Printed in the United States of America
Bloomington, Indiana

This book is printed on acid-free paper.

ACROSS THE BARBED WIRE

Is dedicated

To the men and women of the Armed Forces of the United States and to their families, past and present.

To my wife, Gloria, who shared many of the experiences from which this novel is drawn, and to my children for the times that military service kept me from them.

To my grandchildren. May this story help you understand this period of history.

ACKNOWLEDGEMENTS

I am very grateful to all those whose contributions, advice, suggestions, and encouragement have improved the substance and accuracy of this book.

First I must thank those who helped me over the difficult hurdle of organizing the plot and getting the first chapters drafted: my wife, Gloria, for her inspiration and comments on every page that was written; my friend and literary consultant, John Doyle, for challenging and constructive criticism; and Nancy Seubert and fellow writers in her Life Stories Class for their interest and feedback. Also my daughter and her husband, Gina and Victor Inzunza, provided invaluable literary and computer assistance; and my son, John Pocock, my sister, Jean Cousins, and George Duncan proofread the early drafts.

Next I wish to acknowledge the invaluable assistance of those with special expertise who graciously helped me with certain technical aspects of the novel. Comrades from the 14th Armored Cavalry Regiment Dr. George Bacon and his wife Grace, Lieutenant Colonel (Ret.) Welborn Matthews and his wife Jean, and Lieutenant Colonel (Ret.) Norman Harms all made helpful suggestions concerning Cold War border duty in Germany. Both Dr. Bacon and Dr. William Oliver reviewed the medical procedures for accuracy. Colonel (Ret) Charley Johnson and Lieutenant Colonel Steve Stewart provided extensive information concerning the activities of the 301st MP Enemy Prisoner of War

Camp during Desert Storm, and Colonel (Ret) Joseph Kopacz helped me recall details of tank gunnery ranges in Germany.

USAF Major Harold Koons and his staff assisted with the description of the terrorist attack at Ramstein AFB. My son, USAF Lt. Col (Ret) Jim Pocock and USAF Major (Ret) Mark Malone offered many useful suggestions about references to Air Force personnel and facilities. Another son, architect Ed Pocock, helped describe the intricacies of a building's air conditioning system. Also I wish to thank Diana Repichowski and Judy Edwards of Lansing, Michigan's Church of the Resurrection School for their assistance with Catholic Litany.

Several professional writers and editors generously gave of their time and knowledge to improve my novel. Specifically, I want to thank Elizabeth Kane Buzzelli and Virginia Bailey Parker from the Oakland Writer's Conference, Literary Agent Simon Lipskar, and Martha Bates of Michigan State University Press for their suggestions.

For putting me in touch with German people who provided details of life in East Germany during the period of this novel I am very grateful to longtime friends Gertrude Strieker and her husband, the late Heinz Jürgen Strieker. Those generous people include Herbert and Herta Löffler who drove me to some of the locations described in the book, Winfried Fiedler and his daughter Maria Fiedler who spent a day showing me around Geise and Bad Salzungen, Roland Strieker for providing a cover photo, and author Klaus Hartwig Stoll for his contributions about border crossings in the sixties.

Other Germans who provided invaluable assistance include: Oberstleutnant Werner Gruhl and Sergeant Major Thomas Zeipesel of the German Army Liaison Office at Fort Knox, Oberstleutnant Pätz of Wehrbereichskommando VII in Leipzig, and Walter Sandler, former civil affairs representative of the 14th ACR in Fulda, Germany.

Finally, I thank Gisela Schild, friend and neighbor, for proofreading my rusty German phrases and for saying that my novel caused her to relive much of her life. That comment and those of others already mentioned encourage me in the belief that my effort at historical fiction was realistic.

PART ONE

JUNE 1964 - MAY 1965

James Pocock

CHAPTER I

Gisela Hurwitz pushed a strand of auburn hair back from her forehead as she watched her children playing on the floor of their hotel room. Dieter was stacking wooden blocks while his baby sister, Anna, sat next to him sliding a single block back and forth. Now almost three, Dieter was born only a week before the Berlin Wall was erected in the summer of 1961. Seated on the double bed, Gisela's eyes were on the children she cherished, but her mind was focused on the danger that lay ahead of them. In days to come, when she thought of her family, she would remember that fateful day when she could have changed their destiny.

The door opened and she looked up to see Walter returning from the bathroom at the end of the corridor in the Gasthaus *Zum Goldenen Stein.* Walter removed his glasses and rubbed his eyes before slipping the dark-framed lenses back on. Without saying a word, he stepped over Dieter and Anna to peer out the window. He seemed nervous, and that worried her. Usually he was so confident in everything he did. For a minute he studied their view of the hill leading to the border. Then he looked at her and said, "The sun is setting; it should be dark in another thirty minutes."

"Walter, what if we're caught?" Her voice was hushed, so as not to alarm Dieter, but her anxiety was evident. "I can't bear the thought of going to prison—being separated from you and the children." She knew as well as he did that the minimum sentence for *Republikflucht,* criminal escape over the border, was three years.

He frowned and walked over to join her on the bed.

"We won't be caught!" She was surprised at the harshness in his voice. Maybe he was feeling the stress of waiting or maybe it was because they had talked this through so many times. His words brought back all those nights they had lain awake reviewing together the possibilities and risks involved! They knew people who had made it with less preparation, but with the time for action at hand, her emotions were beginning to take control.

"We already are living in a prison," he continued. "I'm fed up with the government telling us what to do and what to think." He rose from the bed and began pacing back and forth. "When you told me about the *Stasi* trying to recruit you as an informant, I knew we had to get away. We don't want the children growing up in this system, and being taught to spy on us!"

Walter was medium height and thin with dark, curly hair. Denied a university education, he was, nevertheless intelligent and practical. He was the one who thought of getting some phenobarbital before they left Berlin to make sure that the children would sleep through the ordeal. No one would call him handsome, but his piercing gray eyes and air of confidence drew people, especially women, to him.

Hearing the resolution in his voice, Gisela felt better. He had that effect on her, and it reminded her of the day she first saw him five years ago in Berlin's Zoological Gardens. She was captivated. When he asked if he could join her at a table, she responded with a smile that he said later made him feel like she had been waiting for him all her life.

"I know. But I can't stop thinking about the children. If we go to prison, they'll take them away from us."

Walter sat back down on the bed and put his arm around her. His voice softened as he stroked her neck. "Gisela, you're always telling me to have faith in God. It's time to put aside your fear and trust him."

She felt a surge of confidence and reached back to take his hand. "Thanks for saying that. It helps to know you believe too." She turned her head and smiled. "And thank you for the wonderful dinner too."

For their last evening in Geise they had used their remaining East German marks to splurge on a big dinner in the Gasthaus. He argued against being conspicuous in clothes that were too fine, but she had insisted on wearing her prettiest blue cotton skirt with the lilac-flowered blouse that he gave her on her last birthday.

Walter gave her a squeeze. "*Ja*, it was nice, and you looked beautiful. I'm glad you dressed up."

"Papa, help me." Dieter's pile of blocks had just crumbled, and he looked at his father in frustration.

Walter gave her another squeeze, and eased himself down next to the children. His hands steadied a foundation of blocks as Dieter began to build them as high as he could. When he placed the last block, Walter said, "*Sehr gut, Dieter!* Someday you might build wonderful buildings."

"*Ja*, Papa. Or I can build a wall."

Walter frowned but said gently, "*Nein, mein Sohn.* We need buildings, not walls." Anna crawled toward the tower of blocks, and before Dieter could stop her, she reached out and knocked it down. Dieter tried to grab Anna and began to cry, so Walter pulled him onto his lap.

"Listen, Dieter. Stop crying. We are going on an exciting trip tonight. While you sleep, your Mama and I will take you and Anna to a new place where you can grow up to be whatever you want to be. It will be like a dream, but when you wake up we will be on our way to a new home."

His bottom lip still quivering, Dieter asked, "Will there be other boys and girls to play with?"

"*Ja*, Dieter. I'm sure there will be. But you need to go to sleep soon. And if you dream that I am carrying you somewhere, don't worry and don't make a sound. We don't want everyone to know where we are going." Walter hugged his son, and sat him down again next to Anna.

Looking at her husband and children, Gisela thought about their picnic. That morning they had hiked a short distance westward out of Geise. It had been serene and peaceful; and when the children napped after lunch, they made love, furtively on a blanket under a tree. Walking back they took turns carrying Anna while Dieter ran ahead, stopping occasionally to throw stones. However their excursion had not been entirely innocent, for they had surreptitiously studied the terrain around them. Walter pointed out where the tree line north of the road came closest to town and described the route they would take.

As they had approached the Ulster Bridge on their way back, they met two Grenztruppen coming out of town. The senior border guard demanded their identification cards and travel documents, and admonished them for being in an unauthorized area. Fortunately Walter bluffed their way through it by acting confused and contrite.

Walter got to his feet and stood in front of her. "We must go tonight, before anyone else becomes suspicious. We only have two more days until our pass expires, and I don't want to take a chance on the weather changing." He didn't need to remind her that it had taken nearly a year to get special passes to enter the five-kilometer Restricted Zone, and then only because Gisela's great aunt Johanna was living in a nursing home in Geise. She wished that they had crossed before the Wall went up in 1961 when it was so easy that thousands fled into Berlin's Western Zones each month!

"On my way back from the toilet I checked the back stairway," Walter said. "The back door is unlocked and there is only one girl left mopping in the kitchen. If we leave after ten o'clock we should be able to get away without being seen."

"Then I'd better change clothes and get ready. I'll take the water bottles with me to the bathroom and fill them."

Time passed quickly as they changed into dark slacks, pullovers, and hiking boots. Even in July the nights could be damp and cold in the foothills of the Rhön Mountains. Walter put the wire cutters in a pocket of Gisela's backpack where they wouldn't be seen, but where they could be easily reached when he needed them. He would carry a compass and flashlight, with a tissue over the lens to subdue the light.

They spent the final minutes studying the map again while the children lay fully clothed, asleep on the bed. Anna was sucking intermittently on a pacifier, and Dieter clutched wooden Rosary beads in his right hand. A present to Gisela on her confirmation, they had become part of Dieter's nightly ritual of prayer. Then they slipped jackets on the sleeping children. While Walter knelt by the bed, Gisela lifted Dieter into his backpack harness, and then changed places so Walter could place Anna into her harness.

Walter turned and embraced Gisela. *"Ich liebe Dich."* He kissed her tenderly. "I love you too," she said. For a moment she forgot what they were doing and thought only about how much she loved him. Then he moved away, switched off the room light and opened the door slightly. Carefully checking that the corridor was empty, he walked toward the rear of the Gasthaus. Gisela took a deep breath, pulled her shoulder straps tighter, and stepped quietly behind him.

Silently they made their way down the back steps. A dim light shown from the kitchen; otherwise it appeared to be closed for the night. Walter eased the back door open and Gisela followed him into the alley behind the Gasthaus. The air was still and cool. Crossing the alley, Walter took a path alongside the river until he saw the Ulster Bridge looming in front of him. A teenage couple, their arms around each other, came across the bridge from the direction of a park on the other side of the Ulster.

Pausing in the shadows while he checked the street, Walter whispered, "We'll wait by that big beech tree near the bridge until we're sure it's safe. Then walk fast across the bridge and back into the park on the other side of the street."

Gisela nodded her understanding, and they moved cautiously toward the tree. So far neither child had uttered a sound. Two or three minutes passed with no sign of a car or any late strollers. Walter stepped into the beam of a streetlight, and Gisela forced herself to move behind him. Her heart was pounding. These fifty meters were dangerous. Anyone seeing them would naturally be suspicious and duty-bound to report them.

Fortunately the street remained deserted, and they reached the park on the far side of the river undetected. Walter pointed to a vacant space between two houses across Papiermühlenweg. "We'll cut through there, go behind the houses, and then there is only one more street to cross before we're out of town. Are you all right?"

"I'm fine, Walter; but let's hurry."

"Ja, of course. Come on."

They followed a path through a vacant lot leading toward the last street. Near the end of the path a garden wall appeared, and on the other side a dog began to bark. They hurried on, crossing Butlar Strasse; not stopping until they reached a small shed on the edge of town.

"Did you see anybody when the dog barked?" Gisela asked.

"*Nein*, but a man shouted something at the dog. Anyway, he stopped barking." Walter pulled a bottle from his backpack. "Do you want some water?"

"*Ja*. My mouth is dry." It had been less than twenty minutes since they left the Gasthaus, but it had seemed like more than an hour to Gisela. Sipping the water, she felt the panic that had gripped her on the bridge begin to subside. Walter adjusted the harness strap that was digging into her left shoulder, and he shifted Anna so her weight was spread more evenly on her back.

Walter checked his compass and pointed in the direction they would follow up the hillside. "Ready?" he asked. Gisela remembered that she had intended to say a prayer before they left the Gasthaus. "*Ja*. Let's go," she said, pushing away from the shed. Trudging behind her husband and son, she spoke softly, "*Der Herr ist meiner Schafer*, I shall not want. Yea though I walk through the valley of the shadow of death, I will fear no evil, for thou art with me. . ."

They cleared the fringe of garden plots behind the last houses, and the gradual ascent became steeper. The quarter moon cast enough light to illumine large terrain features, but not so much as to make walking figures visible beyond a few meters. On the lower level the grass was short but slippery in spots where cows had grazed and left their droppings.

Gisela tripped and grabbed for Walter's arm, bumping into Dieter. The boy made a small whimper but continued sleeping.

Walter helped her regain her balance. "What's wrong?" he asked, holding her tightly. "Is Anna too heavy?"

"I stumbled over a rock," she panted. "I can carry her, at least until we get to the woods where we can rest."

"Lean forwards a little as we go up the hill. It makes the climbing easier. It won't be long till we get to the woods."

They walked more slowly as their breathing became labored. There was no path, and Walter stopped often to refer to the phosphorescent arrow on the compass. She knew he was worried about drifting to the north, which would cause them to make a harder and longer climb than needed. From what she could see they were close to the planned route, but it was taking longer than she expected.

Gisela was tiring but glad now that Walter had insisted on carrying the children while hiking around Geise. Besides convincing them that the more gentle approach to the border through Wiesenfeld was too far, the conditioning helped prepare her for this steep climb. Finally they came to the edge of the woods. Walter took Anna and helped Gisela slip out of her harness. As she slumped down against the base of a tree, he laid Anna in her lap.

"I'm going to look for a trail," he whispered. "You rest. I'll be back soon."

It was much darker in the woods. She heard him bump into a tree and then proceed more slowly. Anna was asleep, breathing regularly. Gisela must have dozed off, for the next thing she felt was Walter shaking her gently. "There's no trail, but there isn't much underbrush. We'll follow the compass through the woods. We've got to get moving."

Covering the flashlight with his hand, he directed a small speck of light toward his wristwatch. "*Verdammt!*" he muttered. "It's eleven-forty. The guards will be changing soon."

Gisela handed Anna to Walter, who used his right hand to help pull Gisela to her feet. Again he placed Anna gently into the harness. "I'm ready. Go on," Gisela said, realizing Walter's urgency.

Their progress was much slower in the woods, hampered by darkness and a continued climb uphill through dense trees. Gisela blindly followed the moving shape to her front and tried to keep the white collar of Dieter's jacket in view. Now and then a branch brushed by Walter and scratched her face. She pressed on, instinctively holding her left arm up in front of her like a boxer.

Suddenly Walter stopped and reached back to prevent her from crashing into him. She could see a glimmer of moonlight through the trees. Holding her hand, he guided her to the edge of the woods. Walter dropped to one knee and pulled her down next to him. About one hundred meters beyond the tree line, silhouetted against a rise of the hill, were two parallel fences of barbed wire, stretching endlessly in both directions.

Pointing to their right, Walter said, "Look. Over there…about three hundred meters. There's the guard tower. If we move on our hands and knees to the fence, they won't see us." Gisela shivered involuntarily. It looked so exposed, and so far, to the other side of the border.

"What if a patrol comes by?"

Walter checked his watch in the faint moonlight. "It's after twelve. The guards have already changed, but we'll have to be careful; they'll be more alert." He put his arms around her and Anna, and hugged them. Gisela looked closely at Dieter who was still sleeping soundly, pulled up his stockings and gently brushed a leaf from his neck. Walter whispered, "Come, before the children stir. We're almost free."

Carefully they began to crawl on hands and knees, single file toward the fenced barrier. After the rustling noise of their progress through the woods, it was deathly quiet in the open. The meadow grass came almost to their waist, and they were getting wet from dew that was forming. Gisela was breathing hard, and Anna's weight was digging painfully into her back.

Walter turned his head. "Can you keep going?"

She gritted her teeth. "*Ja*. Don't stop."

They continued the macabre game of "ride the horsy", and Gisela imagined that they were back in their Berlin apartment playing on the floor with the children. Her arms and legs were aching and the pain in her back was worse, but she kept on doggedly following the sliding legs in front of her. Again Walter stopped. Raising her head, Gisela could make out the first fence about twenty meters in front of them. Walter hissed, "Wait here while I check for trip wires." He crawled forward awkwardly, Dieter's one arm dragging on the ground, while Gisela fell flat on her stomach.

After a moment she watched Walter ease his way toward the fence. Then he stopped, probing the ground for tripwires. The fence in front of him was about seven feet high with twisted bands of barbed wire parallel to the ground about a foot apart. A long diagonal band of wire connected the fence posts. As best she could make out, the farther fence was the same. A strip of ground about ten meters wide separated the two fences. Then she saw a sign on the closer fence that sent a chill through her body. *WARNGEBIET MINEN!*

They had heard a rumor that the Grenztruppen were going to place mines along the border strip. After some discrete questioning of their Gasthaus proprietor, Walter had dismissed the rumor as propaganda. Now she wasn't so sure. Her mind was racing. What should they do? To come this far and turn back was unimaginable. And she wasn't sure she could make it back.

Walter was crawling back toward her. Reaching her he whispered, "There is a tripwire. I marked it with a couple of rocks."

"But what about the mines? Didn't you see the sign?" Her hushed voice couldn't conceal a tone of panic.

"I saw it, but those bastards couldn't have planted mines here already. The sign is just another one of their tricks. We'll be all right!"

Anna whimpered, distracting them. From her position Gisela couldn't reach her. "I think the grass tickled her face. Help me find her pacifier."

Walter knelt over them and groped through the pockets of Gisela's backpack. Finding the wire cutters first, he stuck them in his back pocket. The pacifier was in the corner of the same pocket, wrapped in a handkerchief. Walter removed it, slipped it into Anna's mouth and stroked her hair. He leaned over and kissed his daughter, watching a moment until her eyelids closed. Then he helped Gisela back up to her hands and knees.

"Stay behind me while I cut through the fence. Then I'll hold the wire back while you go through first. Understand?"

"*Ja.* Be careful, Walter."

They crawled a couple of minutes more until they reached the first fence. Walter began clipping away the bottom strands of wire. He made an opening wide enough for them to crawl through and motioned Gisela to move ahead while he held back the sharp edges of wire. Suddenly she heard a popping sound, and a flare burst overhead outlining them in a flash of white light. One of them must have hit a trip wire!

Walter scrambled through the opening and ran past Gisela to the second fence. He was right, she thought, following him. There were no mines after all! Frantically Walter cut at the wires. Shouts came from the direction of the guard tower, and she heard dogs barking. The wire cutters were not designed for barbed wire, and each successive wire was taking longer. Stepping on the bottom wire, Walter grabbed Gisela's arm and pushed her through the small opening he had made in the two strands above his foot. When she was nearly across the bottom strand, his foot slipped and he lost his balance. Twisting to his right, he staggered backward.

A loud explosion rent the air amidst a swirl of grass and dirt. Walter was blown sideways. He and Dieter landed in a crumpled heap against the fence. Gisela and Anna were lifted up and thrown forward. Gisela felt pain in her legs, and heard her voice scream, "Walter." She had a sensation of being outside her body, seeing Anna and herself beyond the barbed wire with Walter and Dieter behind her. Before blacking out she struggled to touch Anna, and felt blood on her hand.

CHAPTER 2

The radio on the platoon net crackled, jarring Lieutenant Parker's concentration as he tried to follow his driver's route on the acetate-covered map in his lap. He and Stroud had just left Second Squad's listening post on Hill 461, northeast of the little village of Gotthards. Parker responded with his call sign and glanced at his watch. It was 0040, forty minutes after midnight.

"This is Echo One One. Somethin's happen'n near the fence about 300 meters to our right front." Staff Sergeant Anderson's usual drawl had a touch of excitement. "We seen movement—maybe a person—through the scope, and the dogs are barking on the other side of the border, over."

"Roger One One, I'm one klick north of OP (Observation Point) Bravo. Should be at your position in one five. Contact me if anything changes, out."

Second Lieutenant John Parker was conducting a routine check of observation posts along a forty-kilometer sector between East and West Germany assigned to 1st Squadron, 14th Armored Cavalry Regiment. His platoon was part of C Troop, on duty along what the world had come to know as the Iron Curtain. For centuries armies had marched across the east-west route through Fulda where they were based; and after World War II this sector had become the first line of defense against Soviet forces massed across the border.

Parker placed the handmike for his platoon radio on a hook welded to the dashboard and picked up the other handmike to call company headquarters. He gave the duty sergeant a situation report for his inspection of the last observation post and his movement toward Echo One One's position. While he was involved in the transmission with Echo Base, he could hear Sergeant Anderson call again on the platoon net. Stroud used his free hand to grab the platoon handmike and respond.

"Send your message. Will copy, over."

"This is One One. A flare jus went off on the other side, but I don' see nobody. No East German soldiers yet, over."

While Stroud was acknowledging Sergeant Anderson's message, Parker wondered if this might be a border-crossing attempt. In the year he had been with the Squadron he had yet to have any direct contact with people fleeing from the East. Not that many were able to make it across any longer. No, he thought. It's probably just another animal that set off one of the East German trip flares.

John Parker, twenty-two, was a graduate of Michigan State University with a degree in business administration, and a Regular Army commission from ROTC. Since age twelve his heart had been set on West Point, a dream unrealized because of faulty eyesight. Nevertheless, he felt good about his assignment to the 14th Cavalry. Known as an elite unit by those familiar with Armor Commands, most of its officers and sergeants were professionals with combat experience—in the Army until retirement. That fit right in with John's career plans.

Moreover, he was happy to be in Germany, the country of his mother's birth and the only foreign country whose language he could speak. It could have been worse. Some of his classmates in Armor Officer Basic had gotten orders for units in Korea. He felt fortunate to have found and married a wonderful woman while he was at Fort Knox, and not to have been sent on a tour of duty that excluded dependents. It was bad enough that due to a delay in dependent travel, Gail had to wait three months to join him in Fulda. When she arrived she was pregnant, and their daughter, Susie, was born five months later.

"Think someone's trying to cross up there by OP Alpha, sir?" Stroud shouted over the noise of the jeep.

"I doubt it. I've only heard of one in the last six months. Some guy who crawled through a culvert that hadn't been closed. Getting across the barbed wire and death strip is something else." Still, anything's possible, he thought.

The jeep was approaching the western edge of Rasdorf when they heard the blast.

John reached Sergeant Anderson on the platoon radio. "What was that noise, over?"

"This is One-One. It sounded like a mine. I'm moving forward to check, over."

"Roger. Make sure you stay on our side of the border. I'll be there in about five minutes, out." Animals had been known to set off trip flares, but John didn't think an animal large enough to detonate a mine could get through the barbed wire.

"Let's go, Stroud. Sounds like trouble."

"Yes, sir." Stroud whipped the jeep around a deserted corner, and shifted into second gear for the hill ahead.

The more he thought about Anderson, the more John began to worry. The squad leader was new to the platoon and not familiar with the border. Did he understand that the fences and obstacles constructed by the East Germans were really a hundred meters on their side of the border? All that designated the actual border were a few stone markers and barriers across roads and paths. Only a few months before one of the regiment's reconnaissance planes flew over the border, and had almost been shot down. John didn't want any of his men captured or hurt.

"When we get to the OP, tell Echo Base I'm checking an explosion at the border, while I find Sergeant Anderson."

"Got it, sir."

They cleared Rasdorf and Stroud switched off the headlights. Using only the jeep's 'cat eyes', he was peering intently into the darkness on his side of the paved road. He spotted the familiar dirt track, slowed for a left turn, and followed hard packed ruts leading to the squad's observation point on the forward edge of a patch of woods. Just inside the trees Stroud stopped the jeep where the trail narrowed. Several yards away from them, backed into the trees, was one of the scout squad's jeeps.

John dismounted and hurried up the trail. Ahead of him a figure stepped out of the darkness, holding a rifle diagonally across his body.

"Halt. Who's there?"

"It's Lieutenant Parker, Wilson. Where's Sergeant Anderson?"

"He's out there by the fence, suh, with Koz. They saw somethin movin and then there was ah big boom." Pfc. Wilson, a skinny black kid from Atlanta, had only recently completed basic training, and his nervousness showed.

"Damn. I hope he isn't that far. Stay here, Wilson, and monitor the radio. I'm going after Anderson and Koslowsky. Keep your weapon on safe, and don't fire at anything unless I give the order. Got that?"

Even in the dark he could see Wilson's eyes widening as he stared at his platoon leader. "Yas, yas suh."

Moving cautiously in the faint moonlight, John followed an indistinct path of bent grass that he thought led in the direction taken by Anderson and Koslowsky. After a few minutes he could make out the outline of two rows of barbed wire. To his right front he saw a couple of helmeted figures crouched by the nearest fence. Coming closer, John recognized the silhouette of his scout squad leader. Sergeant Anderson was lifting a body on to Koslowsky's broad back.

"Sergeant Anderson," he hissed. "It's Lieutenant Parker. What are you doing? This fence is in East Germany."

"Yes sir. But when I left the OP I saw this woman lying here. I couldn't let her bleed to death."

John opened his mouth to remind him of standing orders to stay on their side of the border, but a whimpering noise distracted him. Then he noticed the crumpled figure by a hole in the fence. A man was lying on his side and above his shoulder was the face of a young boy looking at them with a frightened expression.

CRACK-BANG, CRACK-BANG! Two shots reverberated in the open space to their front. Near the East German guard tower John spotted two guards running toward them. Anderson whipped his M-1 up to his shoulder and took aim, but John grabbed the rifle and pushed it down.

"Don't shoot." he cried. "Those were warning shots. Move back, Koz, as fast as you can. Cover him, Anderson, but don't shoot unless they fire at you. I'll bring up the rear."

They took off, and John looked more closely at the figure by the fence. The man wasn't moving, and the lower part of one leg was missing. The boy was maybe two or three, and strapped to his father's back. They were by the hole, only a few steps away, and the boy was crying now with a terrified look on his face. John could hear the guards shouting, and he hesitated, measuring duty against compassion.

A quick glance told him the guards had closed to 100 meters. "Should he risk it?" A voice in his head was screaming, "Go get him," but could he drag him through the hole before the guards arrived? If he didn't, he'd be in one hell of a mess. Another flare went off behind the guards, and he could see that the bottom strand of wire was cut. Perspiration was running down his back, as he willed himself to rush forward and reach for the kid. But in the seconds it might have taken, he couldn't move. Another shout from the Grenztruppen cleared his head. He took a step backwards, then another, all the while looking into the eyes of the little boy. Then he turned and ran, catching up with his men as they entered the tree line.

When John reached their OP, Anderson and Koslowsky were setting the woman on the ground. Wilson shined a filtered flashlight so Koslowsky could see to remove an infant from her harness. The child was awake and holding tightly to her mother's neck.

"Mama, Mama, Mama," she wailed.

"It's a little girl, sergeant."

Koslowsky fumbled with the harness, unbuckled the straps, and gently pulled the backpack and child off the woman.

Sergeant Anderson held the woman in a sitting position while Wilson removed the poncho from his belt and spread it on the ground behind her. As he eased her down on the poncho, he told Wilson, "Go back to the jeep and bring me a blanket out of the duffel bag."

Koslowsky, a burly coal miner from Pennsylvania, didn't seem to know what to do with the crying child. "Let me have her, Koz." Lieutenant Parker shifted his binoculars out of the way, and cradled the little girl in his arms. "I've got a daughter. Maybe I can calm her down.

Check the backpack, and see if there's a bottle or a toy." He rocked her back and forth, and murmured, "Hush, little one. Don't cry. Hush, hush." He felt something wet on the infant's legs and was afraid that she had a leaking diaper until he realized that it was sticky, like blood.

"I found a bottle with some juice." Koslowsky handed the bottle to Parker. The girl stopped crying and eagerly reached for the familiar bottle. Holding her, John leaned over Sergeant Anderson who was bandaging the unconscious woman.

"How bad is she hurt?"

"Both legs got cuts and punctures. Her left leg is bleeding bad below the knee." He looked up at John with a worried expression. "We need to get her to a medic quick."

John laid the baby next to her mother. "Right. I'll get on it. See if you can rig a tourniquet to stop the bleeding, and check the baby too. I think she's bleeding." He got to his feet and nearly bumped into Stroud coming from the other direction.

"Sir, Echo Six wants a complete report from you right away. He asked how close Sergeant Anderson got to the fence." John's muscles tightened and he felt drops of sweat trickling down his sides. Echo Six was the radio call sign for Captain Collins, the troop commander, and Stroud's tone implied that the "Old Man" wasn't happy about what he'd heard.

"Thanks, Stroud," "I'm on my way." Several quick strides brought him to the jeep where he pulled his map case out from under the seat and grabbed the handmike.

When Echo Base answered, John recognized the voice of Captain Collins who had obviously been awakened while the incident was developing. John immediately transmitted his SitRep.

After completing the coded details of the report he added, "We rescued a woman and baby. The woman is bleeding badly from wounds to her left leg, and the baby is wounded also. We're giving first aid, but they need a doctor ASAP, over?"

"Roger." "What were you doing at the fence? Over." Even over the radio his tone sounded ominous.

"The OP leader heard the woman crying and went to help. I got them back as soon as I arrived. Over."

"We'll talk about that later. Echo Base will set up a medevac. Are any Bundesgrenzschutz at your location? Over."

"Negative. Over."

"Roger. I'll handle their notification. Wait, out." Captain Collins was probably alerting the squadron commander about a possibly serious situation. John knew that it didn't take much to create an international incident along the border, and figured that he was in for a grilling by the Bundesgrenzschutz too. He was familiar with their two man walking patrols along the border. They were a federal police force, equipped with small arms and radios, and represented West Germany's presence along the interzonal border.

After several minutes John wondered what was happening with the medevac, and considered risking Captain Collins' wrath to make a call and ask. A break in the radio's background squelch noise interrupted his thoughts. It was Echo Six.

"There's a chopper on the way to pick up the woman and child. Meet them on the road at coordinates November Bravo, Six Two Three, One Nine Zero. Turn your headlights on and pop smoke when you hear the chopper, over."

"Wilco. We'll be there in one five, over."

"Roger. You come with them. I need a more detailed report, over."

"Wilco. Anything further?" He waited for his commander to end the transmission.

"Negative. Six, out."

Stroud had listened to the radio traffic and began backing the jeep closer to where the woman was lying. John walked ahead to guide him as close as the trees and scrub brush would allow. As they came closer, he could hear the woman's alarmed voice and Anderson trying to calm her in a mixture of English and fractured German.

"I put a bandage on the kid, lieutenant. Think she's okay, but I can't make out what the woman's sayin."

She was struggling to get up, and John bent down to help. *Wo ist Walter? Wo ist Dieter?* Her voice verged on panic.

Even in the darkness John could see her wide-eyed expression. Raising her to a sitting position, he kept an arm around her shoulder.

As she turned toward him, her beauty, despite disheveled hair, dirt, and scratches, struck him.

"We are American soldiers. Do you speak English?"

"Nein." She continued in German. "My husband, Walter, was carrying Dieter. Where are they?"

Switching to German, John struggled to explain. "They didn't make it across the border. A mine exploded and knocked you unconscious." Motioning to Anderson and Koslowsky, he continued. "These men found you and carried you here." Groping for words, he hesitated. "The Grenztruppen started shooting, and…and we couldn't get the man and boy."

"NEIN, NEIN," she screamed as the meaning of his words registered in her mind. Next to her the little girl whimpered, "Mama, Mama," and she reached out and gathered the infant in her arms. "Oh, Anna, Anna…" Her shoulders shook as she rocked her child. "I've got to go back," she cried, trying to stand. "I've got to find them."

John held her by the shoulders. "It's too late. The Grenztruppen already have them. If you try to go back, you'll just be arrested." He was surprised at her strength. Somehow she made it to her feet, still holding the child. Her face was deathly pale.

"Get out of my way. I've got to…" She wrenched herself free, and took a couple of steps before collapsing. Koslowsky alertly caught her and dragged her and the baby back to the poncho.

While Anderson worked on the leg that was bleeding again, John raised her head and wet her lips with water from his canteen. Her eyes opened, and after a moment, the impact of what happened showed in her face. She pulled her daughter closer, sobbing as she stroked her hair.

John was in a quandary. He wasn't sure how to deal with the emotional scene unfolding in front of him. A family had just been torn apart, and his orders were not to interfere. They told him to avoid a confrontation that might have international repercussions. Now he had a hysterical woman on his hands who was badly wounded. Could she stand the knowledge that her husband might be dead, and her son trapped?

Although he wanted to comfort her, he knew they had to get moving to meet the medevac. Gently he put a hand on her shoulder.

"We need to get you to a doctor."

She looked up frantically. "What happened to Walter? Is Dieter all right? Her voice became a shout, "Tell me. Where are they?"

John blurted out the words. "He stepped on a mine. He's badly hurt, but I think the boy is all right." There was anguish now in his voice. "I...I couldn't get him. The Grenztruppen were too close."

"Lieber Gott. NEIN. NEIN."

He waited a moment, listening to the woman's heartrending cries. At last, he said, "We're going to carry you to a jeep." He turned to Sergeant Anderson. "Help me move them."

With an arm from each around her back, Parker and Anderson joined hands under the woman's legs and lifted her while she held her child. As they set her in the jeep's front seat, blood was seeping from the dressing on her leg.

"What is your name?" She looked ahead blankly, and he repeated the question.

"Gisela," she said in a low voice. "Gisela Hurwitz. What is happening?"

"You have a bad wound in your leg, and we made a tourniquet to stop the bleeding. Can you hold this stick to keep the tourniquet tight?"

With a vacant look in her eyes, she held the stick with one hand and her daughter with the other, while John tucked the blanket around them. "Where are we going?"

"We're taking you and...and Anna to a hospital."

He climbed into the back of the jeep and wedged himself between the radios and the back of the passenger seat. Stroud drove slowly in four-wheel drive, following the speck of light from Sergeant Anderson's filtered flashlight leading them out of the woods. As the jeep bounced along the rutted path back down the hill, John held the woman's shoulder to prevent her from being tossed around. Reaching the paved road, Stroud shifted to standard drive and headed west toward Rasdorf.

John pulled back the sleeve of his field jacket to see the luminous dial of his watch. It was 0205 when they reached Rasdorf. He sat back in his seat, relaxing a little as he saw that they would reach the rendezvous point on time. He began to think about what he would say to Captain Collins, but he couldn't get the look on that boy's face out of his mind.

CHAPTER 3

"Echo One-Six. This is Magic Two-Seven. Inbound your location in zero-five, over." The strong signal on the company radio net indicated an aviator's radio transmission.

John reached over Gisela to grab his handmike.

"Roger, Two-Seven. I'll pop smoke, over." Parker's jeep roared out of Rasdorf following county road B-4 in the direction of Hünfeld.

"Slow down, Stroud. The pick up point is just beyond the next curve."

The jeep continued to climb the curving incline on the west side of the village. Reaching the crest of the hill, they could see the two lane road extending straight for another three hundred meters. It was generally clear of trees along the shoulders. At this time of night in the border zone there was no other traffic. John tapped Stroud on the shoulder, and the jeep pulled over and stopped.

"Leave the headlights on," John directed. In the distance the thumping flutter of helicopter blades could be heard.

"Gisela, a helicopter is coming to take you and your daughter to a hospital. I will go with you. Do you understand?"

She said nothing, but he saw a slight nod of her head.

John reached into a canvas bag behind the driver's seat, pulled out a metal cylinder, and used his flashlight to verify the color markings. He climbed over the side of the jeep and walked down the center of the road toward the end of the light beam. Setting the can in the road, he pulled a metal pin and released the retaining clip. A reddish billow of smoke quickly began to form, rising and spreading away from him, carried by the wind. The jeep headlights seemed out of place in this tense situation, but Standard Operating Procedure (SOP) called for all possible recognition means to prevent a border overflight.

"Echo One-Six…Magic Two-Seven. I have you in sight. What color smoke, over?" The pilot was obviously going by the book to counter any attempt by East Germans to lure him into a border violation.

"This is Echo One-Six. Smoke is red. Over." John could see the helicopter rapidly approaching the road. The Huey came straight toward them, pulled up, and hovered briefly before settling on its skids. John waved for Stroud to move the jeep closer, and ran over to the side of the jeep. With Stroud's help he carried Gisela, holding her daughter, under the moving chopper blades and set her on the cargo floor.

John shouted to Stroud, "Drive back to headquarters and meet me at the dispensary." Then he climbed into the helicopter and, with help from the crew chief, lifted Gisela and Anna on to the canvas seats, fastening seat belts around them. Anna scrunched close to Gisela who put an arm around her. They were in the Army's new Iroquois helicopter. Although John had seen them at the regiment's small airstrip, it was his first ride in a Huey; and he was surprised at the amount of room in the cargo area.

After slamming shut the side door, the crew chief handed him a radio headset, motioning to a toggle switch that connected the headset to the pilot's intercom. Depressing the switch, John addressed the pilot whose helmeted face was framed in the dim red glow of the Huey's instrument panel.

"We're ready. The woman is bleeding from a bad leg wound, and I think she's in shock."

"Roger. The dispensary has been alerted."

John felt a slight shudder as the pilot increased power and rotor-blade pitch. The Huey accelerated forward, gaining altitude rapidly. Still climbing, the pilot banked the chopper sharply to the west. The noise inside was deafening. Anna cowered in her seat, hands covering her ears, and snuggled close to her mother. Gisela held Anna tightly, her eyes wide and frightened. John put a hand on her arm and shouted in German, "Don't worry. We will land soon and take you to a doctor."

Gisela's tourniquet was loose again, and blood was dripping on the chopper floor. Looking for something to tighten the pressure, John took off his web belt and, through gestures, showed Gisela what he intended to do. Then he wrapped the belt around her thigh, and cinched it tight through the buckle. The crew chief handed him a first aid kit, and he found another compress bandage that he used to replace the soaked one.

When he settled back into the web seat next to her, John thought Gisela's face looked whiter than it had in the jeep. He could see beads of perspiration on her forehead.

"Are you all right?"

Gisela mumbled something unintelligible and closed her eyes.

"Hold on. We'll be there in a few minutes."

From his door window John could see a glow of lights, and from the other side window he could make out the twin spires of Fulda's cathedral. As they flew over the sleeping city, the helicopter gradually descended while the pilot scanned the morning twilight for signal lights on the parade ground. John felt the forward motion slow, and saw headlights below and the outline of maintenance buildings on the edge of the parade field. A minute later the Huey's skids settled on the graveled surface, and the crew chief opened the left side door.

A box-shaped ambulance moved alongside, just beyond the dying orbit of the chopper blades. The crew chief helped John unstrap Gisela and Anna and move them to the open doorway. Two medics appeared with a stretcher, and carried Gisela to the ambulance. John walked beside them, carrying Anna in his arms. Gisela seemed too dazed to notice the separation from her daughter. John followed them into the back of the ambulance, placed Anna in Gisela's arms, and sat on a stretcher next to one of the medics.

Two minutes later they were at the back door of the dispensary where a staff sergeant in hospital whites helped move Gisela and Anna into an examining room. Coming toward them down the narrow hallway was a lanky, sandy-haired captain with a stethoscope around his neck.

"Sorry to get you out of bed so early, George." Captain George Baker, MD, Assistant Regimental Surgeon, was John's apartment neighbor and friend.

"No problem. I'm used to it. The duty officer said a woman was injured. Who's this?" John was holding Anna who was sucking her thumb and nearly asleep.

"Her daughter. The woman is in there."

Glancing into the examining room where a wiry, black sergeant was cutting Gisela's pants leg, Captain Baker asked, "What's it like, Sergeant Johnson?"

"Back of her left leg's cut bad, Cap'n, and it looks like she's in shock."

The doctor glanced quickly at the drowsy child in Parker's arms. "What about her?"

"Nothing serious that we could find," John answered.

"Good." Pointing to an adjoining room, he said, "Take her into the next room. I'll have someone look her over."

Captain Baker strode purposely into the examining room. "Sergeant Johnson, take a blood pressure reading. Then get an I-V ready."

One of the medics came in with Gisela's backpack. The doctor turned to him and said, "Rogers go into Room Two and check the little girl carefully."

Specialist Rogers, whose blonde hair and good looks had earned him the nickname, "Hollywood," was one of the medical company's most experienced medics. He crossed into the other examining room, and with John's assistance, laid Anna on a table. Rogers carefully removed her jacket and slacks, pulled up her shirt, and softly felt her limbs. Anna opened her eyes, a frightened look on her face. Rogers patted her head; her eyes closed, and she began sucking her thumb.

He called through the open doorway, "No broken bones, Captain. Just some cuts on the back of both legs and a bruise on her left ankle. I don't see anything that needs stitches. Just bandages."

"Okay. Clean the cuts and apply antiseptic. I'll take a look in a few minutes."

Baker concentrated on the semi-conscious woman as he removed the blood soaked dressing and examined the wound. Sergeant Johnson unwound the blood pressure cuff and said, "It's low, Cap'n. Sixty over ten."

"She's definitely in shock. Get the I-V started."

His brow wrinkled in concentration as he probed the deep wound with gloved fingers, Baker was worried about damage to an artery. Trained for general practice with only brief exposure to surgery, he was drawing on a surgical course he took at Fort Sam Houston when he entered the Army. With Doctor Cook away on leave, he would have to send the woman to a German hospital if difficult arterial surgery was required.

"We're in luck, Johnson. There doesn't seem to be any damage to the artery, and the bleeding has nearly stopped. As soon as you have the I-V going, take a blood sample and then get a match for a transfusion."

Johnson checked that the I-V was dripping properly, drew the blood sample, and hurried down the hall to another room containing the dispensary's limited laboratory equipment.

A stocky figure in a starched, olive drab fatigue uniform appeared in the doorway. Captain Collins, C Troop Commander, directed his attention to the table where Baker was beginning to suture Gisela's torn leg. "George, how long will it be before we can talk with the woman? I've got a German officer out in the waiting room who wants to question her.

"Damn it, Charley! Tell him to keep his shirt on. She has a bad wound that needs stitches, she's lost blood, and she's in shock. She's gonna need some rest. He'll just have to wait until she's fit enough to talk."

"Okay, George," he said, backing out of the room. "I get the picture. I'll check with you later." He poked his head in the room where Parker sat and said, "Lieutenant, come out to the waiting room with me and tell this German captain what you know."

"Yes, sir. Let me get her backpack. There might be some identification in it."

John followed his troop commander down the hallway to a small waiting room at the other end of the building. As they walked into the room, a tall, thin man wearing a dark green uniform and shoulder boards of a Bundesgrenschutz Hauptmann rose from a gray metal chair. While they exchanged greetings, John noted that the German seemed old for a captain, probably in his early forties, and spoke heavily accented English. He had a prominent scar on his forehead. John found it difficult to avoid staring at what he assumed was a war injury, and momentarily thought about the World War II battles he had studied. He guessed that the German had seen a lot of combat; maybe even against Americans.

"As you know," Hauptmann Voight began, "the *Bundesgrenschutz* is responsible for making a prompt report to Bonn on all border crossings. I must question the woman about the details of the escape, and how the"…obviously groping for the word fugitives, he gave up and said, "*Fluctlinge*…got through East German security."

"I understand," Captain Collins replied. "But the doctor is still treating her. Lieutenant Parker was at the scene. Let's sit down, and he'll tell you what he knows about the incident." The three men sat in a corner of the waiting room and John described the border crossing as fully as he could. When he finished, Hauptmann Voight asked, "What are their names, and where are they from?"

"She said her name is Gisela, and her daughter is Anna. I'm not sure about her last name." John handed Gisela's backpack to Voight. "I haven't had a chance to look yet, but you might find some identification in there."

Voight opened the backpack, pushed aside some clothing, and pulled out a red, leather wallet. He set the backpack on the floor and began examining the contents of the wallet. Holding a plastic card up to the light, he announced, "Her name is Gisela Hurwitz, and her address is 50 Karl Marx Strasse, Apartment 805 in East Berlin."

Continuing his search, Voight pulled out two photos from a plastic sleeve, perused them, and passed them to the American officers. John recognized Anna in the photo with a boy whose face was beginning to haunt him. Did he do the right thing? he wondered. Should he have risked getting the boy across too?

The other photo was a family scene, the two children with their father and mother. It made him think of his wife and daughter, and brought Gisela's plight closer in personal terms. He handed the photos back, and asked, "Hauptmann Voight, what's going to happen to them now?"

"After I finish talking to her, she and the girl will be sent to the Refugee Center in Giessen. They will stay there until they can be re-settled in West Germany."

Captain Collins interrupted. "An American Military Intelligence representative may also want to speak to her before she goes on to Giessen."

"How will she find out about her husband and son?" John asked Voight.

"The East Germans are usually slow to announce anything about border crossings, if at all. My government will make inquiries through diplomatic channels. They might also release information to the press about the escape to put pressure on the DDR to make an announcement."

"So it may be weeks before she knows what happened to them?"

Voight made a snorting sound. "Unfortunately, that's how things are when we are dealing with the communists."

The three men sat in silence several minutes. Dawn was breaking and daylight was beginning to brighten the shadows of the waiting room. The notes of *Reveille* came over the post loudspeaker system, and John realized that his platoon would soon be relieved by the second platoon.

The hallway door opened and Captain Baker came over and sat down wearily. He held out his hand to the German officer and said, "Hello. I'm Doctor Baker."

"Hauptmann Voight! A pleasure to meet you."

Baker's face showed none of his earlier annoyance, and his response to Voight was relaxed and friendly.

"Look, I know that you want to speak with this woman, but she and her child are both sleeping soundly. I had to give her a blood transfusion, after closing her wound and getting her stabilized. She was in shock."

"*Ja*. I understand. When will I be able to talk to her?"

"We're not set up to keep patients here, so we'll have to move her to the German hospital in Fulda later this morning. I suppose you could visit her there this afternoon."

"Very well." Hauptmann Voight stood and handed the backpack and wallet to John. "I was hoping to speak to her earlier, but I did not know how bad her injuries were. However, the lieutenant has been most helpful, and I have obtained some information from her wallet."

The others stood also. John had a sudden thought. "Would it be all right if my wife and I visited them later—to see if they need anything?"

Baker shrugged, and Collins said, "It's up to you, lieutenant; when you're off duty. But first I want to talk to you… in my office."

"I will stop by the hospital early in the afternoon to speak with her," Hauptmann Voight said. "After that I have no objection to anyone visiting her."

As John walked down the steps of the dispensary, his mind was preoccupied with concern about his summons to the troop commander's office, and he failed to notice Stroud until his jeep pulled up beside him.

"Want a lift, sir?"

"Oh! It's you, Stroud. No. Just go on to the motor pool, and you can take off after you finish maintenance on the jeep. I've got a meeting with Captain Collins."

Stroud rolled his eyes, but only said, "Roger that. Good luck, lieutenant." He accelerated slowly and drove away in the direction of the motor pool.

Twenty minutes later John knocked on the door of the C Troop Commander's office, entered in response to a gruff command, and remained standing while Collins continued writing at his desk. After a few moments Captain Collins looked up, unsmiling, and motioned for John to take a seat. What hope remained in John's mind that the captain wasn't angry was erased when Collins described the heat he was catching from the squadron commander over his men's movement into East German territory. When he finally asked for an explanation, John made the mistake of trying to defend Sergeant Anderson's actions. This brought a blistering lecture from Collins, concluding with a question about whether he understood what it meant to follow orders.

Normally slow to anger, John was stung by Collins' demeaning question, and felt the color rising in his face. "Yes, sir. But we couldn't just leave the woman there to bleed to death? That was the point of the USAREUR Fact Sheet about the Berlin Brigade soldiers who failed to rescue the German who was shot and left lying by the Wall."

It was evident from Collins' silence that he had forgotten the story that had made front pages in newspapers around the world and caused major embarrassment to the US Army in Europe (USAREUR). His attitude softened slightly and he said, "Well, I'll check out that fact sheet. Maybe it will get us off the hot seat. But remember, Parker, orders are orders!"

John left feeling that he was out on a limb with no support. He found himself doubting his prospects for an army career. Over six feet tall and muscular, John had been a fine athlete in high school, but he didn't look like it as he walked with heavy steps and slumping shoulders toward the housing area. Somehow his gloomy thoughts turned toward his first fascination with soldiers: the day he watched his cousin march in a veterans' parade in Dearborn after the Korean War. Later his cousin had showed him around the Tank Automotive Command in Warren where he worked, and let John drive one of the prototype tanks. From then on he was hooked on the Army. His commissioning ceremony in front of Demonstration Hall at Michigan State, attended by his parents and cousin, was one of his proudest memories.

He suppressed a yawn as he returned the salute of the MP on the main gate at Down Barracks. He hadn't slept much in the last twenty-four hours, and he was hungry. In less than ten minutes he reached the steps to their third floor, two-bedroom apartment. It was built in the fifties with Marshall Plan money, and the Post Quartermaster provided most of the furniture. Although they didn't have many household goods of their own, Gail had used her ingenuity to decorate in a style that made their standard apartment appear different and comfortable.

"Hi, honey, I'm home."

An attractive blonde woman in her early twenties came out of a bedroom, carrying a baby girl sucking a pacifier. Gail Ann Taylor had seemed like everything he expected in a Southern Belle when John first met her at on a blind date. She was vivacious, yet warm-hearted, with a passion for art and music and a teaching degree from the University of Kentucky. Sometimes he wondered why she was willing to marry him, leaving her family and a host of college suitors, to become an Army wife. Raised in genteel surroundings in Louisville, Gail was still adjusting to the military.

John walked across the room, embraced his wife, and touched his daughter who grabbed one of his fingers with one hand while waving the other.

"She's happy to see her Daddy," Gail said. "Here, John. You hold her a while." She handed the baby to him, and he lifted her up above his face for a moment. "How's my Susie? Do you have a smile for Daddy?"

Susie gave a little squeal of pleasure, dropping the pacifier which Gail alertly caught before it hit the floor. John lowered the baby into his arms and sat down on the sofa.

Gail followed him and sat down next to him. "I didn't think you would be home this early."

"Neither did I. But we had a border-crossing incident last night. I came back early on a chopper with an East German woman who needed medical care. By the time I finished briefing Captain Collins and writing an incident report, my platoon was already relieved by Second Platoon." John decided not to bring up his run-in with Collins. It would only upset her and leave her less enamored with the Army. "When the captain heard that I'm scheduled for Officer of the Day tomorrow, he told me to take the rest of the day off."

"That's mighty big of him, considering that you work about seventy hours a week," Gail said sarcastically. John winced at her dig at the frequency that he was required to pull extra duty on evenings and weekends.

"Yeah. Well, nobody ever said troop duty on the border was going to be easy. Anyway, I'm hungry. How about some breakfast?"

"Okay." Gail smiled. "Eggs and bacon coming up. I'm sorry if I sounded cranky, but I wish we could have more time together. I mean just by ourselves, and not at some Army function."

"I know. So do I. Maybe we can get some leave after tank gunnery next month, and take a little vacation."

"I'd like that John. We've been in Europe for almost a year, and we haven't gone further than Frankfurt." Gail got to her feet and headed for the kitchen.

She had a point, John knew. Frankfurt was only sixty miles away. But he didn't have much money or leave time accumulated for a longer trip. Nor was there much opportunity to get away with all the mandatory duty requirements. He set Susie in the corner of the sofa, and arranged a pillow to keep her from falling. Then he bent over and began unlacing his boots.

Soon there was a smell of bacon frying in the kitchen where Gail was bustling about. She came into the dining area with a place mat and silverware, and looked at her husband with alarm as he carried Susie to the table. "John, you've got blood on your sleeve. What happened to you?"

John recounted the story of the failed escape attempt, and described what happened to Gisela and her child. Gail listened intently, almost burning the bacon. When he finished, she said, "That's terrible. Where will they go?"

"George Baker said they were going to be moved to the Fulda hospital today. After that they'll probably go to a refugee center. Maybe we should visit them this afternoon, after I get some rest."

"Good idea. Did you say they only have the clothes they were wearing and a backpack?"

"Yeah. And the medic cut off her pants leg."

Gail had driven to the border once with John, and had seen the fence, and watchtowers. She was quiet a moment and then shuddered.

"What's wrong?"

"I was just imagining being in her situation, trying to crawl through barbed wire with Susie on my back. While you're sleeping I'll go to the Thrift Shop and see if I can find some clothes for them. Do you have any idea what size she is?"

"I don't know. She's probably an inch or two shorter than you, and about average weight."

Their conversation shifted to household matters while John ate his breakfast. A few minutes later, John finished eating and yawned. "Thanks for the breakfast, Gail. It hit the spot," he said, getting up from the table and heading toward their bedroom. He stripped off his dirty fatigue uniform and crawled into the bed. Yet, as tired as he was sleep didn't come easily. It took a long time to sweep the disturbing images from his mind: a frightened boy across the barbed wire; the woman's anguish over her missing husband and son; and the chewing-out he got from Captain Collins.

CHAPTER 4

Otto Huber thought Major Müller looked worried when he sauntered into Muller's Grenztruppen office in Geise, East Germany. Hauptmann Huber was the Grenztruppen political officer, technically under Müller's command, but with a reporting channel of his own.

"Otto. The Adjutant just called. We must send the guards who were on duty during the escape to headquarters on Monday. The Kommandant is placing them before a tribunal." Müller shook his head dejectedly. "The guards, their sergeant, and us! I'm afraid we're in for it."

"*Verdammt!*" Huber grimaced. He had expected an angry reaction from their superiors, but now he felt frustrated and threatened. Major Müller was a promising officer, although not strict enough, especially in matters of ideology. Otto often had to remind him of his responsibilities to the Communist Party. Now this unfortunate escape would probably result in Müller's being relieved of command, and a black mark on his own record.

"The guards must have been asleep," Huber said. "If the mine hadn't exploded, they wouldn't have known someone escaped until the cut in the wire was discovered."

"I'm afraid you're right," Müller reluctantly agreed. "That's why we're meeting tonight with the junior officers and sergeants." With renewed vigor he sat up in his chair and slapped the top of his desk. "It's going to take more than your lectures about why soldiers need to protect the country from the actions of dissidents. I am going to make it clear and simple. A soldier's duty is to obey orders. If they disobey, there will be severe punishment, and that will include the responsible leader."

"I hope we get another chance to show we can be relied upon," Huber responded, a frown on his pudgy face. "Those damned deserters! They had a good life in Berlin. How could they think that living in a capitalistic society was worth the risk of sneaking across the border?"

"And why did they have to try their escape in our sector?" Müller groaned.

"Apparently the woman had an elderly aunt living in the nursing home in Geise. The investigators checked their travel documents, and the aunt was the reason their travel in the Restricted Zone was approved."

Müller leaned back in his wooden office chair and stretched his legs. Even in the late afternoon his calf-length jackboots had a bright shine. "Have you learned anything from the man who stepped on the mine?"

Huber looked disgusted. "He's still unconscious and in critical condition. I don't know if we'll ever get anything out of him."

"Too bad! Especially for the boy. Where is he?"

"He's in the hospital also. No serious injuries, but he's too young to give any useful information. Someone from the state welfare office will be looking after him."

Gazing wistfully out his window at the distant hills along the border, Major Müller sighed. "Aren't there any relatives willing to take him?"

"Not that we know of. I suppose he will be placed for adoption somewhere." Huber knew of other families caught escaping, and young children were adopted. It made sense. The parents were going to prison and could no longer be considered reliable citizens. So the state takes over.

"They probably never thought about the consequences for their children and the rest of society. These dissidents think only about themselves." Major Müller stood abruptly, and reached for his cap.

"Come. Let's get something to eat. Then we'll come back and prepare for the meeting."

Gisela lay on a blanket spread on the grass of Treptow Park gazing at Walter throwing a red ball to Dieter. Anna was asleep on the blanket beside her. The sky was filled with puffy white clouds, and bright sunshine made this one of Berlin's warmest summer days. The remains of their picnic lunch were still uncollected by the basket at her feet.

Everything was peaceful as she lay back looking at the sky. Suddenly the wind began to blow and dark clouds moved across the trees. Gisela sat up, alarmed. She opened her mouth to warn Walter about the approaching storm, but her words made no sound. Walter and Dieter took no notice of the change in weather or her attempt to get their attention.

The sky was growing dark quickly, and Gisela became frantic with concern. Then a burst of thunder jolted her. Before she could react, a bolt of lightning struck the ground next to Walter and Dieter. Gisela screamed and struggled to get to her feet, but somebody was holding her. She began crying, and shouted, "Walter, Dieter…"

"There, there, my child. You're safe. You must have been dreaming." Gisela heard soothing words and felt strong arms holding her as her eyes focused on the white uniform of a middle-aged woman who resembled her Aunt Johanna. Her eyes darted around the room, and she became aware of her surroundings. She was in a single bed in a small room, sparsely furnished. Anna was asleep on a cot between her and the window. Late afternoon sunlight streamed through the open window, and she could hear the chirping of nearby birds. The walls were painted light green, and through the open door was a corridor. The woman who had been holding her was tall and heavy-set, wearing a white cap trimmed in blue. Her uniform was crisply starched.

"You are in the Fulda Krankenhaus, and I'm your nurse." She was confused, thinking she was with Americans, but the voice was speaking German. "My name is Martha. The military brought you and your daughter here this morning. The little girl is fine." She glanced over at the child. "Sleeping soundly."

Gisela fell back against the pillow, aware now of a dull pain in her left leg. Her body ached, and she felt weak. Her mouth was dry, and she ran her tongue over chapped lips. Martha lifted a pitcher from the nightstand, poured water into a glass, and handed it to Gisela. "Here. Drink this and rest a little." She waited as Gisela drained the glass. Then she poured more water into the glass and handed it back, but Gisela waved it away. Placing the glass on the table next to Gisela, she said, "I will see about some food for you." With that the nurse walked out of the room leaving the door partially open.

Gisela leaned over and touched Anna who stirred slightly. Removing her hand, she rolled back onto the pillow. Visions of the night flooded her mind: trudging through dark woods behind Walter carrying the children on their backs, crawling through barbed wire, an explosion and soldiers around her. Then the realization hit her. Something had gone terribly wrong. Walter and Dieter were missing; she was injured and alone with Anna. Gisela lay back on the pillow, tears flowing down her cheeks. She pulled a blanket over her face to muffle the noise of her sobbing from her sleeping child.

A short time later the nurse appeared with a tray. "*Hier ist etwas Kartoffel Soupe und frisches Brot.*" Gisela didn't feel like eating, but the smell of potato soup and the sight of fresh baked bread were appetizing. Martha helped her sit up in bed and set the tray over her. Gisela tasted a spoonful of soup and realized how hungry she was. She hadn't eaten since…? Then she remembered a wonderful dinner at the Gasthaus with Walter and the children, and stopped eating.

Martha may have sensed her anguish, or it may have been her nurse's training that took over. "Come now, there's no time for moping. You must be strong to take care of your child." She took the spoon from Gisela, and placed another spoonful in her mouth. "This will make you feel better."

Next to them, Anna was stirring. The aroma of food and the activity in the room was waking her. Martha watched now as Gisela finished feeding herself.

"Ah… my dear. There's a *Bundesgrenschutz Officier* and another man waiting to see you. The doctor told them they could talk with you after you woke. I will take your daughter and get her something to eat while you and the officers talk."

Gisela nodded. She didn't feel like talking, but she was eager to know something about Walter and Dieter. After holding Anna, and reassuring the groggy child that the nice nurse would bring her back to Mama soon, Gisela handed her to Martha who carried her out of the room.

Gisela's mind returned to fearful thoughts about Walter and Dieter when there was a knock at the door. She looked up to see a tall German officer in a green uniform standing in the doorway. Behind him was a man of medium height wearing a dark business suit and tie.

"Excuse me, Frau Hurwitz. I am Hauptmann Voight of the Bundesgrenshutz, and this is Herr Smith from the American military authorities. The doctor said it would be all right if we talked to you for a few minutes. May we come in?"

"Ja, bitte." Gisela pushed herself up in bed, and her face brightened with anticipation. "Tell me, please. What happened to my husband and my son?"

"I'm sorry. I just don't know." Voight stepped into the room and pulled a chair over to the bed. "We don't have any information from the East Zone yet." Mr. Smith followed, but remained standing near the end of the bed.

"I will tell you what I know about other border escapes and what we can expect in the way of communication from the other side," Voight continued. "Also I must ask you some questions concerning your border crossing and about security measures in the DDR. "Herr Smith's interested in the same information for the American military. The more we are informed, the better we can exert pressure on East Germany to provide information about missing relatives over there."

Gisela slumped against her pillow, and the light seemed to fade from her eyes. Hauptmann Voight was speaking about the difficulty in communicating with the East Germans, but Gisela wasn't listening. Her mind pictured Walter and Dieter, badly injured, perhaps in a hospital as she was. She could see Dieter crying, and tears ran down her cheeks.

The captain noticed Gisela's distress and stopped talking. He handed her a tissue from the bedside table. He waited a minute and said gently, "I know this is hard for you, but the sooner we know your story, the sooner we can help you learn something about your husband and son."

Gisela sighed and wiped her eyes. The captain's words made sense. She needed help, and she would gladly tell them whatever she could to learn about Walter and Dieter.

"*Ja. Natürlich.* I...I don't know where to start. There were four of us. My husband, Walter, and I, and our two children, Dieter and Anna. And...and we went to Geise, and..."

"Maybe it would be easier if you begin with your life in Berlin, and what caused you to flee to the West," Mr. Smith said in fluent German.

"Well, Walter and I lived in a small apartment on Alexanderstrasse. It was only one room, and we shared a kitchen and bathroom with another family; but we were lucky to have it. I met Walter in the summer of 1960 when I moved to Berlin from Dresden." Gisela's eyes shifted from the faces of the two men to the bare wall above their heads, and her expression became wistful.

"He lived in East Berlin and worked in a large bookstore in the west zone, and I was a secretary in the Ministry of Agriculture. We met at a cafe in the Zoological Garden." A note of bitterness crept into her voice. "Of course that was before the Wall was built, and we could travel into West Berlin to work and shop."

"Walter was older, and I was impressed with his ambition and intelligence. And he wasn't afraid to speak out against things that were not fair. He told me that he had taken part in the 1953 uprising and narrowly escaped being arrested. You know, that's when the Russian Army killed hundreds of construction workers."

"*Ja.*" Hauptmann Voight said. "We remember those days very well."

Gisela continued. "Because Walter wouldn't join the Party, he couldn't get admitted to a university. He wanted to be a writer, but his independent attitude kept him from being published. Yet he could be charming, and very considerate. When we met he bought me a bouquet of flowers, and we sat on the terrace, drank *Berliner Weisse,* and talked for hours. Before the day ended, I knew I was in love with him, and six months later we were married. Dieter was born the next year, and Anna two years later."

"It sounds like you were happy," Mr. Smith said. "Why did you flee to the West?"

"We were happy as a family, but Walter resented a system where the Party controlled your life. We could see the freedom and opportunity that existed in the West, and we wanted that for our children and ourselves. We talked about crossing over to the West, but I became pregnant with Dieter. He was born in July of '61."

"And a few weeks later the Wall was put up," Hauptmann Voight interjected.

"That's right. On August thirteenth. I'll never forget." Gisela's voice became agitated. "It was on a Saturday night. The next morning we were going to take Dieter to Canisius Church to be baptized. But you couldn't take the subway into the West Zone anymore. We were shocked to find out that we were completely shut off from the West. Walter was out of work, and we were very discouraged. It took him months to find a job, and then only as a waiter."

"Why did you pick this time to leave?" Mr. Smith persisted.

"Last year when the American President, Kennedy, came to West Berlin to see the Wall, Walter got into trouble. We were still angry with Ulbricht for building a Wall that made us feel imprisoned. Kennedy's visit excited us, and we listened to his speech on the West German radio station, even though it was forbidden. Walter got into an argument with one of the neighbors who defended the need for the Wall. Walter mentioned something that Kennedy said. The neighbor reported it to the police, and the Volkspolizei questioned Walter. Luckily he persuaded them that he was just making a joke that the neighbor misunderstood."

Gisela paused and took a sip of water. "This spring I was approached by one of the supervisors at work who wanted me to be a spy for the Stasi. She didn't say I would be a spy, only that I should inform her about Walter's activities, since he was considered a potential security risk. It was my duty, she said, for the protection of the State and of my children to report any subversive remarks by him. She even hinted that I might be promoted if I cooperated. I kept putting her off, but she began to pressure me. When I told Walter, he was furious."

"So why did you cross the border in this region? Wasn't it difficult to get a travel permit?"

"*Ja, gewiss!* But my great-aunt was living in a nursing home in Geise. We applied for a travel permit before Walter got into trouble. Somehow it continued through the system and was approved."

"Wouldn't it have been easier to try to escape into West Berlin?" Mr. Smith asked.

Gisela closed her eyes, remembering their long discussions about the best way to cross the border. After a few moments she responded. "Walter didn't think so. All the buildings along the Wall are sealed with bricks and are off-limits. We heard about tunnels, but that seemed too difficult with children. Besides the rumor was that it would cost five thousand marks, and we didn't have that kind of money."

"How much did you know about the border around Geise?" Hauptmann Voight asked.

"We knew that there was a fence with watchtowers, and that it was patrolled by soldiers. There were articles in the paper about how dangerous it was because of American weapons and troops there. But we thought that was just propaganda."

Hauptmann Voight pulled a map from his briefcase. "Tell us, please, other places where you considered crossing and what you remember of your escape."

Gisela leaned over to look at the map, supporting herself on an elbow. She told the men what she and Walter had planned and what had happened the previous night. As she spoke, it seemed like she was describing a bad dream; it seemed so distant, and yet so real. When she finished, she sat back and looked directly at her interrogators.

"What are you doing to find out what happened to Walter and Dieter?"

Hauptmann Voight answered. "We don't have any official communication between the Bundesgrenschutz and the Grenztruppen, but occasionally some of our patrols can get an East German soldier to talk if he trusts his partner not to report him. I'll brief our men to try to make contact with guards on the other side and ask about your husband and son. Of course there will be an official inquiry from our Foreign Office based on information from my report."

A frantic look came across Gisela's face. "How long will it take to get an answer?"

"From my patrols maybe a few days or even longer. It depends on how tight the East Germans clamp down on their guards. Usually after an escape they put the squeeze on discipline and inspect the guards more often. As for the bureaucracy, we may have an answer in a week or two, but it may only be partially true. Unfortunately, relations between East and West Germany have been especially strained lately."

Gisela slumped back in bed, utterly dejected. Hauptmann Voight stood and said, "Thank you for your help. You have our best wishes that things will turn out all right. As soon as I have any information, I will contact you. *Auf Wiedersehen.*"

The two men left the room quietly. Gisela closed her eyes. In her despair she did what she normally did in a time of trouble; she prayed.

It was late afternoon when the Parkers climbed into their Chevrolet and drove out of Downs Barracks married housing area along Haimbacher Strasse into the central part of Fulda.

"I think the hospital is near where we lived before we moved into quarters on post," Gail said.

"That's right. It's on Edelzeller Strasse, a couple of blocks from where we lived. We've driven by it on the way to Edelzell."

"You know, Jean Ferris almost had her baby delivered there. It was during that snowstorm last winter, and Dr. Baker wasn't sure they could make it through the storm to the 97th General Hospital in Frankfurt. They got there all right. It was their first child, and she had a long labor."

"So why didn't they use the Fulda hospital?"

"George didn't think they had an incubator that was working. Also he had a closer working relationship with the doctors at 97th General. Jean said it was funny when they stopped twice to fix the chains on the ambulance, and Ralph, who was following in their car, came rushing up thinking that she was delivering in the ambulance."

As John turned into the hospital parking lot, he said, "What's in the shopping bag? Did you find something to bring them?"

"Yes. I went over to the Thrift Shop on post and Elaine Thompson let me take a couple of skirts, some blouses and a dress for her. And we found something for the little girl."

John parked the car and walked around to open Gail's door. She handed Susie to him, while she got out of the car with the shopping bag. Then she took the baby in her arms and gave John the bag to carry as they walked up the hospital steps. Inside John asked in German if they could visit Gisela Hurwitz, and was relieved to find that they were within prescribed visiting hours. John was wearing dark slacks and a light blue, open-collar shirt. Nevertheless, from his short haircut and the difference in clothing styles, it was obvious that the visitors were American. Following the receptionist's directions, the Parkers proceeded to the third floor and located Gisela's room.

Anna was sitting in bed with her mother who was reading her a story. When John knocked and stepped into her room, Gisela looked apprehensive.

"Excuse us, please," John said in German. "I am Lieutenant Parker. My soldiers found you, and I rode in the helicopter with you." Stepping aside, he motioned to Gail who came through the doorway with Susie. "This is my wife, Gail, and our daughter, Susie. We just wanted to see how you and Anna are doing."

Gisela reached with her free hand to pull up the top of her hospital gown, as Anna shrank back until she could scarcely be seen. As John stood next to Gail he felt her elbow poke him. "You didn't tell me she was so pretty," she muttered.

John ignored Gail's comment and brushed past her.

"*Ach, Ja*, Gisela said slowly. Now I remember. But I didn't recognize you; you're not in uniform."

"No. I like to wear civilian clothes when I'm not on duty. How are you and Anna feeling?"

"We're all right." With an anxious expression, she hurriedly asked, "Have you heard anything about my husband and son?"

John dreaded the question, knowing it was coming. If only he hadn't been frozen with indecision, he might have gotten them across to safety! He couldn't look her in the eye as he answered.

"I'm afraid not. But I know the German and American authorities are working on it. I hope you will have an answer soon." He thought it best to change the subject, so he turned to Gail and said, "My wife has something for you."

Gail took the bag from John and left him holding the baby. She walked over to the bed, and used a few words she picked up from a German language class she was taking. *Wir haben kleider fur Sie.*

Setting the bag at the foot of the bed, Gail pulled out a skirt and a blouse to show Gisela. Switching to English she said, "These are gifts, *Geschenken*, from the officers' wives. Excuse me. I don't speak much German, but we thought these might help until you are able to go shopping."

Gisela's face brightened as she held up a white cotton blouse for Anna to see. *"Sehr schön. Vielen Dank."*

"We also have *Geschenken* for your daughter. Gail reached into the bag and pulled out a small doll that she held out toward Anna. Gisela had to coax Anna to take the doll. Anna touched the doll's hair tentatively, and then held it as if she was afraid to play with it.

Gail pulled out a child's blouse from the bag. "Here are a few things that might fit Anna." Gail continued speaking in English with John doing his best to translate as she displayed more children's clothes. Although Gisela appeared somewhat overwhelmed by their attention, she thanked them again for the gifts. As they were getting ready to leave, Gail asked, with John interpreting, "When do you expect to be released from the hospital?"

"The doctor said that in a few days I will probably be sent to a refugee center. But I want to stay in Fulda where I might hear something about Walter and Dieter."

"I don't know what the West German regulations require," John said, writing on a card he took from his wallet. "But if we can help in any way, here is a telephone number where you can reach me." He handed it to Gisela who looked at the card and then at John and Gail.

"*Vielen Dank.* And please thank the other Americans for the clothes."

CHAPTER 5

Major Erich Burchert was tired and his leg hurt when he arrived at his home in Dermbach, twelve kilometers east of the Interzonal Border. He opened the door, limped into the living room, and set his high peaked hat on a bureau. It had been a long day, and that combined with the wet weather, had caused the shrapnel wound from long ago to ache again. The green border and piping on his shoulder boards denoted his position as a staff officer in the East German Grenztruppen. Specifically he was responsible for compiling intelligence reports at Grenzregiment 3 Headquarters. Inge, his wife, came out of the kitchen when she heard the door close, and switched on a light.

"Where have you been, Erich? I thought you would be home by seven."

"There was a court martial at Regimental Headquarters, and it took longer than I expected." Removing his wide black belt, he set it next to his hat and loosened the top buttons of his tunic. Erich was a stocky man in his mid thirties with thinning brown hair. He crossed the small living room, and sat wearily in a big armchair. He took off his glasses and rubbed his eyes.

"Three guards in Mueller's company were being tried for a border escape a few days ago."

Inge sat on one of the chair arms, and put her arm around Erich's neck. Inge was a pleasant looking woman of about thirty who prided herself on her appearance. Shortly after her arrival in Dermbach she told him that even in this farm town there was no reason she shouldn't look fashionable. Taller than Erich, she wore a light blue dress with a silver necklace. Her blonde hair was pulled back, revealing a smooth forehead and wide blue eyes.

"Can I get you something to eat?"

"Just some cold meat and bread, with a beer. I had a big lunch."

Inge slid off the armchair and walked toward the kitchen. "It will only take a minute. Just lean back and relax."

Erich rested his head on the back of the chair and closed his eyes. But he couldn't relax. He needed to talk with Inge. He began reviewing the events of the day in his mind. The entire regiment, except for duty personnel at key border sites, had been assembled in the headquarters auditorium. Bernhard Mueller and Otto Huber sat in the front row, while Erich was in the row behind with other senior officers. Two soldiers and their post leader sat at a table in the front of the hall. The adjutant read the charges: gross inattention to duty while on guard, and failure to prevent an escape in their sector.

One post leader from each company came forward and read a statement of condemnation. For over two hours the three accused endured the painful humiliation in front of their fellow soldiers. Finally they were adjudged guilty of the offenses by a tribunal of senior officers, and the Regimental Commander, Oberst Stoph, announced the sentences. The two guards were demoted and sentenced to three months in military prison at Schwedt, while the post leader was stripped of rank and jailed for thirty days. Major Mueller and Captain Huber were reprimanded for deficiencies in training and discipline in their company.

The sentences didn't surprise Erich—they were to be expected under the collective discipline of the DDR. He felt a twinge of sympathy for his friend Bernd Müller. They had been through a lot together since, as schoolboys, they were compelled to join the Home Guard during the bitter fighting of 1945. But Bernd was too easy going—too concerned about his soldiers' feelings. If this country was going to succeed against the forces trying to drain away its life's blood, it needed firm discipline. That was the message of the tribunal, and Erich supported it.

Afterward there was a meeting with company commanders and political officers to review training procedures. Oberst Stoph stressed the importance of collective thinking and the need to develop greater zeal among soldiers on guard duty. He informed them of a new policy to avoid ideological contamination from the West by sealing off border guards from any outside contacts, other than their families. Monthly political training about the Anti-Fascist Protective Barrier would be increased to eight hours. In addition, political officers were to deliver a weekly current events lecture to reinforce the need for constant vigilance.

The tribunal highlighted Erich's frustration. More than ever he saw himself in a dead-end position, his abilities wasted in the boring task of guarding the border. Worse, he was now concerned about being identified with a regiment that had failed to prevent an escape.

Erich was one who had thrived under Russian occupation. When they learned that his father was one of the early members of the *Kommunistiche Partei Deutschland*, he was quickly released from a prisoner of war camp and allowed to resume his education. He was clever and ambitious, but most importantly, he was an ardent believer in Marxist-Leninist ideology. Following university graduation, he was selected for officers training. He rose rapidly in the NVA until he made the mistake of criticizing an incompetent superior in public. The fact that he was right didn't matter, and within days he found himself transferred to this isolated Grenzpolicei post in Thüringen.

That was four years earlier, shortly before Inge's second miscarriage. In many ways this reversal of fortune had been harder on Inge than himself. A vivacious woman who was a passionate believer in communism, Inge loved the parties, concerts and theater of a big city. There was little of that after she had joined him, and he felt guilty. Inge had enriched his life with the refinements he lacked: an appreciation of music and art. Erich knew he owed her...owed her more than he had provided.

When the meeting ended, Erich was asked to stop by the deputy commander's office. It was that conversation he wanted to discuss with Inge. Before he had time for further reflection, she was back with the food, setting it on a small table in the corner that served as their dining area. Erich crossed the room and sat down, while Inge joined him. He ignored the food and looked at her seriously.

"Inge, something came up today that I want to ask you about. After the tribunal, the deputy commander called me to his office. The family that was trying to escape didn't all make it across the border. The father was badly injured by a mine, and may not survive. Even if he does, he'll be in prison a long time. He was carrying a three year old son who is being placed for adoption."

Erich hesitated before continuing. "Oberst Leutnant Edinger wanted to know if we would like to take the boy."

He started to say more, but he knew with one look at his wife what the answer was. Her face seemed to light up and tears glistened in her eyes. In nine years of marriage they had tried everything to conceive a child. Nothing worked, and they had discussed adoption. Inge was an intelligent woman who wanted to continue her teaching career, but childcare was easily available. Yet Erich was uncomfortable with the thought of raising someone else's biological child, and swayed the debate with the prospect of conception by the use of a new drug, which had been suggested. Two years passed with no pregnancy, and Erich realized that there was no alternative to adoption.

"Oh, Erich, yes! I want a child and we have waited so long. I know you have doubts, but my heart tells me that this is right."

"That's true," he said slowly. "There doesn't seem to be any other way." Erich thought a moment, and his voice became more determined. "He's only three, and the memory of his parents will fade quickly. With thorough training we can raise a son who will make us proud and be a credit to the State."

Inge reached over and took Erich's hand. "Thank you, dear. This makes me so happy!" She jumped up and looked over the small house obviously thinking about changes they would have to make. "I can hardly wait to see him. How long will it be, do you think?"

"I'm not sure. I suppose a few days. I'll have to go through Oberst Leutnant Edinger, and he will make arrangements with the State Adoption Office." He stood, and put his arms around her. "I hope we won't have to live here much longer. If I can get transferred, we can raise him in a decent city."

On a sunny morning six days later Inge and Erich walked out of Bad Salzungen Hospital with their new son and placed him in the back seat of their automobile. Dieter was clutching a teddy bear with *Berlin* embroidered on its blue jacket. The new shirt and shorts Inge brought were a little large, but the green Tirolean hat fit and would have given him a more jaunty appearance if he wasn't so somber. The nurse told them that Dieter was listless and had eaten very little in the week he stayed in the hospital. Physically Dieter appeared to be well. His injuries from the explosion were healed, but Inge was surprised to discover a scar on his left thigh, which the nurse said was from some earlier accident.

Inge climbed into the back seat of their small Trabant so she could sit next to Dieter. As they drove west out of Bad Salzungen on Highway 62, Inge tried reading to Dieter from a book with pictures of farm life, but he showed no interest. Then she pointed to various animals in the fields they passed, asking Dieter their names. He didn't respond. He simply gazed out the window with vacant eyes. The only time he showed any expression was when they passed a bus, and he looked intently at the faces in the windows.

When they reached Dermbach, Dieter suddenly turned to Inge and asked, "Are you taking me to my Mama?"

For a moment Inge didn't know what to say. Then she said abruptly, "I'm very sorry, Dieter, your Mama and Papa are gone. They are never coming back. We are going to be your Mama and Papa now."

"Nein! Nein! Nein!" Dieter shrieked. "I want my Mama. I want Papa."

Inge put her arm around the weeping child, and tried to console him. He pulled away, crying loudly.

Less than fifty miles away, but in a different world, Gisela and Anna sat in a reception room of a large building that once was a sports hall for Hitler Youth. The Center For Refugees at Giessen in the West German State of Hesse had plenty of room. Since 1949 when the Bonn Government instituted the Emergency Admission Procedure, more than 2,600,000 East Germans had taken refuge at centers in Giessen, Welzen, and Berlin. After construction of the Berlin Wall and sealing of the border, however, the number of escapees dwindled.

Gisela read in a folder of instructions that the center's mission was to provide temporary housing and assist in resettling fellow Germans within a burgeoning West German society. In addition to processing applications for identity cards and other documents, the center helped locate friends and relatives who might help the newcomers with their transition.

Gisela and Anna spent their first night on cots in a partitioned area of a former exercise room. There were only two other families, and about fifteen adults, being housed in the large facility. Neither mother nor child had slept well, and now Gisela was nervously undergoing an initial processing interview.

A fat man wearing a coat and tie sat across the table from them, perusing a file through bifocal glasses. Anna sat on her mother's lap holding her doll in one hand and sucking her thumb on the other. Herr Mathias Gauck was in his fifties and nearly bald. He must have heard the stories of thousands of refugees, Gisela thought. At first he seemed unsympathetic to her plight. But after his abrupt response that there was no news about Walter or Dieter, she sensed a softening in his attitude.

Reading from a paper, he said gently, "So you have no living relatives in the West. Is that correct?"

"*Ja.* My father was a prisoner of the Russians in the war, but he never returned. My mother died when I was sixteen." Saying the words made her recall the sadness of her mother's funeral and the end of her childhood.

"What about your mother's family?"

"She was an only child, and we lived in Fulda near my grandparents. After they were killed in an air raid in 1945, we moved to Dresden."

"And your husband's family?"

She stared at him a moment and then said bitterly, "They were Jews who died in the camps."

Herr Gauck cleared his throat. "I see. Ah…why do you want to resettle in Fulda?"

"I want to be near the border, where I might be able to get word about Walter and Dieter." She was silent a moment and stroked her daughter's head. "Also I was born in Fulda, and the cathedral meant a great deal to my mother. She talked often about the wonderful services there.

"It must have been difficult for her to find a church in the East, wasn't it?"

"*Ja.*" Her tone was resentful. "Although the government said there was religious freedom, they did everything to discourage it. Even in school the teachers ridiculed religious ceremonies." In a more determined voice she added, "Despite the tragedies in my mother's life, her faith in God was strong."

Herr Gauck stood and walked to a file cabinet. Returning to the table with a thick file folder, he leafed through several papers that were clipped inside.

"There are no job postings for secretaries in Fulda at present, and there is not much available housing either. But I will see what I can do. In the meantime, be patient and relax with your daughter."

Gisela remained sitting, and for a moment didn't respond. Hesitantly she said, "An American officer said he might be able to help us. May I use a telephone to call him?"

"I doubt that the Americans can find you work any faster than my office can." His tone suggested that he considered this an affront to his efficiency. "Still, if that will make you feel better, you can use the phone on the desk in the corner."

Gisela found the card in her backpack, and dialed the number scrawled on it. When a voice answered in a rattle of unintelligible words, she said, *"Leutnant Parker, bitte."* She repeated it twice, and after a long wait, heard another voice.

"Lieutenant Parker speaking." The connection wasn't very clear, and it took several repetitions before Parker understood what she was asking. He said he would contact someone, asked for a number to reach her, and promised to call back within a day.

That afternoon, after Anna's nap, Gisela borrowed a baby stroller from the center for a short walk around town. This was her first opportunity to look in store windows outside East Germany since her early days in Berlin. In those days she believed government claims that West Berlin shops were special showcases of capitalism, and not representative of life in the West.

As they strolled by the first few shops, Gisela pointed excitedly at vacuum cleaners, television sets, refrigerators, shoes, and brightly colored coats and dresses. "Look, Anna," she said. "Look at what they have!" Giessen was not a large city, and Gisela knew she had been deceived. Standing in front of a grocery store, her eyes were drawn to a display of fruit.

"Oh, Anna. Look at the fruit. And the bananas! See the yellow bananas!" While she showed her child things that would have been wonders in East German shops, anger began to build in her. She clenched her fists and pounded the stroller handle.

"Walter was right. They lied to us! Her voice quivered with emotion. "They lied to us, Anna."

A middle-aged woman was about to pass by, but took a second look at the scene and stopped. "Is something wrong? Can I be of any help?"

"Nein, danke." Gisela was embarrassed, and made an effort to control her feelings. "I was just talking to myself."

On the walk back to the center, Gisela began to calm down. In a way, she realized, this was what they expected to find in the West. "If only things hadn't gone so wrong with their escape," she thought. With an effort she forced her mind away from self-reproach and set off on a brisk pace.

When they reached the center, there was a message for her from Hauptmann Voight with a number for her to call. Conflicting emotions of hope and fear caused Gisela's fingers to tremble as she dialed the number. When Hauptmann Voight came on the line, his first words dashed her hopes.

"Gisela, I'm afraid that I have bad news. Yesterday's edition of East Berlin's *Neues Deutschland* had a short article about Walter. I will read it."

"Walter Hurwitz, 29, died yesterday in Bad Salzungen from wounds…"

"Lieber Gott, Nein. Nein," she screamed.

Voight waited. For a few moments Gisela could do nothing but sob as she held on to the receiver. At last she managed to gasp, "What… What does it say about Dieter?"

"Unfortunately nothing. He is not mentioned."

"Oh, my God. What have they done with him?"

"I'm very sorry. I don't know. Let me read the rest of the article; it's short."

"…from wounds he received when he stepped on a mine laid by Imperialist Forces along the West German border near Geise in Thüringen. Hurwitz was lured to the border region by Western provocateurs who managed to escape back across the border."

"Lies," Gisela shouted. "Those are lies. Maybe Walter and Dieter are in a hospital or in prison."

"No. I don't think so." Hauptmann Voight spoke firmly. "Despite the propaganda, when the communist press reports a death, experience has shown them to be accurate." Gisela brushed aside the tears as she listened intently. "Unfortunately I don't know anything yet about your son. My border patrols are still trying to get information, but their contacts are being very cautious. I promise to call as soon as we know something. I am truly sorry to bring you such tragic news. *Auf Wiederhören.*"

Gisela hung up the telephone and slumped back in the chair, crying softly. Herr Gauck came into the room, saw Gisela and started to speak, but then thought better of it. After a minute she looked up. A look of resolution came across her face, and she pulled herself out of the chair.

"I must tell Anna," she said haltingly, "that her Papa is dead. Then I have to find a church! Can you please give me directions to a catholic church?"

The next morning after a breakfast that she hardly touched, Gisela heard a loudspeaker announcement directing her to the office for a telephone call. When she answered the phone, Lieutenant Parker was speaking.

"Gisela, I checked with the Civil-Affairs Office. There is a job available as a maid and baby-sitter with room and board. It doesn't pay a lot, but it could lead to something better. And you wouldn't have many expenses. Are you interested?"

The words came slowly. "My husband is dead. Hauptmann Voight called yesterday and read me a report of his death in the Berlin newspaper."

"Oh, I didn't know. I'm very sorry. Perhaps I should call you later about this job?"

There was a moment of silence. Finally Gisela took a deep breath. "*Nein*. I want to go to Fulda, and what kind of work doesn't matter. I'm sure Dieter is alive. Somehow I will find him!"

CHAPTER 6

Gisela stood in front of the cash register at the cosmetics counter of the Downs Barracks Post Exchange (PX). There was less than an hour before the PX opened, and she was apprehensive about her first day as a sales clerk.

"You learn quickly, Gisela," her manager, Frau Bishof said.

"*Ja*, the machines are *leicht*. I forget the English word, but I hope my little English is okay for people."

"Easy. *Leicht* is easy. Don't worry. You'll be fine and we need your help. This is the busy season. You will be surprised at how fast your English will improve. Here is a pamphlet on PX procedures. It's in English and German, so it will be a good review of what we talked about and it should help with your English vocabulary. Take the time until we open to study it."

This was the last morning of training for a part time job, which she hoped, would become permanent. The pay was more than double what she was making as a *Putzfrau*, and the work was more dignified than cleaning toilets and changing diapers. It was not that she was ungrateful for the position that the Parkers found for her. It had gotten her back to Fulda where she stayed in touch with Hauptmann Voight. The work was not that difficult, and it kept her mind occupied and enabled her to care for Anna and save a little money. But as the weeks passed, she began to consider how she could best provide a living for Anna and herself.

She had inquired about secretarial positions in Fulda, but realized that temporarily she was better off with the Americans who offered a free room and minimal living expenses. Then Gail suggested that she contact the Civil Affairs Office where German nationals could apply for a variety of civilian jobs on the military post. She spoke with the office manager and learned that occasionally secretarial positions came open at higher pay than in the German economy, although English language proficiency was required. A path toward that goal, she was advised, was to take an entry-level job where she could improve her language skills and obtain some references.

The proximity to the border did bring some news about Dieter. In September a Bundesgrenschutz patrol made contact with an East German border guard. In exchange for American cigarettes, the guard said that a small boy had been transported with his father to a hospital after a failed crossing attempt that summer near Geise. The guard heard that the father died, but he didn't believe the boy was badly hurt. Gisela was elated. Despite the lack of confirmation, she was convinced that it was Dieter and he was all right.

Marina Roberts, one of the women she worked for who was German, helped her with her English. Marina loaned her an English language textbook and dictionary that she studied at night in her small room on the top floor of the married officers quarters. Other than baby-sitting, there was little else to do in the evenings. So she studied diligently, practicing her pronunciation with Marina, Gail Parker, and three other wives who shared her services. Caring for Anna wasn't a problem, since all the ladies she worked for had pre-school children. Anna simply accompanied her to whichever apartment she was cleaning, and played with that woman's toddlers.

Across the border in Dermbach, Inge Burchert was meeting with the director of Dieter's day care center. Frau Grubel asked her to stop by to discuss a problem with Dieter. As a teacher, Inge was used to being in control, but she was apprehensive when she sat down and had difficulty keeping eye contact with the older woman

"Something is wrong with the child, Frau Burchert. He often sits by himself. It's like he's in a trance, either looking out the window or just staring at the wall. When I try to get him to join the other children in their play, he gets angry and throws things."

The adoption was not going well, and Inge was frightened. After all it was her idea. She had been so sure that she could handle a three-year-old as easily as she handled her own class of third year students. But Dieter was different, and he made her feel vulnerable. As a mother, she should be able to control her child. What would people think of her, especially Erich? He had been noticeably distant since Dieter had come into their house.

"I know he is troubled, but I hoped he would improve by being around other children."

"You told me he was recently adopted. Is there something about his previous situation that could still be affecting him?"

"*Ja*. It must be that. You see, his parents were dissidents who tried crossing the border to the West. His father was carrying Dieter, and was killed by a mine. The mother and another child escaped. He still has nightmares."

"So! I thought it had to be something traumatic. I care nothing about politics," Frau Grubel confided. "I am only interested in helping to nurture these young children." She sat back and thought a moment.

"Well, let's see what we can do to help him. I will give him some special attention. Also it might help if you and your husband talk with the boy to reassure him that you won't be leaving him."

"*Ja*. We did that after we brought him home, but we should probably tell him again. If he doesn't show some improvement soon, I wonder if we should take him to a child psychologist."

"He's still a little young for that. Let's see how he does over the next few weeks, and meet again in February."

Inge agreed and set up another appointment. However, as she left the Day Care Center, another idea began to form in her mind.

Gisela found that she was enjoying her first day of work in the PX more than she had expected. The women customers were patient with her halting English, and she appreciated the interaction with adults. Over the noon hour a couple of soldiers tried to strike up a conversation with her, but she followed her supervisor's guidance to politely discourage flirting GIs and concentrate on helping customers.

Late in the afternoon the small exchange became busier as more soldiers came in. She finished a rather difficult transaction with the first woman who was not friendly, and she was bothered by the experience, wondering if she had done something wrong.

"Excuse me." Gisela turned to find a young officer with a crew cut and crooked nose standing at the counter. He was only a few inches taller than her, and his powerful build would have made him intimidating except for an engaging smile and soft eyes. "I won't be that hard to please," he said, chuckling.

"How, please? *Ich meine...* I mean," she stammered. "I don't understand."

He leaned over the counter and said in a low voice, "You just waited on Mrs. Granger, wife of Colonel Granger the post commander. She sometimes acts like she is the commander."

"Oh, *versteh ich.* I understand. But she is mad at me, no?"

"I don't see how she could be. You were polite and helpful. But you must be new here. Mrs. Granger was probably just trying to impress you with her importance. What's your name?"

"*Gisela. Ja.* I am only one day here." She noticed the nametag on his field jacket and the silver bar on his collar, and asked in her practiced English, "How may I help you, Lieutenant Newman?"

For a moment he was unsure of what to say. Standing in front of him was the prettiest woman he had seen in the sixteen months he had been in Fulda. His duties as tank company executive officer didn't leave much time or opportunity to meet attractive women, and clearly this was someone he wanted to know better.

"Ah…you can help me pick out a bottle of perfume to send home for Christmas."

"Certainly. For who do you buy it?"

"My mother. She lives in Kentucky. I have to mail the package tomorrow so it will be there by Christmas. I'd like something nice; something expensive that she wouldn't buy for herself."

Gisela placed some perfume bottles on the counter. "This is *Joy*, the most expensive. Here also is *Channel #5* and *Miss Dior*. They are very popular, too. I show you." Taking the first bottle, she sprayed a few drops on her hand, and held it up to him.

He leaned forward and smelled her hand, conscious of both the fragrance and the closeness of her body. "Very nice. Can we try another sample?"

"*Ja.* That was *Joy.*" She put a few drops on her other hand. "And here, *Channel #5.*"

He lingered a moment over her hand, and smiled again. "They both smell fine. I don't know. What do you suggest?"

"I can't say. *Frau Grubel* say to me *Joy* is most popular with American *Frauen.*"

"Then *Joy* is what I want. I'll take the large bottle, please."

While she wrapped the package, he counted out money from his billfold. As he handed it to her he asked, "Do you work here every day?"

"Only Thursday, Friday and Saturday. Other times I work for Frau Parker and some ladies. I hope your mother is liking the perfume. *Auf Wiedersehen.*"

"Yes. Thank you." He started to leave and then turned back. "Gisela, my name is Fred Newman, and I look forward to seeing you again." As he left the store he resolved to do some more shopping at the PX and to talk to John Parker about the pretty woman who was working for them.

December 5th in Germany, both East and West, is the night St. Nicholas brings gifts to good little children. It is said that those who are bad receive a bundle of tree branches that can be used as switches by their parents to punish them until they are good enough to warrant a gift. As temperatures grew colder and December daylight shortened, many in East Germany still prepared to observe the birth of the Christ Child, especially in Western fringes of Thüringen. There was no official recognition of the religious holiday. Yet some churches were open; and despite government repudiation, a few of the older generation still attended services. Others, like the Burcherts, were more focused on a visit from St. Nicholas.

Inge had decorated their small home with holly branches and pinecones. Also for the first time in their married life, she persuaded Erich to buy a Christmas tree that she decorated with ornaments and small candles in tiny holders. For several weeks they told Dieter stories about St. Nicholas and the presents he would bring to good little boys. Yet they were discouraged that he showed little interest.

They were finishing supper in the kitchen when Inge set dishes of apple strudel in front of Dieter and Erich. As usual Dieter was just picking at his food.

"Finish your dessert while Mama goes to see about something." She went into the living room, took some brightly wrapped packages from a closet and placed them under the tree. Then she took some matches from her apron pocket and carefully lit the candles on the tree before returning to the kitchen.

"Dieter, come see what St. Nicholas has brought." Obediently the boy slipped off his chair and followed her into the living room. The Christmas tree, lit with two-dozen miniature candles was a beautiful sight, and Dieter's face shown with wonder. Erich watched from the doorway a moment. Then he crossed the kitchen and went out the back door, picking up a large carton on his way out. He circled the house and left the carton at the front door, returning the way he came. When he reappeared from the kitchen, Inge was showing Dieter the packages under the tree.

"Here is a present with your name," she said, handing him a small box. With Erich's help, Dieter opened the package and found a model of an army truck, which he rolled back and forth a few times and then ignored. Two more presents, a plastic airplane and a picture book of fairy tales, produced the same reaction.

"Listen, Dieter. I think St. Nicholas might have left something outside the door. Go with your Papa and look."

Erich took Dieter's hand and led him to the front door, which he opened. On the doorstep was a box with two paws and a black head hanging out. Erich reached into the box, pulled out a German shepherd puppy and held him in front of the boy. "Look, Dieter. St. Nicholas has brought you *einen jungen Hund.*"

Dieter reached out and patted the dog's head tentatively which caused the puppy to respond by licking his hand. Erich handed the bundle of fur to the boy who laughed and hugged the puppy. Dieter turned and ran back into the living room, still holding the squirming dog.

"Mama, see what I have," he said excitedly. His face came alive as he looked at the dog. "St. Nicholas brought me a puppy."

"*Ja.* I see." Inge's eyes glowed with pleasure. "St Nicholas has brought you a puppy to be your friend."

The rest of the evening Dieter was animated as he played with his puppy. He set a dish of water in a corner of the kitchen for the dog, and Inge showed him where they would feed him. They fixed a bed out of a shallow box with an old blanket, and placed it next to Dieter's bed. As Inge was tucking him in for the night, she asked whether he had thought of a name for the dog.

"Nicki," he said without hesitation. "I want to call him Nicki because St. Nicholas brought him."

Downs Barracks was a quiet place on Christmas Eve. The usual contingent of personnel was on hand to perform essential tasks: border patrol, guard duty, headquarters and troop staff duty, meal preparation, etc. Yet passes and leaves were granted liberally, and many single soldiers were passing the lonely hours in nearby bars.

Fred Newman had finished a duty tour as Officer of the Day, and went into the headquarters building to retrieve his portable radio. As he walked down the darkened corridor, he noticed a light burning in the office of the Regimental Adjutant. He looked in the open doorway and saw a young soldier typing furiously on a manual typewriter.

"Specialist Lane," he said "What are you doing here so late?"

"I'm finishing a Report of Survey for Lieutenant Parker. I'm going on leave tomorrow, and it's overdue. Our orderly room typewriter is broken, and First Sergeant Brown told me to use this one." He pulled the last sheet of paper from the typewriter and thought a moment.

"Sir, I was wondering if you would be seeing Lieutenant Parker tonight or tomorrow? He wanted to review the report before turning it in, and Major Turner told him to have it on his desk by 0800 Monday."

Specialist Lane was the orderly room clerk in Troop C, and had a reputation for reliability. Why not? Fred thought. Lane deserved a favor, and maybe he could find a way to see Gisela. John Parker had told him her story. Instead of being put off by her situation, Fred became more determined. On his third visit to the cosmetics counter he asked her to have dinner with him, but she politely refused without giving a reason. She fascinated him, and he didn't believe that her refusal had anything to do with him specifically.

"Sure. No problem. His apartment building is near the BOQ. I'll drop it off on my way."

"Thank you, sir. I've got a bunch of things to do before I leave tomorrow, and that will really help." Lane stapled four copies of the report, slipped them in a large manila envelope, and handed them to Newman.

It was after five o'clock and almost dark when Fred left Regimental Headquarters for the short walk through the married housing area. It was snowing softly with more expected the next day. We should have a white Christmas, he thought. He could see lights on Christmas trees and other decorations in apartment windows. As Fred walked along the sidewalk, he thought about Christmas in Kentucky with his mother and sister. A sense of homesickness came over him, as it often did at Christmas.

Ten years since I left, he thought, and his fingers tightened into fists as his mind focused on the vision of a drunken stepfather belting his mother in the face on Christmas Eve. In his stupor the brutish policeman that his widowed mother had mistakenly married forgot that Fred had put on 30 pounds and two inches in his sixteenth year. Involuntarily Fred scowled as he remembered spinning the bigger man around and pummeling him until he was unconscious. He spent the holidays with a friend's family, and after returning home briefly when his stepfather was at work, he left for good. Looking back Fred realized that the Army had become his family when a hard-pressed recruiting sergeant had taken his word that he was eighteen and he had boarded a bus for basic training. He had only gone back for one Christmas since then. That was just before his present assignment, and after his long-suffering mother had finally summoned the courage to leave his abusive stepfather.

The Parkers lived on the third floor of the last building in the row of apartment houses. Climbing the stairs Fred could hear the sounds of children crying and smell the aroma of food cooking. He knocked on the door of Number 3-C, and was surprised when the door opened and he stood facing Gisela.

"Ah...Hello, Gisela. I wasn't expecting to see you. Is Lieutenant Parker here?"

She smiled, opening the door wider. "Please come in."

When he stepped into the living room, John Parker rose from an easy chair. "Hey, Fred. Merry Christmas. Take off your coat and have a seat."

"Merry Christmas, John." Fred hesitated as Gisela moved into the kitchen. "I just stopped by to drop off a Report of Survey for Specialist Lane."

"Terrific! Lane promised to finish it before he left. I knew I could count on him. Major Turner has been on me to get that wrapped up before the holidays. Please sit down and stay a while. How about a beer?"

"Well, if I'm not interrupting a meal or anything, a beer would be great. I just finished twenty four hours as OD."

Gail Parker stepped out of the kitchen and exchanged greetings with Fred while John opened a couple of bottles of Becks. "Fred, if you're not busy, why don't you stay for dinner? We've invited Gisela and Anna, and we would love to have you join us. We're having a roast and there is plenty."

"Gee, Gail. I don't know. I have such a hectic social life with so many engagements on Christmas Eve," Fred grinned. "But honestly, it would be a real pleasure."

Fred followed John into the living room and sat down. While he sipped beer and talked with John, Susie and Anna played with dolls near a small Christmas tree.

In the kitchen Gisela was preparing a plate of relishes and thinking how grateful she was to John and Gail. At times she felt overwhelmed in her grief. She had been dreading the Christmas holidays, the first without Walter and Dieter. Gail's invitation was a welcome diversion, and now she began wondering about the unexpected arrival of Fred Newman. She turned to Gail. "What you know about Lieutenant Newman? Is he good man?"

"Well, he's from Kentucky like I am, so he must be good," Gail laughed. "Seriously, I know John looks up to him. He's been in the Army longer than John and should be promoted to captain soon. John told me he left home when he was in high school. He joined the Army, became a paratrooper, and did so well that he got an appointment to West Point."

"What is West Point?"

"It's the Army's military academy, a four-year college. Most graduates make the Army their profession." Gail gave her a sly look. "How come you're interested in him?"

Gisela blushed and recounted their contacts in the PX. "He said I was pretty."

"Did he?" Gail exclaimed, "Well you are, but I'm surprised he noticed. Since we've been here, I've never seen him with a date at the Officers Club."

A timer on the stove buzzed, interrupting their conversation. Gail opened the oven and removed the roast. Gisela couldn't remember when she had last seen a sirloin roast, and this one looked delicious. As she helped Gail place the roast on a platter, she said, "Thank you for asking me and Anna to dinner. I don't know what we…" She couldn't finish speaking her thought.

"We're happy to have you join us," Gail interjected quickly. "Try not to think about what's happened and enjoy the evening. Now let's get these dishes on the table."

The bustle of bringing plates of food from the kitchen broke her mood, and soon she heard Gail say, "Dinner is served." Gail's announcement stopped the men's shoptalk and everyone came into the dining room. "Fred, you sit over there next to Susie, and Gisela can sit across from you with Anna."

Gisela got Anna seated and adjusted her bib. When she straightened up, she was surprised to find Fred holding her chair to assist her. When everyone was seated, Gail said, "It's Christmas Eve. John, would you say a blessing?"

For a moment John looked flustered, but managed to stammer a few words of thanks to God. Gisela crossed herself and looked up to see Fred smiling at her. Is he really seriously interested in me? She wondered. Before this evening she thought he was just looking for a passing fling, but now she found herself returning his smile. These Americans are much more friendly and open than what she had expected.

She was reminded of that as she watched Fred during dinner. He laughed easily and was attentive to the children, patient even when they became noisy and fidgety. The conversation took her mind off her troubles. In a mixture of German and English, they talked about life in America and East Germany, Christmas traditions, and even religion. She was a little disappointed to find out that Fred was not Catholic.

After dinner Fred read a story to Anna and Susie while Gail and Gisela cleaned up. She helped Gail put the children in bed, and then they returned to the living room where Fred and John were talking.

Fred addressed both women. "John says that he was going to drive Gisela into town so she could attend midnight mass at the cathedral. Why don't I give her a ride? I'd like to attend the service also, and I can bring her back here."

Gisela had mixed feelings. She wanted to be alone in church to focus her prayers on Dieter and on Walter's soul. But something in Fred's eyes made her hesitate.

"That's very kind of you, Fred," Gail chimed in. "It saves a trip for John and it's more convenient for Gisela. Is that all right with you, Gisela?"

"Ja. Danke."

"Okay," Fred said quickly. "Just let me go to the BOQ and change clothes. I'll be back in a few minutes."

The Fulda Cathedral, or Dom as Germans called it, was only a mile from Downs Barracks but the freezing temperature and biting wind made it tough on anyone who had to walk. Fred was grateful to Gail for convincing Gisela to accept a ride in his warm Porsche convertible. He had changed into a coat and tie and wore a gray Loden overcoat.

Fred spoke to her in German. "That's a pretty coat you're wearing." It was a long black wool coat that matched her calf length boots.

"It's Gail's. She insisted that I wear it. But the boots are mine," she laughed, extending a leg so he could see. "I'm still buying clothes for Anna and myself." She gave him a quizzical look. "You speak German well. Where did you learn?"

"At the military academy. We had to study a language for two years, and I chose German. I thought I would be stationed here sometime."

Fred turned right on Leipziger Strasse and maneuvered the car through the one lane opening of St. Paul's Gate. Before them, bathed in spotlights, was a breathtaking view of St. Boniface Cathedral, or *Dom*, flanked by its distinctive twin obelisks. Fred drove slowly past the cathedral square that was filling with people hurrying toward the *Dom*. A light coating of snow covered the ground, and they could see the frosty breath of nearby walkers.

"Oh, how beautiful!" Gisela exclaimed.

"Wow! I haven't seen it lit at night before."

Fred found a place to park on a side street a few blocks away, and they joined the throng of people walking rapidly to get out of the wind to find a choice seat. They didn't say much, as they walked through the bitter cold. By the time they reached the entrance, Gisela's cheeks were rosy, and there was a tingling in Fred's ears. The cathedral was nearly filled, and they were directed down a side aisle.

In contrast to the outside lighting, the interior was illuminated with hundreds of candles. Incense was strong and mixed with the smell of pine boughs laid at the base of each stained glass window. On either side of the altar were two enormous Christmas trees, also decorated with lit candles. A high dome accentuated the fullness of light surrounding the altar. The effect, further highlighted by white walls with gold trim, was one of majestic dignity.

"I've only been in one cathedral," Fred whispered. "St. Patrick's in New York. But this is awesome!"

They found seats a few rows back from the ornate pulpit attached to the north pillar. Further down the aisle Fred noticed huge statues that adorned the walls of the long nave. He motioned to them, and Gisela said, "They are statues of the apostles." Fred continued to gaze around while Gisela knelt in prayer. After a few minutes, she made a sign of the cross, and sat back on the bench.

"Look up there," he said. Above the four main pillars were gorgeous fresco paintings.

"I think they are the four evangelists." When he didn't respond she added, "You know, Matthew, Mark, Luke, and John."

"Oh, I see." He was about to say more, but the service began with a procession of priests and a robed choir. When they stood during the processional, Fred recognized some Americans scattered among the congregation. Standing on the stone floor, he could feel his feet getting cold. Whatever heating system was used for the ancient building was at a low level, and most people kept their coats on.

Fred had difficulty following the spoken portions of the service that was mostly in Latin, so he remained a silent observer. He found comfort in the service, and also with the thought that his mother was probably attending another midnight service, although far away in a small town Methodist Church. At one point he was moved by a theatrical performance of *Ave Maria* by the choir. They began softly, and the interior lights of the Cathedral were gradually turned up until the choir reached a crescendo, when they burned brightly; then the lights slowly dimmed again as the anthem ended.

"That was beautiful," he murmured.

Gisela heard him and nodded her agreement. She had stayed on her knees until the *Ave Maria*, and he could see that she had been crying. Once he had been on the verge of putting a comforting hand on her shoulder. But he was afraid to intrude, not wanting his gesture to be misinterpreted either. By now the size of the crowd had pushed the people in their pew closely together. The warmth of her body made him conscious again of how much he was attracted to her. Despite the solemn occasion, he enjoyed the feeling and found his mind wandering to thoughts of a more intimate relationship with this captivating woman.

The service concluded with the congregation joining the choir in the familiar hymn, *Silent Night*. Fred could hear a few voices singing the English words, but what seemed more remarkable was how all voices blended into a harmony that transcended nationality. Afterward Gisela went to one of the side altars and lit three candles that she said were for Walter, Dieter, and the third for her mother. He stood by as she knelt and prayed for several minutes.

When they left the cathedral, Gisela was quiet, and Fred waited a while before speaking. Halfway to the car the words of a poem he had memorized for a German class came into his mind. He recited the first stanza aloud,

"*Wo man singt, da lass ich nieder; böse Menschen haben keine Lieder.*"

(Where one sings, I will stay; angry people have no songs.)

Gisela looked at him inquisitively. "German poetry. How do you know that?"

"It's something I read in college. I don't remember the poet, but I thought of it when we were singing *Silent Night*. The service made me wonder if we will ever really be able to live without the threat of war."

"I wonder too." There was a note of bitterness in her voice. "I wonder if that terrible wall will ever come down."

Fred regretted his comment that broke the hopeful mood of the service. Not sure what to say, he put his arm around her as they walked back to the car, thankful that she didn't pull away.

CHAPTER 7

"Gentlemen, let me remind you that the classification of this briefing is Secret." Lieutenant Colonel Hampton's brief statement and serious expression stopped the buzz of conversation, and grabbed the attention of First Squadron's officers. Buck Hampton was tall and imposing. He had the build of a football lineman, which he was during the glory years of Army football in the late forties at West Point. Now he commanded 900 soldiers organized into three cavalry troops, a tank company, an artillery battery and headquarters elements.

"The purpose of today's meeting is to review some aspects of the world situation which will affect us this year, and to make you aware of some changes in our wartime mission."

John sat up in his seat and exchanged glances with Fred Newman. It was the first duty week of the New Year, and since notice of a classified Officers Call was first circulated, rumors were flying. Word that an officer in Third Squadron and several soldiers had just received orders for Vietnam spread rapidly, adding to the anticipation surrounding the meeting.

"Intelligence sources tell us that we can expect some relaxation of tensions in Europe resulting in part from the ouster of Khrushchev as Soviet Premier last October. Unannounced alerts of NATO military units will still occur on a monthly basis, but Fifth Corps tactical nuclear weapons will not be brought as close to the border as they were previously."

That was good news, John thought. Since the Cuban Missile Crisis fourteen months earlier, threat levels had kept everyone in the squadron on edge. Even wives and children were affected, as evacuation procedures were discussed and practiced. Every family had emergency bags packed, and private automobiles were always kept full of gas and backed into parking spaces, ready for a rapid get-away.

The squadron commander uncovered a map of Southeast Asia propped on an easel. "However, I'm sure you know that international tensions are increasing in other areas."

John was well aware that the number of military advisors to Vietnam had increased steadily since the Gulf of Tonkin Resolution six months earlier. The Pentagon was no longer relying on volunteers, and they all faced the prospect of future assignments in a combat zone.

Using a pointer to focus attention on several circled areas of the map, LTC Hampton continued. "Within the next few months Marine and Army combat units are expected to be deployed to protect U.S. bases at Danang, Bienhoa, Hue, and Vung Tao. USAREUR (US Army in Europe) is warning us that some key positions, especially junior officers, infantry NCOs, medics, and communication specialists, may remain unfilled for lengthy periods. This means we need to emphasize cross-training of personnel, so that we have someone as a backup who can fill the gap."

There was a stirring in the room, and Colonel Hampton paused. "Before we talk about our war plan, are there any questions on what I've covered?"

Sam Erwin, the artillery battery commander stood. "Sir, are there any indications that duty tours in Germany will be shortened?"

"No. I haven't heard anything like that yet." Seeing another raised hand, he said, "Yes, Tom."

Tom MacAfee, the S4, or supply officer, asked, "What about the replacement of major items of equipment? Recently it's been taking longer to get requisitions filled."

"Yes. I'm aware there has been a problem in receiving M113 personnel carriers, and I expect that to continue until production increases. Also the Corps G4 says that radio repair parts will be in short supply for several months."

Seeing no other questions, Colonel Hampton crossed the room to another easel. "Now I want to direct your attention to our role in the current NATO War Plan." He unveiled a map of Central Germany with an acetate overlay depicting the area southwest of Fulda to the border and beyond. Red symbols on the acetate represented enemy units capable of attacking in their sector. John was awed by what faced them. He knew that they would be outnumbered, but seeing the amount of red squares on the map was sobering.

"The threat remains the same: elements of two armored divisions of the Soviet Sixth Guards Army, supported by one East German motorized rifle division. As the Corps Covering Force, our mission is to delay any attack, and to impede the enemy's advance while withdrawing to successive phase lines until we pass through Third Armored Division defensive positions."

John watched as Hampton slapped his pointer on wavy black lines, roughly parallel and identified as PL Ohio, PL Kentucky, and PL Kansas. He tried to visualize his platoon emplaced along one of those Phase Lines: tanks in defilade, infantry nearby in fox holes, two squads of scouts trying to locate the enemy's first echelon, and his 4.2 mortar squad behind the tanks in a firing position to support the scouts. They had rehearsed the tactics often, but what would it be like with enemy artillery, missiles, and tank projectiles coming at them? With an effort, John jerked his attention back to the Squadron Commander.

"Changes since our last briefing are shown on the overlay. The Fourteenth Cavalry's sector has been expanded, so our area of responsibility is now about ten klicks (kilometers) wider. When I finish I want troop commanders to pick up copies of this map overlay to use in making adjustments to your initial delay positions. Any questions?"

Captain Collins asked, "Does this change in our sector require any adjustment in our Passage of Lines with the Third Armored Division?"

"That's a good point, Charley. I've looked into that with the S3, and we don't think so. But he's going to take that to the Regimental S3, and make sure we're still on the same sheet of music with Third Armored. If the balloon ever goes up, and we're shagging ass in front of the Russians, we damn sure better know where we're going."

His comment drew nervous chuckles from the group. Whenever leaders in the 14th Cavalry gave serious thought to a Russian assault, they faced the grim prospect that in carrying out their mission they would be lucky to reach Third Armored's battle positions with half their force.

Colonel Hampton ended the briefing by saying, "Those of you who might be wondering how armored officers would be utilized in Vietnam as advisors, should talk to Fred Newman. He's been there, and can fill you in."

It was dark outside when the meeting ended. John listened to Fred describe his experience as an advisor to several officers clustered around him. Finally the group broke up, and John walked down the stairway with Fred. When they emerged from the building, Fred asked, "Can I buy you a beer, John?"

"Sounds fine, Fred. I'll take you up on that."

One of the nice features about Downs Barracks was its small size. Five minutes later the two friends were seated at a table in the Officers Club. John took a drink from a bottle of Löwenbräu, and asked, "How long do you think American combat troops are going to be in Vietnam?

"I'm afraid we'll be there longer than most people think. The Viet Cong are no pushovers. From what I saw they're better motivated than the ARVN (Army of Vietnam) soldiers. As long as they keep getting support from North Vietnam and Russia, this conflict may last several years."

"I'm not sure what I should do." John knew it would be important to have combat experience on his record. "I'd like to volunteer for Vietnam, but I don't think I should at this time. We're expecting another child."

"Really? Congratulations! When's the baby due?"

"Not until August. Gail just found out a week ago."

"That's great! Don't be concerned about volunteering for Vietnam. If it lasts as long as I think it will, we'll all be going, like it or not." He looked at his beer for several moments, as if he was contemplating something. "You know, John, I envy you. You have a lovely wife and a growing family. The Army may keep us away from home a lot, but at least you have someone waiting for you when you return. I'd like that." Fred scratched his chin, and grinned, like he had just decided something. "I think I'm going to pursue that objective."

"Are you talking about Gisela?"

"Yes, hopefully. She's beautiful and I'd like to date her, but it may be too soon for her."

"Maybe Gail could speak to her and be able to share some thoughts about that." John drained his beer, and pushed back his chair. "Speaking of Gail, I'd better be going. Thanks for the beer, Fred."

As much as Fred wanted to spend time with Gisela that winter, the Army, as so often is the case, had other plans for him. First there was the annual field exercise, Winter Shield, which took the squadron for two weeks to the open terrain bounded by Hohenfels and Grafenwöhr. From Winter Shield, he was sent to a three-week course for maintenance officers at Vilseck. Tank Gunnery qualification followed in March and April, when Fred was detailed to Grafenwöhr Training Area, filling in for his commander who had broken a leg.

In the few days between training events, Fred saw Gisela whenever he could. On two occasions he took her with Anna on sightseeing drives through the Rhön Mountains outside Fulda. Yet whenever he sensed that she might have serious feelings toward him, he had to leave. He wrote her letters, both in German and English, and received first a short note and then a warmer letter during his long stay at Grafenwöhr. He learned that she was working full time at the PX, and was spending some of her free time looking for an apartment in Fulda.

John Parker was also at Grafenwöhr in April. As a reconnaissance platoon leader he was responsible for the performance of his two M60A1 tank crews. He had done his best to get his crews up to speed for this critical test of proficiency. He was acting as commander of his first tank, but despite the extra time spent on the miniature range in Fulda, his second crew had him worried. The tank commander, SFC Nelson, had arrived three months earlier from a desk job at Fort Hood, Texas. Sergeant Nelson put up a good front, especially in his appearance, but he was brash and relied too much on the other three members of his crew. It was troublesome that the early days of practice firing on Grafenwöhr's ranges revealed deficiencies in his knowledge of tank gunnery.

SFC Nelson wasn't the only weakness in Parker's two crews. The constant rotation of draftees, as well as frequent absences for guard, barracks orderly, and other administrative activities, limited the effectiveness of their training. Lack of nearby range facilities was another disadvantage for armor units along the border. But John wasn't concerned about other tank units, he just wanted to be at the top of the competition in First Squadron.

The night before they were scheduled to fire Table VIII, the Tank Crew Qualification Course, John walked back to his temporary barracks with another platoon leader, Jim Johnson. Johnson, an ROTC graduate from Howard University and the only black officer in the squadron, had a high score in last year's competition. Already tapped to move into the troop executive officer spot, this would be his last gunnery competition.

"How's Specialist Rivera working out on Nelson's tank?" Johnson asked.

"He's made an improvement, but I'm still worried about Nelson. I hated to move Rivera from my tank, but he's fast and accurate. Now if Nelson can just locate the targets for him, and give correct fire commands, the move might be worth it."

"It's always a gamble to move people around at the last minute, but I had to do it last year when my gunner went home on emergency leave. I was lucky his replacement turned out to be the best gunner in the squadron. Anyway, good luck tomorrow."

"Thanks, Jim. I'll see you later. I've got to meet my guys in the training room for one more review. We're giving it our best effort. Good luck to you too, not that you need it."

Table VIII at Grafenwöhr was a demanding course. Each tank drove separately along a prescribed route, and engaged a series of infantry and combat vehicle targets at various ranges. A second phase of the course was repeated at night where the crew utilized the powerful Xenon searchlight with its infrared capability.

On the last night of firing John stood with his crew around a small pile of burning ammunition containers waiting for SFC Nelson's tank to complete the course. The night was damp and cold, with a chilling wind that penetrated their field jackets. John was disappointed in his crew's performance. They had qualified, but fallen short of the prestigious designation of Distinguished Tank Crewmen when his .50 caliber machine gun jammed on a truck target, and his gunner missed a tank target at 800 yards.

Sergeant Nelson's mud-spattered tank came around the final turn of the two-mile course with its main gun tube elevated and a green "All Clear" flag mounted on top of its turret. It slued to a halt in a row of C Troop tanks, and the loader began tossing spent 105-millimeter shell casings over the side of the turret. John walked toward the tank as Nelson and the range scorer were dismounting.

"How'd it go, Sergeant Nelson?"

"Not so good, sir." For once Nelson's bluster was absent. "We missed getting three rounds off in the required time, and I messed up a couple of fire commands."

"They were a hundred points short of qualifying, Lieutenant," the scorer said bluntly. "It's too bad, because your gunner nailed all the targets; but target acquisition was too slow. Crew coordination needs some improvement also."

"Thanks for letting me know, sergeant." John turned his attention to SFC Nelson, as the range NCO moved off to turn in his scorecard.

"I'm sorry, sir." Nelson looked down at his boots. "I know I let you down, but I just ain't had much time in a tank in the last three years."

John was tired, frustrated and in no mood for excuses. "Damn it, Nelson. You're supposed to be the best-trained man on that crew. I don't care about the last few years. I want to know if you're the right man for the job now."

Nelson raised his head, and his eyes met Parker's. I ain't gonna bullshit you, lieutenant. I never TC'd a crew through tank gunnery before, but I'm gonna do my best to prove I can."

"We'll see. I'll have to talk to Captain Collins about that, but I'm willing to give you a couple of months to show some marked improvement. Now go help your crew clean the gun tube." Nelson saluted and headed back to his tank.

Two hours later John was sitting on a bunk in his room shining a pair of boots when Fred Newman walked by his open door.

"Say, Fred. Do you have a minute?"

"Yeah. I guess my mail can wait. What's up?"

"I wanted to ask how my platoon's crew scores were, compared to the rest of the squadron?"

"I don't remember exactly, but somewhere in the bottom half. Sergeant Nelson's score was near the bottom, but there were at least two other bolos with scores worse than his. So among recon platoons, yours was a little below average."

"That's what's bothering me. Captain Collins is going to have a fit. He was really pushing to have all his tank crews qualify, and it looks like my platoon didn't make it." Knowing this would probably show up on his efficiency report was even more galling.

Fred moved across the room and sat down on a footlocker. "John, don't let this get you down. There's a lot more to running a recon platoon than tank gunnery. Sure it's important that our crews are well trained, but Collins must realize that your new tank commander was a problem. Maybe that's why he put him in your platoon, where there was the best chance to get him up to standard quickly."

"If Collins has that much confidence in me, he sure doesn't show it. Besides, that's where the vacant position was."

"Collins is kind of a hard nose guy. No question about that. But your platoon did a great job in Wintershield, picking up that night flanking move by enemy tanks; and everybody knows it, especially the squadron commander. Don't forget that Colonel Hampton was singing your praise to Collins after Wintershield.

He stood and slapped John on the shoulder with the letters he was holding. "Don't sweat it, John. No one expects lieutenants to get perfect efficiency reports. Put it out of your mind, and have a good trip back."

"Thanks, Fred. That helps. I just hope you're right."

Although John's troop was leaving the next day for the return to Fulda, Fred remained several more days to supervise the cleaning and turn-in of equipment and billets he had signed for from the Grafenwöhr Supply Office. Then he led a column of jeeps and supply trucks on the long road march back to Fulda. By the time the last vehicles were washed and secured, Fred was exhausted. It was late, and Gisela didn't have a phone. So he went to his BOQ room, dumped his duffel bag in a corner, and crawled into bed.

The next day, after a retreat formation, Fred stopped by the PX and saw Gisela showing some perfume to a lady. He stood patiently by the magazine rack until the woman left. Before another customer could get in his way, he stepped quickly over to the counter. Gisela had her back to him. When she turned around, she seemed surprised but her face lit up in a smile. She looked prettier than ever, and Fred knew then that she was a prize worth winning.

He spoke hurriedly. "Gisela, it's great to see you again. I've really missed you. I'm sorry I've been gone so much."

"*Ja.* I understand."

He hoped she hadn't lost interest in him. While she acted pleased to see him again, she didn't seem to want to talk. Maybe it was because the manager was looking in their direction.

"Did you get my letters?"

"Only one before I moved."

"So that's it. I didn't know how to get in touch with you. Where are you living now?"

"On Petersburger Strasse. We have a small flat across from the cemetery." She leaned closer and lowered her voice. "I'm sorry, Fred. When I found a place, I had to move fast, and there was so much to do, I didn't have time to write you my address."

A sergeant and his wife were standing at the end of the counter, and Fred was beginning to feel self-conscious. He decided to plunge ahead. "Gisela, I really want to spend some time with you—alone. Will you let me take you to dinner this Saturday?"

Now it was Gisela who was flustered. Glancing at the customers down the counter, she stammered, "I…I don't know. About Anna… what to do. I can't answer now."

"Okay. Don't worry about Anna; we can find someone to watch her. Please think about it. I'll see you tomorrow when it's not so busy."

Saturday it was still light at six o'clock when Fred parked his car on Petersburger Strasse and climbed the stairs to a second floor apartment above a gravestone monument office. Gisela and Anna were ready, so they didn't linger in the cramped apartment. Gisela wore a red print dress and had her hair pulled back in a tight bun. She even had some lipstick on. The effect made an impact on Fred. There was something about her—a self-assurance that he admired. He could visualize himself escorting her to a dance at the Officer's Club. Heads would turn. It wasn't just her beauty; she had a style and elegance that seemed natural.

First they drove to the military housing area, and took Anna to the Parker's. Gail had readily agreed to Fred's request that Anna spend the evening with Susie. John was away serving as Squadron Duty Officer, and Gail was obviously hoping to encourage a budding romance.

It was warm for early May, so Fred parked on Kanal Strasse; and they walked a few blocks to the *Zum Ritter*, a small hotel in the city center known for its excellent restaurant. For once Gisela seemed lighthearted, her eyes sparkling as if she was a new person, forgetting the past.

A waitress wearing a colorful dirndl dress led them to a table in the corner of the walnut paneled dining room. Fred examined the menu until he noticed that Gisela was silent. He followed her gaze and saw that she was staring at frescos painted on the opposite wall above a mantle display of porcelain pitchers.

"What's wrong, Gisela?" Tears were forming in her eyes, which were focused on the cherubic figure of a small boy in the central fresco.

"I'm sorry." Her voice was choked. "That picture! It reminds me of Dieter...my son."

"Oh. I never thought about the paintings. I shouldn't have brought you here. Come. We'll find another restaurant."

Outside, on the sidewalk, Gisela said, "I didn't mean to spoil the evening, but I couldn't get my mind off Dieter and what is happening to him."

Fred took her arm and looked into her eyes. "As long as I'm with you, the evening can't be spoiled." He smiled and gave her a little hug. "Let's walk over to the *Hauptwache*. They have a good menu."

They walked past several shops without speaking. Fred could tell Gisela was thinking about something, and he was unsure of what to do. Finally she said, "While you were gone, I got a message from *Hauptmann* Voight. When I called, he told me that there was another report about the boy involved in the border crossing. An East German guard said that the boy was not hurt seriously, and he was taken to a hospital in Bad Salzungen."

Gisela stopped walking and looked directly at him. "I'm so torn, Fred. I know he's alive; but I don't know where he is or whether I'll ever see him again. I've even thought about going to the border post at Helmstedt and trying to cross back into East Germany. But *Hauptmann* Voight and others have warned me that I would probably be put in prison, and that I could lose Anna too."

"Gisela, we can't be sure of the future. Anything can change. It's even possible that the border might open again." He took her hands in his. "Remember, what you told me? God answers prayers."

She looked into his eyes, apparently considering his words. "You're right, Fred. Thank you." She smiled and seemed to unwind. "I'm sorry to talk so much about my problems when I'm with you. From now on I promise to be cheerful." She swung around gaily, still holding his hand, as they stepped off briskly toward the *Hauptwache*.

CHAPTER 8

In medieval times the *Hauptwache* was the main guardhouse of the city wall. It survived as a small building with stone arcades and a large terrace, the inside converted into a charming restaurant. When they arrived, it was early enough to find a table alone in one of the smaller rooms, which offered a degree of privacy. An old man in a worn formal jacket and bow tie came over and asked if they wished to order anything to drink. Fred looked at Gisela inquiringly. Her response surprised him.

"Fred, have you ever had a *Nicolaschka*?" A mischievous smile creased her face.

"No. What's that?"

"You'll see. "*Herr Ober, zwei Nicholaschka, bitte.*"

A few minutes later the waiter brought their drinks, two large shot glasses of amber liquid, with saucers containing slices of a lemon and a small container of ground coffee.

"What you do is to put the coffee on the lemon, and chew it. Then finish your drink all at once. Like this." Gisela sprinkled the coffee on the lemon like an expert, and chewed it with her eyes fixed on Fred. With a flourish she downed her drink in one swallow. She grinned. "Now it's your turn."

Fred looked dubious, but he wasn't about to back down. Following her example, he held a slice of lemon between his index finger and thumb as he applied the coffee, and then popped the concoction in his mouth. He grabbed his glass and took a big gulp, emptying it. His eyes were watering when he gasped, "Wow. What's in that drink?"

"Cognac. Only cognac. Did you like it?"

"Well, it certainly wakes you up. Where did you learn about this… this Nicholaschka?"

"Oh, I had a few dates before I was married," Gisela said coyly.

The waiter returned to ask if they were ready to order dinner. After listening to his recommendations and conferring with Gisela, Fred said,

"We would both like Rhönforellen (Mountain trout), and bring us a bottle of your best wine." When the waiter asked about their taste preference, Fred hesitated. He was more used to beer than wine. Gisela suggested a Reisling, and the old man hurried off to place the order. He was back soon with a bottle of Berncasteler that he showed Fred before giving him a sample. It tasted dry, he thought, but smooth. When he nodded his approval the waiter poured a glass for each of them.

Fred raised his glass to make a toast. "To happier days."

Gisela paused, and then touched her glass to his. "Yes, hopefully."

An awkward moment followed as Fred tried to think of something to say while Gisela seemed to be studying him. Fred broke the silence. "I've been meaning to mention that your English is really improving."

"Thank you. I have been getting much practice working at the PX. Frau Bishof lets me go to an English class for German employees two hours a week." He could see that his complement pleased her. With a note of pride in her voice, Gisela continued. "When she found out I could type, she gave me some monthly reports to do. So now I am getting paid more."

"That's great!" He couldn't help admiring her determination and hard work. "You've done a lot on your own."

She made a self-effacing gesture. "*Ja*, this last year was difficult, but people have been good to me here. A woman at the PX even found someone to care for Anna when I work."

"I'm glad for you. You've been through a lot." His mind returned to the scene at the *Zum Ritter*, and he rubbed his finger around the lip of his glass while he considered how to put into words what he was thinking. "I know that you think about Dieter every day. But you need to think about yourself—and Anna."

Their eyes met and they were silent for a few moments.

"There has not been time to think."

The food arrived and the waiter set the steaming dishes in front of them, making a grand show of service. With their permission he removed the fish skin and backbone and squeezed a few drops of lemon juice on the trout. Then he carefully ladled a creamy sauce over the fish, explaining the mixture of herbs that went into it. Finally he refilled their wine glasses before departing.

The second glass of wine helped restore Gisela's festive mood. Fred loosened up when he saw that she was enjoying herself. The food was delicious and their conversation was animated. He was surprised at how easily he was able to talk to her about his childhood, the pain of his father's death, and the problems with his stepfather. He joked about the struggle he had with academics at West Point, and the punishment hours he walked when he rebelled against silly hazing from upperclassmen who knew less about leadership than he did. He wanted to tell her about his time in Vietnam, but he held back concerned about how she might react.

Gisela shared happy memories of long walks with friends in the wooded hills of the Erzgebirge, the loneliness she felt when her mother died and she went to live with her aunt, her love of literature and art, and her disappointment when she dropped out of the university. Despite her setbacks she showed a sense of humor and laughed often, especially when he told her about trying when he was eleven to walk a bulldog that dragged him, running behind, around the neighborhood.

After the main course they ordered coffee and shared an *Eisbecher* of vanilla ice cream, chocolate sauce, nuts, cherries, and whipped cream. They lingered over coffee, continuing to laugh about silly things they had done in the past. It was dusk when Fred paid the bill and they stepped outside. Streetlights popped on as they stood on the steps of the restaurant, and Fred thought it was as if someone had taken a flash photograph to keep this night living in his memory.

They strolled along Friedrich Strasse until the lights of the Union Theater came in view. Gisela said hesitantly, "I haven't seen a movie in a long time."

"Well, I think you might like this. It's a comedy with Peter Sellers, in English with German subtitles. I've heard its funny, and it's another way to learn English."

The movie was *A Shot in the Dark*, and Gisela laughed so hard that she had to wipe tears from her eyes. Coming out of the theater she said, "That was wonderful. Thank you. I had a lot of fun tonight."

"So have I. I like watching you laugh. You are even more beautiful then."

She looked away and didn't reply. He took her hand and they started walking back to the car. Gisela turned her attention to the shop windows and began chatting about all the products that were available in the West. Fred nodded, finding it difficult to concentrate on anything but her. When they reached the car, he held the door while she got in. Then he walked around the car and sat behind the wheel, not starting the engine.

He turned and looked directly at her. "Gisela, there's something I want to tell you." There was a pause, and he cleared his throat. "I think I'm falling in love with you." In the streetlight's shadow he couldn't see her eyes clearly, but he felt her body stiffen. "I know," he added quickly. "It's too soon for you, but I just wanted to tell you how I feel."

She reached over and put a hand on his arm. "I feel strongly about you too, but I'm afraid to think about love. Each day I have to remind myself that Walter is dead and I won't see him again. I loved him, and I don't know if I can love again."

"You will! Anna needs a father, and your life can be full again. I need someone too, and I think I've found her."

Her response was disheartening. "Fred, you're a good man, and I like being with you. But I don't know. It's hard for me to think about the future. I keep dreaming about having my family back together, even though I know Walter is gone."

"I understand," he said slowly. "Until now there hasn't been much time in my life for a serious relationship. You've done something to me.

I love just being near you. And when I am away, I can't stop thinking about you."

He took her hand in his. "I'll be staying in Fulda for another year, so I can be patient. I'll do whatever I can to help you find Dieter. I just want to continue seeing you as often as possible."

Suddenly Gisela threw her arms around his neck. He wanted to kiss her, but before he could react, she moved away. She took a handkerchief from her purse and wiped her eyes. "You are the best thing that has happened to me here. I want to keep seeing you too. Thank you for understanding."

Lying in bed later Gisela couldn't sleep. When Fred brought her home, he kissed her. It wasn't a passionate, bursting-fireworks type of kiss; but it frightened her, not because of what he did, but because she was afraid to respond. The evening, and the kiss, had aroused feelings she couldn't suppress. Fred wasn't handsome, yet his enthusiasm was engaging. He was fun to be with and he made her feel secure. He was different from Walter who had been serious and intense in most things. His complements pleased her, and she realized that what he thought of her had become important. She could remember only three men who had ever told her that they loved her. One was a fellow student who was simply trying to get her into bed when she was seventeen; then Walter, and now Fred.

And what about her future? She was still young; but not many German men her age would want to marry a woman with one small child who was pining for another one.

Whenever these thoughts crossed her mind these past months, she pushed them aside. But Fred's words brought feelings alive that she couldn't ignore. Having him hold her felt good, and she missed that intimacy. He seemed to like Anna and was very attentive to her. And he was willing to help her in her quest for Dieter. Did that mean he would leave the Army and remain in Germany?

Most of all, did she love him? She knew it would never be the way she had loved Walter. Still she had to admit that she often found herself thinking about Fred. What if he grew tired of waiting and found someone else? For a minute she fantasized about being married to him and living in a nice house with Anna and Dieter. Then she drifted into a fitful sleep.

Across the border in Dermbach Erich and Inge Burchert were also considering their future. Erich had come home a little early from the Army Kaserne with an announcement.

"Inge, Oberst Leutnant Edinger telephoned to tell me that I have been selected for special training in chemical engineering at the Humboldt University in Berlin. It begins in August and would take two years."

"Eric, that's marvelous." Inge gave a squeal of delight, and kept smiling while Erich continued to explain.

"You know, this could be an important stepping stone for me. Only one officer a year from the Volksarmee is picked for this course." As he heard his own words, a new thought crossed his mind. It might even mean he was on a path to becoming a general some day.

"How exciting, *liebchen*." As if reading his mind, she said. "Now you are marked for promotion. No one is more dedicated than you. Even Honecker knows your name."

Ja, Honecker knows my name because of my father, he thought poignantly. They were in the Brandenburg Görden Prison together. His father was frail and no match for the Gestapo, so he didn't survive the war. But Honecker somehow managed to last for ten years until Soviet soldiers liberated him. Now he was the deputy premier.

"Maybe that helped in my selection, but I like to think they recognized my abilities."

"Of course they did," Inge said, as she took off her apron and joined Erich at the kitchen table. "What would you do when you finish the course?"

"I would probably be assigned to the Volksarmee staff to advise on the design of protective equipment and the use of chemical and nuclear weapons."

Inge was silent a moment, obviously thinking. "Where do you think we would live?"

Erich smiled confidently. "They tell me there's a new apartment complex near the university, and we should be entitled to a large apartment."

"Oh Eric, that sounds marvelous. Berlin will be much more exciting. Just think, operas, concerts, big stores, and nice restaurants. There is so much more to do there."

Just then Dieter came running in from the bedroom with Nicki bounding along behind him. "Hello Papa," he said sliding to a stop in front of Erich's chair. "Look what I have!" He held a stick in front of him. "I taught Nicki how to fetch. Look!" He started to throw the stick toward the living room, but Inge yelled, "Not in here, Dieter. You must play those games with Nicki outdoors."

Dieter lowered his arm, and Erich reached out and pulled the boy up on his lap. "Your Mama is right. But you are a good animal trainer and I am proud of you. I have a surprise to tell you. Soon we are going to move to a big city where you can see many animals in a wonderful zoo. They have lions, and tigers, bears, elephants, and even giraffes."

"Do they have monkeys?"

"*Oh, Ja*. Lots of monkeys, and gorillas too."

"Can we take Nicki, please Papa?"

Erich put a hand on Dieters shoulder, caressing him gently. "*Ja*. Nicki is a good dog and we will bring him to Berlin too. It's a big city and you both will like it."

At the mention of Berlin, Dieter looked momentarily confused. Erich and Inge exchanged worried glances. But with no further questions he slipped off Erich's lap and knelt in front of the dog. "Did you hear Nicki? We're going to Berlin. It's a big city and you're going to like it there."

On Saturday, John Parker returned to his apartment shortly after one o'clock in the afternoon. His uniform was rumpled and there were dark circles under his eyes, but he seemed quite chipper for someone who had worked through the night.

"Hi, honey." Gail kissed him as he came into the living room. "I thought you were coming home after you were relieved as staff duty officer."

"Well the old man had his own inspection laid on to get us ready for the Command Maintenance Inspection, and I thought I should be there. My platoon was in pretty good shape, and Captain Collins complemented us."

"This is a rare day, isn't it?" Gail said dryly.

"That's not all," John continued. "Afterward Captain Collins called me into his office and showed me my efficiency report. It was better than I expected. He had me next to the top block for potential, and his written comments were all positive."

"That's wonderful, John." Gail's tone was genuine. "I know how stressed you've been."

John collapsed into an armchair. He was surprised that Gail had sensed his anxiety. Collins didn't give much positive feedback, and with plenty of good lieutenants in the squadron, John had been worried. Until this day it was hard to know where he stood. "Anyway I feel a lot better about having an Army career."

"Is that what you still have your heart set on?" Gail had perched on the arm of his easy chair, and began rubbing his neck.

"Oh, that feels good," he said, stretching his arms and relaxing. "Yes I do. When I was a kid, it was the uniforms, the parades, and the war heroes that attracted me. Now it's the challenge of being in charge of a group of men, and keeping them motivated to follow me."

"What about your Dad's business? I thought he wanted you to join him after a stint in the army."

"Yeah, he's mentioned that a couple of times. I know he wants to retire or at least only work part time sometime soon. He's getting up in years. But that's not for me." Gail stopped the massage, and he turned to look up at her.

"You want to know what I think? Promise you won't laugh?" Gail's eyes widened, and she nodded.

"Remember what President Kennedy said when he was inaugurated?"

"Uh…something about what you can do for your country?"

"That's it. 'Ask not what your country can do for you, but what you can do for your country.' It might sound corny, but those words have stuck with me—especially after he was assassinated. I think the best way I can contribute, is by serving in the army."

Gail stepped away from the chair, and looked out the window. After a minute she turned to face John with a look of concern.

"That's what worries me, John. I dread the thought of you being gone, and in danger, while I have to be both mother and father to the kids."

"I know Gail." He reached out and took her hand. "I don't know when and if it will happen, but that's part of being in the Army. Look, we know lots of couples who have been through these separations and who still have strong marriages."

He stifled a yawn. "Let's not try to figure out the future right now. I'm just relieved to know I'm doing okay. Even though I didn't get much sleep as SDO, I feel like celebrating. Why don't we go out to dinner or to a movie tonight?"

Gail looked like she wanted to say more on the subject, but then her expression changed. "I'd like that, and you deserve a celebration. I'll see about a baby-sitter."

"Speaking of babies, is Susie taking a nap?"

"Yes. She was up late last night when Anna was here, so she will probably stay down for a while."

John pulled his wife onto his lap. "Then why don't we take a nap together?"

PART TWO

APRIL 1966-JULY 1968

James Pocock

CHAPTER 9

When John Parker pulled into the driveway of his duplex in the Godwin Housing Area of Fort Knox, it was growing dark and he was bone tired. The WHAS radio announcer was giving a follow-up report to the April 15th anti-war parade in New York, which attracted over 100,000 people the previous day to hear Martin Luther King and others protest US policy in Vietnam. John was angered to hear that 200 youths had burned their draft cards in Central Park. Since his arrival at the Armor Training Center six months ago, he had become fed up with anti-war demonstrators and draft dodgers.

As he stepped through the front door, he could see a light in the kids' room and hear Gail's voice. He was relieved to make it home before the kids were asleep. He had been up since 0500 when he joined his drill sergeants for the morning run with their new recruits. Tossing his field jacket and cap on a chair he hurried down the hallway.

He pushed open the door of the children's bedroom, and saw Gail rocking eighteen month old, Matthew, on her lap as she read to him. Susie sat on the bed next to Gail.

"Daddy! Daddy!" Susie ran across the hardwood floor in her stocking pajamas and John knelt to give her a hug. "Daddy." She pulled on his arm. "Read us a story."

John picked her up and carried her to the bed. "Sure, Susie, but let me rest a minute first." He bent over, kissed Gail, and tousled Matthew's hair. "Sorry to be so late, honey. Had a couple of problems that needed fixing at our evening training meeting."

He pulled off his dusty boots and lay down next to Susie. "Let Mommy finish the story and then I'll read you a short one."

Ten minutes later he joined Gail in the living room. "I almost fell asleep reading *The Three Bears*."

"I'm not surprised. You're not getting much sleep on this job. Do you want something to eat?"

"No thanks, I'm fine. I ate in the mess hall with the troops." He eased into the armchair next to hers. "But I have some news I think you'll like."

Gail took another stitch in Susie's pants, and looked up expectantly. John was beaming with pleasure.

"I talked to a major from Armor Branch Office in the Pentagon this morning. He said they have me slated to take the Armor Officers Advance Course next fall. So the end is in sight for me as a basic training commander."

Gail put down her sewing. "I'm glad to hear that. Maybe we can have more time together as a family." She didn't seem very excited, as if her mind was on something else. "How long does the course last?"

"About six months, if I'm selected for the nuclear weapons phase. And you're right. It's pretty much an eight hour training day, Monday through Friday, with almost no weekend duty." He was disappointed that Gail didn't share his enthusiasm.

"And then what happens? Will we stay here or will you be sent to Vietnam?"

"It's hard to say. There are nearly 400,000 troops over there now. Unless the country mobilizes the reserve, everyone on active duty is going to end up in Vietnam. So it's not a question of will I go, but rather when."

She looked up at him hopefully. "John, you don't have to go to Vietnam. Your obligation is almost up. Why not take your Dad's offer, or find another job?" She leaned forward and spoke excitedly. "I don't mind moving to Michigan or anywhere that we can have a normal family life. You could help build up your Dad's business or work for Ford or GM. You're a good manager, and you'd make more money than you ever will in the Army. We could buy a house, and the kids wouldn't have to change schools every couple of years."

John was taken back by her reaction.

"Gail, we've talked about this before. I'm not interested in a civilian job," he said wearily. He thought a minute. "I've got an obligation to serve in Vietnam just like any soldier. When that time comes you can move near your folks, and you'll have family and friends around to help you. So in the meantime let's make the most of the time I'll be in the Advance Course."

Gail lowered her head. "I'm sorry honey. I just get lonely when you're gone so much. I'm afraid it'll be much worse when you're away for a year, especially worrying if you'll come home in one piece."

John slid off his chair to kneel in front of her. He reached out and lifted her chin with his hand. "Don't be down now. Things are going to be better for a while, and we shouldn't worry about what we can't change." He kissed her, and stood up, pulling her up with him. "I love you, Gail." He held her close, not letting go.

"Oh, John. I love you too."

Later, John had trouble falling asleep. It bothered him that Gail had tears in her eyes when he knelt by her chair.

In the fashionable Potsdam district of East Berlin, Erich and Inge Burchert were getting ready to leave their apartment. Inge wore a long green dress set off with a strand of pearls, and Erich had changed into a dark civilian suit with a maroon tie. It was early evening and Frau Gruber had come from an upstairs apartment to care for Dieter. While Inge went over instructions with the baby sitter, Dieter came into the living room carrying a piece of paper. Erich stood near the door.

"Look what I did in school, Papa," Dieter said, holding up the paper.

The paper was lined and filled with upper and lower case printing of the letter A in a child's hand. "We are learning how to write, Papa. See what the teacher said."

"This is something, Dieter. The first paper you wrote. And your teacher wrote *Sehr Gut* on the paper. Well done." Erich leaned down and put his hand on the boy. "I'm very proud of you, Dieter. How do you like school?"

"Um—I like it. I like playing with the other boys and girls."

"That is good, but you must pay attention and do your best on everything the teacher tells you."

Inge walked over to Dieter and tucked in his shirt. "Isn't he doing well, dear?" The pride she felt for her son took a somewhat different form than her husband's. It was part contentment and part relief that Dieter had come to accept them as parents. She took his hand, leading him to a place on the sofa where her neighbor had taken a seat.

"Now Frau Gruber is going to read to you until it is time for bed. Mama and Papa are going to be out until after you are asleep. But we will be back soon after that to kiss you good night. Do what Frau Gruber tells you and remember to brush your teeth."

"Yes Mama." Dieter obediently climbed onto the sofa and looked at the picture book Frau Gruber spread open in her lap while Inge and Eric walked out the front door.

As Erich drove their Trabant out of the apartment complex, Inge said, "I'm so happy that Dieter is adjusting better. I believe he doesn't think so often about his real parents."

"*Ja.* He is doing better. It helps that you only work mornings and can spend more time with him. Of course, the dog made a difference. He seemed to improve after Nicki arrived."

"Oh, Erich, everything is better in Berlin. Imagine, going to the opera again like we did when we were first married!"

"*Ja,*" Erich said slowly. "Those were good years. But I have a confession...I don't like opera, especially Wagner."

"Erich, many of the generals and government ministers will be there with their wives. It's important that we be seen and make some contacts." Besides, she thought, I like operas and concerts, and the chance to see some of Berlin's social life. "And I've always wanted to see *The Flying Dutchman*. It has such beautiful music. What's wrong with Wagner?"

"He may be German, but I don't like him." When she looked perplexed, he continued. "It's because of Hitler. He identified Wagner so much with the Third Reich that I can't listen to Wagner without thinking about the damned Nazis. I prefer good socialist composers like Prokofiev or Stravinski. When their operas are playing, you'll really see a lot of the party big wigs."

"Well we can save those for another time. Anyway, I'm sure important people will be there who we can talk to. I just wish you would wear your dress uniform."

"I'm here as a student, not as part of a military unit," he protested. "I want to relax and not be conspicuous."

"It's good for you to be noticeable, dear. You're going to be one of the top leaders in this country, and I want to see you there sooner, rather than later. And mark my words! Dieter will follow in your footsteps some day!"

The day after John quashed her idea of leaving the Army, Gail sat alone in the living room folding laundry while Matt napped and Susie played in the bedroom. With the hours he's working we don't seem to have time for each other any more, she brooded. Why can't he be more sympathetic? She yearned for the cuddling intimacy of their early months of marriage. And while it may seem noble to him, she was frightened at the prospect of him going to Vietnam.

There was another concern that worried her. She was more than a month late for her period. If she were pregnant, she would have three young children on her hands while John was in Vietnam. The more she thought, the more depressed she became. Suddenly the tears started, and she buried her face in a towel to muffle her sobs.

It took several days for Gail to regain her positive view of life, aided by two surprises. The first was when John came home early on Friday with a bouquet of flowers, and took her out for supper without the children. Then on Saturday John took advantage of the end of a basic training cycle by taking the family on an excursion to Bardstown where they toured My Old Kentucky Home and had a picnic in Bernheim Forest.

The other surprise was news from Fulda. Gail read the letter twice and couldn't resist the urge to call John at work. He wasn't in the office, but the orderly room clerk said he would leave a message for him to call home. About an hour later her phone rang.

"I got your message Gail. What's up? Are you and the kids okay?"

"We're fine, honey. But we got a letter with some wonderful news and I just couldn't wait to tell you. Gisela wrote that she and Fred are getting married."

"Wow, that is something. When is the wedding?"

"Next month in Fulda. She says it's just going to be a small affair in St. Michaels with a few friends, and Fred's family. Oh John, I wish we could go."

"So do I, dear. But I can't get leave now, and besides we don't have the money for a trip."

"I know, but it's exciting to dream about it anyway."

"Well, let's send them a nice gift and welcome Gisela into the ranks of Army wives. Maybe we'll see them in the states. I don't think Fred can extend much longer in Germany." There was a pause and Gail could hear John talking to someone. "Sorry, the Colonel is on the other line. I'll talk to you more when I get home. Bye."

The following Wednesday, Gail returned from her appointment with the obstetrician at Ireland Army Hospital with mixed feelings. He had confirmed her earlier fear; she was definitely pregnant. But after she thought about it she was happy to know they would have another child. They had always wanted more than two; and even though the timing wasn't perfect, she was beginning to feel confident that she could handle it. John would be there the first few months after the baby was born, and her parents and friends could help later. Besides, she loved babies, and knew that Susie and Matt would too. How John would react was another matter. The first thing she did when she was home was to arrange for a baby sitter that evening. Then she called John. She was doubly lucky: he was in the office, and he said he could get away in time for dinner at the club.

"But what's the occasion?" he asked. "We just went out last Friday."

"Well, it's a surprise," she laughed. "So you'll just have to wait to find out."

By the time they were seated at a table at the Brick Club, officially called the Fort Knox Officers Open Mess, John was almost out of patience with Gail's evasiveness.

"What is it, Gail? I thought we might be meeting someone." A waitress came up to their table with his drink order before she could answer. "Are you sure you don't want a glass of wine, or something?" he asked.

"No, dear," she smiled. I'm watching my figure."

"Well, as far as I can see you don't have a problem there."

"That's part of the surprise, John." She reached out and took his hand. "I just found out today. We're going to have another baby."

For a moment John was speechless, and his expression was blank, as if his mind wasn't processing what he'd heard. Then he smiled—not his triumphant I've just hit the jackpot smile—but a sincere, comforting smile that made her know it would be okay.

"That's wonderful, honey," he said looking into her eyes. "When?"

"In November—around Thanksgiving. Oh John, I know we weren't planning to have another one this soon. A few weeks ago I was afraid that I forgot to take a birth control pill, and now I know for sure." She saw a look of concern in his eyes and added quickly. "I'm happy about it John, and I'll be fine. Don't worry if you have to leave."

"I'm happy too, Gail. And let's be optimistic. Maybe the war will be over before I have to go."

Gail knew there was little chance of that, but at the moment it didn't matter.

CHAPTER 10

In the late afternoon of a warm spring day in 1967 Gail looked out the kitchen window and saw a blue Porsche pull up and stop in front of their quarters. She dropped the head of lettuce she was washing into the sink, and reached for a towel to dry her hands. At the same moment Susie banged open the front screen door and yelled, "They're here, Mommy! They're here!"

"Yes, honey. I see." She lifted her slumbering baby from his infant seat on the counter, thinking how much she had been looking forward to this day. John was buttoning his shirt as he followed a toddling Matt down the hallway. As Gail reached the front step she saw a smiling woman coming toward her with outstretched arms. A little girl was shyly holding on to the woman's yellow pleated skirt. John was moving toward the far side of the car to greet a familiar figure dressed in slacks and a polo shirt.

"Gisela," she said, giving her a hug with one hand while holding the baby in the other. "It's so good to see you again. Congratulations on your marriage. And Anna, how much you've grown. You remember Susie, don't you? She pushed her suddenly timid daughter toward Anna.

"It's wonderful to see you too Gail." Gisela leaned over for a closer look at the little one. "*Und das kindchen*. What a beautiful baby!"

Fred came up and, after embracing Gail, joined Gisela in admiring the sleeping infant. John greeted Gisela with a hug and said, "Welcome to Fort Knox, Mrs. Newman."

Gisela tossed her head back and laughed. "Hello, John. I'm still getting used to my married name. So many changes these last months… it's good to see friends from Fulda." Still holding Paul, Gail took Gisela's arm and they walked slowly toward the Parker's side of the duplex.

"We spent a few days in New York, so I could show Gisela and Anna around the city and West Point," Fred said to John. "After that we drove on to Kentucky. We stayed with my mother in Jeffersontown for another week, and then visited my sister in Lexington."

"Where will you be assigned?"

"I'm going to be working at the Armor Agency on new tank development. So I'll be away from troops for a while."

"Sounds interesting." John opened the screen door and Gail led their friends inside. Susie and Anna rushed by with Matt tagging behind. Susie shouted, "Come on, Anna! See my Barbies."

Gail showed Gisela the kitchen and living room before taking her down the hall to Susie and Matt's bedroom. As the children sat on the floor playing, Gisela said, "May I hold the baby?" Paul opened his eyes when Gail placed him in Gisela's arms. Instead of crying, his mouth opened in what appeared to be a smile. It might have been a gas pain, Gail thought. Whatever the case, Gisela was delighted.

"Oh, Gail. He's so sweet. Like an angel." She put a finger on his mouth and made cooing sounds.

"He has been an angel—at least so far. Much easier than Susie. Of course it's harder with the first one—being new and everything." After a few minutes Paul began fussing, and Gisela handed him back to Gail.

"You're lucky, Gail—to have two boys and a girl! We're hoping to have a child of our own," she confided. "No sign of one yet, unfortunately. Fred really wants a son."

"You've come to the right place then. Lots of babies are born at Knox, and they have a fine maternity ward."

John and Fred stayed in the kitchen talking while John got a couple of beers out of the refrigerator.

"So you've got orders for Nam already," Fred said. "What unit?"

"Headquarters, MAC-V (Military Assistance Command-Vietnam) in Saigon, but from what I hear, I'll probably end up in one of the provinces. There aren't that many armor units in Vietnam, so a lot of us are being sent over as advisors to the Vietnamese." John motioned for Fred to follow him into the large room that served as living room and dining room, and they settled into armchairs.

"In '63 all we had there were advisors and aviators." Fred set his beer can down, and looked wistfully past John out the window. "I had just finished Ranger training and was gung ho, so I volunteered for Vietnam. I spent a year with an ARVN ranger battalion at Tay Ninh in the Delta. Learned a lot about Vietnam, but it was pretty lonely with only two other Americans for company. Even got so I liked *Ncoc Mam* sauce before I left."

Turning back to John, Fred smiled. "By the way, congratulations on your promotion. Saw your name on the list in *The Army Times.* You're moving right along."

"Thanks, Fred. I'm indebted to you." He ignored Fred's protestations, adding, "Hey. You're my mentor. And I wanted to ask if you think I need to get more command time for promotion to major. After I get to Vietnam, I might try to get transferred to an American unit where I could be a company commander."

"Hm. How does Gail feel about that? You might have to extend your tour."

"I haven't mentioned it to her. I'm afraid it would upset her."

Fred leaned forward in his chair. "One of my best friends did that. Extended his tour to get a command. Two months later he was killed leading an attack. Sometimes its not worth trying to push fate."

John started to say something in response, but at that moment the ladies walked into the living room.

"I'm sorry to hear that you're leaving for Vietnam. And so soon," Gisela said to John.

"I am too—especially now that you and Fred are here. But Gail will be staying on in Louisville. We've found a place to rent not far from her folks. Anyway, we'll have a few weeks before I go. Maybe we can help you move in, and then you can give us a hand on our move to Louisville.

"I don't know how soon we'll be able to get quarters on post," Fred said. "I called when we were in New York, and I was told there was a three-month wait. But they said things might change when your Advance Course graduated."

"Where are you staying tonight?" Gail asked.

"We're checked into the post guest house for tonight, and I'll stop by Billeting first thing in the morning to see what's available. If it will only be a few weeks for government quarters, we'll probably stay at my mother's and I'll commute."

John turned to Gisela. "So what do you think of America, Gisela?"

"Oh, it's so big… many houses with nice yards. And Kentucky is lovely in the spring—flowers blooming, and everything is green." She gestured toward the row of flowers along the patio divider that could be seen through the back window. "Also I like the people. They say *honey* to me in the shops. 'Have a nice day, *honey*,'" she mimicked, and then laughed.

"Gisela, what have you heard about Dieter," John asked.

Gisela's smile faded, and she turned toward John with such a serious expression that he regretted the question.

"*Ja.* We know for sure that he is alive. For two years I got no reply to any letters that I sent to the East German government. I wrote everyone I could think of, including Ulbricht." Her voice was strained, and John noticed her hands were twisting and untwisting a tissue. She paused for a moment. "A day doesn't go by that I don't think about him." She stopped talking and seemed to be making an effort to control her emotions. Fred glanced at her and picked up the narrative.

"I suggested that we see a lawyer, and we found one who had a contact in the Foreign Office in Bonn. Through him, West Germany made a formal request for information about Dieter, and about two months ago we finally got an answer. They said that because Dieter's father was dead and there were no known relatives living in the DDR, Dieter was a ward of the state. He was placed for adoption, but we can't get the name of his new family."

Gisela stood and began pacing in front of Fred. "I get so angry every time I think about what they have done to Dieter…and to me. I want to go back and confront the rulers and make them listen to reason." Her hands were clenched, and her voice was rising. "Ulbricht and his henchmen are cruel monsters."

Fred put his hand on her arm and said soothingly, "At least we know that Dieter is being cared for. In the meantime our lawyer is going to keep trying to find out where he is through informal contacts."

"What a heartless system," John looked at Gisela sadly. "If only I had been able to reach him. I've re-lived that night over and over. If I could have just…"

They were all looking at him. From Gail's expression John realized it was the first time she understood the depth of his anguish. Fred was first to speak.

"You did all you could, John. You had already exceeded your orders. Anything more could have made things a lot worse."

Gisela added quietly, "Don't feel bad, John. Fred told me what happened with the Grenztruppen shooting, and you being on the wrong side of the border. No one blames you for what happened to Dieter."

"We're not giving up," Fred said. "I've promised Gisela that we'll go back to Germany on future assignments. And if anything changes while we're in the states, we'll take leave to go there."

For a few moments no one said anything until Gail changed the mood in a cheerful voice. "How is Anna adjusting to her new life?"

"She loves Fred," Gisela relaxed and sat on the arm of Fred's chair, her arm on his shoulder. "He has been wonderful to her, and she thinks of him as her papa. But she has been moved around a lot, and I think it will be good for her to live close to other children. She seems lonely sometimes."

Someone else was thinking about Anna that day. After school Dieter had been invited to a birthday party for Karl Schneider, one of the boys in his school. At the party Dieter needed to use the toilet, and when he came out of the bathroom, he saw a familiar figure in the adjoining bedroom.

He stepped into the room and said, "Anna? Anna?"

A little girl with short dark hair was in a crib, her hands clutching the top rail as she rocked back and forth. She was about a year and a half old, and looked at him quizzically. She made some talking sounds, but all he could understand was, "Mama."

Dieter stood looking at her for a minute. Confused, he backed out of the room and walked back to the party in a daze. When Karl opened his gifts, his mother carried the little girl into the living room and sat down holding her on her lap. Dieter couldn't take his eyes off her. Moving over to where Karl was unwrapping a toy truck, Dieter asked, "Who is she?"

"Who? Oh, her. That's Brigitte, my sister."

"I have a sister too. Her name...her name is Anna," Dieter mumbled. But Karl had picked up another package and wasn't listening. None of the other boys paid any attention to Dieter either.

Later, as he was walking home with Inge, Dieter asked, "Where is my sister?"

"What?"

"Where is Anna?"

The questions jolted Inge. It had been more than a year since Dieter had made any reference to his birth family. Even then she couldn't remember his talking about a sister.

"I don't know Dieter. You remember we told you about your mother and father. They are gone forever and your sister is gone too."

"Are they dead? Is my sister dead too?"

"*Ja.* I don't know the details, but she may as well be dead too."

"Was her name Anna?"

"I don't know. I would have to go to some office and look at documents to find out." She stopped walking and turned to face him. "Why are you asking all these questions, Dieter?"

"I saw a little girl at Karl's who looked like…" His voice trailed off, and he looked down. Quietly he said, "But she was Karl's sister, and then I thought that I had a sister, too."

"Well you don't now." Inge bent down in front of him and pulled his chin up so she could fix his eyes on hers. "I'm sorry you have had to go through this turmoil, Dieter. Your parents were bad people who were trying to harm this country. But that was long ago, and they are gone forever. Now forget about them. You have your papa and me, and we are your parents. Your name is Dieter Burchert. We are going to help you grow up to be a great man. You will be someone who everybody will be proud to know."

Inge straightened his shirt and stood. Taking his hand she said, "Now put those thoughts out of your mind, and hold your head up. We must hurry. Your papa will be home soon, and I need to fix dinner."

Alone in his bed that night, Dieter had trouble sleeping. He missed the wooden beads that Inge had taken away, but she said that he was a big boy and didn't need them. After a long time he fell asleep, and dreamed of being in a room with another mama and papa, and playing blocks on the floor with his sister, Anna. She knocked over the blocks, and he woke up sobbing. Nicki climbed onto the bed and nuzzled his head next to Dieter who hugged the dog and finally stopped crying. Dieter still had his arm around the dog when Inge went into his room in the morning to wake him.

John Parker drove up in front of the terminal at Louisville's Standiford Field, stopping near the TWA sign. He was wearing a freshly starched khaki uniform and overseas cap. Gail got out of the front seat and helped the children out of the car while John got a duffel bag and worn suitcase out of the trunk. He stood for a moment looking at Gail in the orange and white dress that was his favorite. She had dressed Susie and Matthew in their Sunday best, but they left Paul with Gail's mother. John felt another pang of regret. He loved them, and the thought of being gone for thirteen months made him feel guilty. He kissed Gail and held her tightly for a few moments.

"Good by, darling. I love you. Remember that always."

"I love you too, John." Leaning back she raised a hand to his cheek. Her chin quivered. "Don't try to be a hero, old buddy. Come home safely!"

They had discussed his leaving and neither wanted an emotional, public scene at the airport. Their farewell took place in the quiet hours of the previous night when their expression of love could be more passionate and lasting.

One at a time John picked up each child.

"Susie, you're a big girl, now. Help Mommy while I'm gone." He kissed her, and set her down.

"Matthew, be a good boy. I'll be back to wrestle with you, and you'll be bigger too." Then his voice caught, and he said huskily, "I love you."

Then he turned quickly before the tears that were forming in Gail's eyes could affect him as well. Picking up his bags he strode into the terminal, stopping briefly by the window to wave good by.

In the terminal waiting room he reflected that the past six weeks had gone by in a blur. There was a graduation party the mood of which wasn't dampened by the fact that most of the class had orders for Vietnam. His fellow officers were happy to be finished with the tedium of classes and studying, and the ladies were excited to have a fine dinner and dancing. The short graduation ceremony the next day had been anticlimactic. He had hoped to be the top graduate among one hundred twenty captains and senior lieutenants, but he was satisfied to be among the top ten.

As expected, the Newman's were put on a waiting list for government quarters at Fort Knox, and moved in temporarily with his mother forty miles away in Jeffersontown. Nevertheless, John and Gail saw them frequently. Gail spent several hours showing Gisela around the post, and one day helped her through the maze at Ireland General Hospital to get immunization shots for Anna. John and Fred found time for a round of golf, neither playing well but enjoying the warm weather. Lindsey Golf Course provided them a unique view of the Gold Vault along the boundary of one hole, while paratroopers jumped from C130 aircraft in the distance.

Gail's mother helped them locate a small, three-bedroom home to rent four blocks from Eastern Parkway near Cherokee Park. Unpacking, hanging curtains, assembling a swing set, and building storage shelves had kept John busy. Still there had been time for a short trip to visit his folks in Michigan and for back yard barbecues with friends and family in Louisville.

As John boarded the jet for the first leg of his flight, he wrestled with a mixture of emotions. There were a few other young men in uniforms aboard, but he was traveling alone. No Army bands or men who had forged close friendships through months of training were there to boost his morale. This wasn't World War II with the whole country mobilized for the cause. Still there was the excitement of embarking on an adventure, which might test his courage and determine his future. But he realized there was no such excitement for Gail or the children. They faced thirteen months of loneliness without the support of a group of others sharing the same burden.

Three months later John shielded his eyes from the bright sunshine outside Tan An when the fluttering sound of helicopter blades focused his attention on several approaching specks in the blue sky. A string of Hueys descended toward the makeshift airstrip outside the capital city of Long An Province. John stood next to his radio operator, Private First Class Cowan, waiting for the airlift that would take them and the Province Reconnaissance Unit (PRU) deep into an area under the control of the Viet Cong (VC). Their leader, Dai Uy (Captain) Minh, a tough looking Vietnamese wearing a black beret, had a map spread in front of him, pointing out positions to his two lieutenants. Cowan couldn't stand still, walking back and forth, checking his radio, and testing the firing mechanism of his M-16 rifle. John was nervous too, but tried not to show it.

PFC Cowan was new to the advisor team, coming to Vietnam directly from a hastily organized basic training program at Fort Hood, Texas. Lanky and awkward, Cowan was one of McNamara's "Hundred Thousand," a recent group of draftees accepted into the Army after

Defense Secretary McNamara lowered the mental and physical standards for classification. A high school drop out from Oklahoma, who had worked at a filling station and lived with his widowed mother, Cowan shunned tobacco and alcohol and wasn't embarrassed to be seen reading the small Bible he kept in his jungle fatigues. He was only eighteen, eager to please, and had taken a shine to Parker.

Cowan said, "Sir, I've never been in combat before. What should I do when we hit the ground?" John put a hand on the young soldier's shoulder and replied, "No sweat, Cowan. Just stay close to me and do what you've been trained to do. After the first few minutes you'll forget about being scared."

John wished he felt as confident as he sounded. This was the first combat operation where they would be inserted into the target area by American helicopters, and coordination would be tricky. He worried about hitting a hot LZ, and whether the PRU force would get too spread out.

In a surprisingly short time ten troop carrying choppers touched down, loaded eighty PRU soldiers with their two advisors and lifted off. As John looked out the door of the lead chopper, the green, fertile landscape fell away beneath his feet. The muddy waters of the Van Co Tay River were visible, snaking northwest of the town into the Plain of Reeds and beyond to Cambodia. Then the pilot banked to the left, beginning a turn to the west. Their destination was a remote spot in the swampy jungle of Can Giuoc District.

In the time John had spent in Long An as S2 (Intelligence) Advisor, he had learned a good deal about the strategically important province lying south and west of Saigon. A vital agricultural region of rice and sugar cane production, its 350,000 people were spread among seven districts from the Rung Sat, (Jungle of Death) on the east coast, to The Plain of Reeds that spread westward to Cambodia. Two important land routes, Highway 4 in the west and Highway 5 in the east, ran through Long An connecting Saigon to the provinces in the south.

Crammed into the cargo space of the Huey with John were PFC Cowan, Captain Minh, four other PRU soldiers, and a guide, Tran Van Dong. The Province Reconnaissance Unit was a mobile strike force, trained to react quickly to hard intelligence about the Viet Cong. The hard intelligence in this event had been developed by interrogation of Tran Van Dong, a Viet Cong deserter. After an aerial recon with John and the Province S2, Dong willingly pinpointed the location of what he claimed was a VC training camp. John and the S2 then went to the Province Chief and, instead of the usual foot-dragging, got immediate approval for an operation against the enemy camp.

Because the regular PRU advisor was on leave, John was taking his place as well as providing liaison for other US support that might be needed. Dong said there were approximately fifty armed soldiers of the 506th VC Battalion in the camp area, and John hoped his force would achieve surprise. Previous efforts had discouraged him about the effectiveness of South Vietnamese intelligence and the prospect of launching an attack that actually surprised the VC. Among advisors there was strong suspicion that there were a number of VC spies within the Province Headquarters. The South Vietnamese didn't seem able to make any contact with the enemy that the VC didn't initiate, usually by over-running an isolated outpost.

Using a spare headset, John listened to the radio chatter between the pilot and copilot as they checked navigational landmarks with their maps. After twenty minutes of flying, he got a cryptic message from the pilot. "We're 2 minutes from the LZ, Captain. Get your people ready."

John poked Dai Uy Minh in the arm to get his attention, and pointed down. Holding up two fingers, he pointed at his watch and shouted, "Two Minutes!" The others were watching and began readying themselves for a rapid exit from the chopper. They were going in cold. There was no artillery preparation of the landing zone, and they had no gunships to suppress enemy reaction.

Their helicopter made a sharp dive and leveled off just above the ground. The crew chief tapped John on the shoulder and he jumped three feet on to a dry rice paddy. Minh, Cowan and the others were right behind him. As he ran in a crouch toward the paddy dike, John was aware of cascades of gunfire above the din of the departing choppers. The PRU soldiers were moving in a fairly decent skirmish line toward the dike and firing as they moved with everything they had. Halfway to the paddy dike, he noticed puffs of dirt erupting in front of him and realized that some of the gunfire was coming from the far tree line. Out of the corner of his eye he saw one of the PRUs suddenly twist around and crumple to the ground. Then they reached the cover of the paddy dike, and he lay panting next to Dai Uy Minh who was shouting to his soldiers and yelling instructions to his radio operator.

John rolled over to reach for his radio, but Cowan was not near him. Glancing back he saw several figures lying immobile in the dry rice paddy they had traversed. A short radio antenna stuck out at an angle from one of them. He yelled, "Cowan, Cowan." But there was no movement from the figure.

He crawled back and found Cowan face down with his helmet askew and a rivulet of blood along the left side of his face. Reaching his arm across Cowan's back, he rolled the motionless figure over. There was a small hole oozing blood above the boy's left eye. His mouth was open, but there was no pulse and no life left in the body of the young soldier whom he had led to his death.

The rest of the action went by in a blur. Somehow he dragged Cowan's body back to the paddy dike. He directed air strikes at the tree line and beyond. The PRUs advanced by using a base of fire and trying to maneuver around the VC. There were more casualties among the PRUs. Medevacs were called for their wounded, and Cowan's body left with them. The VC broke contact and melted into the jungle, taking most of their casualties. A base camp was found with two VC bodies. Like Cowan, they were just teenagers. The Hueys came back, and he clambered aboard with the rest of the PRU force.

The return to their Tan An base was depressing for John. Although the province chief claimed victory, he knew otherwise. It was clear the VC had been tipped off. They knew about the attack, and were ready. Not only was it a failure, it was Cowan's wasted death that made him begin to doubt their purpose in Vietnam. A young life cut short. Cowan never had a chance to experience the deep love of a woman, to marry, or to raise children. He may not have been brilliant, but he was a good man and deserved to live. What a waste!

The failed attack made John question the commitment of their Vietnamese allies. Until now he had ignored reports of corruption and cronyism in the Vietnamese chain of command. Apparently some province officials were willing to accommodate the VC as long as their positions were not threatened. Although he had no doubts that Thanh and Minh were fighters, John was aware of advisors' complaints that some Vietnamese officers were content to sit back and let the Americans fight their war. He began to doubt the cause that brought him to Vietnam. Was it worth risking his life and the lives of Americans like Cowan, he wondered?

CHAPTER 11

Ring! Ring! The noise of the telephone increased the throbbing in Gail's forehead, and she hurried into her bedroom, trying to reach the phone before the next ring that might wake the children. She had just gotten them all down for naps, including Susie who, at four and a half, usually put up a fuss about even a brief rest period in the afternoon. A virus had been going around that seemed to have reached each of them at different stages, and just after lunch Susie had thrown up and complained that her head hurt.

Gail grabbed the telephone receiver just as the next ring was starting, and breathlessly answered it.

"Hello, Gail. How are you and the children?"

"Oh. Hi, Gisela. Not so good. Now Susie is sick, and the boys aren't any better. I'm trying to get a doctor's appointment."

"Well, I'm driving into Louisville tomorrow to do some shopping, and I thought I might stop by with Anna to see the baby. But it sounds like this is not a good time, with the children feeling sick."

"I really would like to see you and Anna, but to be honest, I think I'm catching the same bug they have. I'm sorry, Gisela. I want you to come. I get so lonely with John gone. It seems like all I do is take care of the kids." She looked out the window and saw that the rain had changed to wet snow that was beginning to make the yard look white, but wasn't sticking to the sidewalks or streets. It was a dreary day that matched her mood.

"What have you heard from John lately? Is he all right?"

"His last letter was about a week ago. It was fairly quiet in his sector over Christmas, and he was feeling better. You know he picked up a case of hook worms—evidently from tromping around in the rice paddies."

For a moment, Gail's mind strayed from the conversation with Gisela to thoughts of John…wishing he was there to help with the kids…missing the reassurance of his comforting arms…hoping for a letter.

Gisela was talking, and Gail made an effort to focus. She was saying something about worrying that Fred might have to go to Vietnam again, and then asked, "How is the baby—other than being sick, I mean?"

"Um…Okay, I guess. I mean…until this week he's been fine. He's almost seven months now, and if I nurse him just before I go to bed, he usually sleeps through the night." As Gail thought about sleep, she realized how tired she was. There were a million things she wanted to talk about, but at the moment the need to sleep was overwhelming.

As if reading her mind, Gisela said, "You sound tired, Gail. Better get some rest. I'll call in a few days, and we'll find another time to get together."

Gail didn't want to end the conversation. But her mind was telling her to get a nap before the children woke, so reluctantly she said good-by to Gisela.

She hung up the phone and laid down on the bed. She closed her eyes, but couldn't shut off the thoughts that ran through her mind. The last time Dad was over he smelled gas, but the furnace repairman checked everything two days ago and couldn't find anything wrong. The dishwasher had broken last week, and they were waiting on a part to get that fixed, and the car kept stalling on her.

And she was bothered about the argument she had with her sister and brother-in-law about Vietnam. It had spoiled Christmas at her parents, and it made her angry every time she thought about it. Her Dad made the mistake of saying that he thought President Johnson was wrong to have gotten the US so deeply involved in what was essentially a civil war in Vietnam. Then Karen chimed in that America had no right to be killing innocent Vietnamese; and Karen's long-haired husband, Bob, bragged about participating in a demonstration against the war at the University of Kentucky. Karen was a secretary in the U of K Admissions Office, supporting them both while Bob worked on a master's degree in economics. It was Bob's fourth year of graduate study, and it was becoming apparent that he was more interested in a draft deferment than the degree.

Gail had watched TV coverage of the demonstration in front of the ROTC offices, and was appalled. Several hippies burned a US flag and spray-painted anti-war slogans on the building before campus police finally managed to arrest a handful and disperse the rest. Bob's smug boasting about his involvement in the anti-war movement lit a fuse in Gail, and she finally exploded in a furious denunciation of his intelligence, his patriotism, and his manhood. Karen came to his defense, and before her parents could calm things down, Gail had told her sister and brother-in-law that they should be ashamed of themselves while John's life was on the line in Vietnam. Then she gathered up the kids, and left the house in tears.

And she couldn't talk to her mother about her problems without getting some sort of lecture. Shortly after Paul was born in November, Gail was feeling depressed and complained about how hard it was to be an Army wife. Her mother's comment, that she should have known what she was getting into when she married a career officer, had stung. Perhaps she had been naive in thinking about the glamour of travel to distant lands, parades, and dances at the officers club, while paying little attention to the hardships of military life. But she had been in love with a person, not a system. Her mother was well meaning and helpful in many ways, but her inability to empathize just added to the strain Gail was feeling. After a few more minutes of troubled thoughts, exhaustion finally took over and Gail fell into a deep sleep.

The meeting of the Province Intelligence Committee was finally over, and John was glad the other advisors and Vietnamese representatives were leaving. He felt rotten, and he had an intelligence summary to write. He had been fighting the effects of Dengue Fever for over a week, and he wasn't sure he was making much progress. The vomiting and diarrhea had stopped; but the splitting headaches still came, although with less frequency. With no appetite, he was barely eating; and until today, he had spent the last six days in his bunk, drifting in and out of a feverish sleep.

He knew that Roger Decker, the team doctor, had been looking in on him; and he remembered being told to rest and drink plenty of fluids. But he remembered little else of the nightmarish bout with the malaria-like illness that felled him like an axed tree. He was fortunate to be with a team of advisors that included a doctor. Otherwise, he would have been med-evaced to an Army hospital in Saigon. John wanted no part of Saigon. If he had to be sick, he'd rather be around friends.

This morning he forced himself to get up and dressed so he could attend the weekly meeting of the PIC, one of his ideas that Dai Uy Thanh had actually greeted with enthusiasm. With the rapid build up of US military units and aid organizations during the past year in Long An Province, sharing of enemy information and coordination of intelligence estimates had been falling through the cracks. The logical solution in John's mind was to get the intelligence officers of all military units and agencies operating in the province together once a week to exchange and verify information. It didn't take much to convince Dai Uy Thanh. Having attended a US Military Intelligence Training School in Okinawa, Thanh knew his business. But convincing his superiors took some time, and they had only been operating out of their new office three weeks before John got sick. Nevertheless, the Tuesday meetings had grown steadily in attendance and development of accurate information.

"Thanks for the scoop on VC re-supply along the rivers," John muttered to a Lieutenant JG in Navy fatigues who was going out the door.

"Yeah. No sweat. The Order of Battle updates helped me. Hope to see you next week." That was the first time John had seen a naval representative in Long An, a province whose two major rivers emptied into the South China Sea. But the meeting had brought face-to-face confirmation of something he'd heard about: a joint US and Vietnamese task force trying to interdict VC traffic on the Vam Co and Nha Be Rivers.

John walked over to the large map board on the wall where MSgt Gonzales was checking enemy unit locations that his counterpart had posted. "So the 506th VC Battalion is supposed to have moved into Tan Tru District?" John asked.

"Yes sir. They haven't done much in the last month. But you heard what Dai Uy Thanh said at the meeting. Looks like something big is going on."

John rubbed his eyes, trying to ease the throbbing in his forehead.

"You still got the crud, Captain? You don't look so good, if you don't mind my saying so."

"Yeah, I know. I'm going back to the hootch and lay down after I finish here. But I've got to get our report up to the Division Intelligence Advisor for their Intelligence Summary."

"No problem, sir. I've already put it together. I was going to send it, if you were still under the weather. You want to take a look at it?"

"Thanks. I should've known you'd take care of it. Lemme see what you've done, so I'm up to date."

MSgt Gonzales pulled several sheets of paper out of a basket on a nearby desk and handed them to Parker. John scanned through the report, and handed it back.

"I just copied your last one, and added a few changes. There hasn't been that much activity this week."

"You did a good job. Thanks for holding things together." John headed for the door. "I hope to be up to speed tomorrow."

When John woke the following day something was different. It took a minute for him to realize his headache was gone and he was actually hungry. He pulled the mosquito netting aside, swung his lean frame out of the bunk, and stood up. The movement was too sudden, and he grabbed the back of a folding chair to steady himself. He was weak, but for the first time in days, his head felt clear. As he fastened the belt on his jungle fatigue pants, he saw the tab end slide an inch further through the buckle. Damn, he thought, he must have lost another ten pounds. A look in the field mirror next to his bed proved his concern. His face was lank, and he could see ribs protruding from his torso. Between his bouts with hookworms and dengue fever, he was beginning to look like one of the Bataan Death March survivors.

An hour later he was feeling much better. A large breakfast of real scrambled eggs and bacon, several slices of toast, canned apple juice and coffee helped bring a surge of energy. He even enjoyed the ribbing he received from fellow advisors about his gaunt appearance and the lengths to which he would go to get a little R & R (Rest and Recuperation). It was good to be back in place as a member of the team. Walking out of the compound toward the Tactical Operations Center (TOC), he took his time and savored the scenery of Tan An that he had taken for granted.

Despite the war and the smell of garbage, Vietnam could be beautiful. The sun was shining, the city was bustling with people heading for the market and making preparations for the Lunar New Year Celebration known as Tet. Laughing children ran by, and made him think of Susie, Mathew, and little Paul, born in the middle of a war his country couldn't understand, with his father gone to fight in it. Suddenly John yearned to be home, to hold Gail again, and have his children around him.

"Hey, GI. Give me Salem, okay?" The voice of a scruffy kid broke his reverie. The boy was about eight or nine, and trotting along side of John trying to scrounge American cigarettes. John didn't smoke, but found a *Tootsie Roll* in his pocket, and tossed it to the kid who laughed and trotted away.

When he reached the TOC, Dai Uy Thanh greeted him warmly. "Ah, Dai Uy Parker, you look better today. You okay now, I hope?"

"Yes. Thank you. I think I'm going to live. Yesterday I wasn't sure." Thanh smiled as John sat down in the seat next to the Intelligence Officer's desk. "I don't remember much of yesterday's meeting, but I got the impression that the VC are planning a big attack soon."

"*Dong roi!* That's right! Many reports from many sources. Here is a document found on a dead VC last week in Tan Tru District that say," Thanh paused to pick up a weathered piece of paper from his desk.

Reading from the paper he continued, "People's Liberation Forces need to gather their strength in all provinces of the South in order to achieve victories early in 1968, essential to gaining prestige and bargaining power."

"What do you think they mean by early in 1968?"

"Not sure, Dai Uy. But you ever hear how Vietnam defeated Chinese invaders in 1789?"

"No. I'm sorry…I don't know much about Vietnamese history." John remembered the advisor course and the longer Vietnamese language class that, at one point, had been a requirement for advisors. But when his orders came, the Army was short on advisors and in a rush to fill quotas. Since it would have added another three months to his separation from the family, it hadn't bothered him to miss the extra training. There were times, however, when it would have been helpful.

"I tell you," Thanh said. "That was when Tay Son leaders moved against Chinese troops occupying Hanoi. They achieved total victory by attacking at most unexpected time—during sacred holiday of Tet."

"But the VC have announced a truce during Tet. It's supposed to last from tomorrow through, ah…February 3rd, isn't it?"

"That is what VC say. But VC many times say one thing and do another."

There was no doubt about the truth of that remark. In the six months he had worked side by side with his tough-minded counterpart, John had grown to admire his professionalism and common sense. Nguyen van Thanh stood out among younger Vietnamese officers, and had been assigned to the province chief's staff after persistent suggestions by the senior American advisor that Colonel Nhu needed more competent officers in key positions.

Thanh more than fit that requirement. The son of a village official who was murdered by the VC, he graduated at the top of his class from the Vung Tau Military Cadet School in 1958. He spoke English well, and had seen combat as a company commander with the ARVN 25th Division in Tay Ninh Province before being sent to the US Intelligence Officers School in Okinawa. More impressive was his knowledge of the VC infrastructure in the Mekong Delta, and his ability to find nuggets of information from the stream of reports flowing into the S2 Office. Because John recognized Thanh's ability, and didn't try to dominate him, they had worked well together. John accompanied the diminutive captain on field operations, and got him the resources he needed.

"Intelligence platoon bringing a prisoner here they capture near Rach Kien. They come in about an hour. You want to talk to him?"

John paused before answering. Despite the question, Thanh's eyes were not inviting. Over six months John had learned when Thanh wanted his help, and when he didn't. Sometimes there was a hard edge to him that made John wonder.

"No. I have a pile of paperwork waiting for me. I'll check with you later."

John moved over to his desk, and began scanning the stack of Periodic Intelligence Summaries from III Corps, MACV, and 25th Division that had accumulated during his absence. Colonel Rogers, the senior advisor, had tasked him to write an estimate of all enemy forces operating in the province, and in adjacent provinces. It was only partly finished when he got sick, and he wanted to complete it as soon as possible.

The morning sped by, and John was surprised at how much he was able to accomplish. However, the more he read, the more alarmed he became at references in other intelligence reports to a VC call for a coordinated attack soon throughout the country. He leaned back in his chair, rubbing his eyes. He felt the beginning of a headache, and realized that he hadn't taken his medicine that morning.

"Sergeant Gonzales, I'm going back to the hootch for some medicine. Be back in about a half hour," John said, as he put on his fatigue cap and headed for the door.

John passed through the fence that surrounded the TOC and the Province Chief's house. Across from the sandbagged guard post was a low building in which some of the province staff offices were located. At the rear of the building was an entrance to a separate office where Thanh sometimes met with informants. John remembered the prisoner, and crossed the street. He was worried about what he read in the intelligence summaries, and wanted to know if the prisoner had revealed anything. As he neared the rear of the building, he heard high-pitched shouting in Vietnamese and a choking cry. A hose from an outside spigot ran along the building and up through a partially shuttered window. John opened the door and stepped inside.

What he saw made him freeze in place. Dai Uy Thanh's back was toward him, but two soldiers from the scout platoon turned to look at him with surprised expressions. The prisoner was a boy of about sixteen. He was naked and hog-tied to a small-backed wooden chair. One of the scouts had his mouth pried open and was tormenting him by forcing water from a hose down his throat. The other soldier had just punched the boy in the stomach as John entered the small room. The eyes of the prisoner flashed a look of fear and hatred at the tall foreigner.

"What's going on?" John cried out.

Thanh whirled around, and glared at him. Then he grabbed Parker's arm and turned him back through the door. "You not needed here, Dai Uy. Better you leave."

The dengue fever had weakened him more than he realized, and he staggered back a couple of steps before regaining his composure.

"You can't do that," John attempted to reason with his counterpart. "It's against the Geneva Convention."

"No Geneva Convention for VC. They kill my father and take his land," Thanh shouted, and the door slammed shut. John turned and walked toward the advisor compound, his face flushed. It wasn't the first time that he had seen prisoners treated harshly, but it was the first time that he had witnessed the torture of a prisoner. Should he keep quiet, or should he report this to someone? What would this do to the relationship he had with his counterparts? John was mulling over what he should do when he reached the compound, and saw Lieutenant Colonel Rogers sitting in the shade of a tree getting his hair cut. It was the noon hour when many of the Vietnamese coped with the heat by taking a siesta. But once a week Mr. Troung, a local barber, showed up with his clippers and his youngest son, Ba, to cut the American soldiers' hair.

"Excuse me, Sir. Could I talk with you for a minute when you're finished?"

"Sure, John. Or you can pull up a chair, and talk now."

John glanced at Mr. Troung. "It's something confidential. I'll wait." While he was waiting, John went into the hootch and came back with some photos. The barber's son, Ba, reminded him of Matthew.

He squatted in front of the little boy, and showed him a picture of Matthew standing in the back yard, holding a child-size baseball bat. "This is my son. This...my Ba," he said gesturing to Ba and his father.

Ba laughed and pointed at the picture, then at John. "Dai Uy's Ba?...Dai Uy's Ba?"

"That's right. He's my Ba. His name is Matt." Then he handed the boy a picture of Susie, and one of the baby. The last picture was the most recent, showing Gail on the living room sofa with Paul sitting in her lap, and Susie and Matthew standing on either side of her. Ba spoke excitedly to his father, and held the picture up so he could see.

"Ah, Dai Uy. Your woman Number One. Nice family."

"Thank you, Mr. Troung." John fished a *Bit of Honey* candy bar from his pocket and gave it to Ba while he retrieved his pictures.

Mr. Troung handed the colonel a mirror to inspect his newly shortened crew cut. Rogers grunted his satisfaction, brushed hairs from his jungle fatigues, and paid Mr. Troung, adding a nice tip.

"Now, what's up, John?" the senior advisor said, leading the way to his room.

"I'm concerned about indications of an enemy attack, and about an incident that just took place."

The colonel took a seat at the desk in his bedroom, which he also used as an office, motioning John to the only other chair. John explained what he had gleaned from the intelligence summaries and the PIC meeting, and then described the brutal scene he had witnessed.

"I'm surprised at Thanh," Rogers said, after a long pause. "I thought he would be above that sort of thing. One thing I've learned though, is to tread lightly about these issues with the Vietnamese. We have to remember that this is their country, and their war. I'll talk to the Province Chief about him, of course, and I want you to write a report which I'll forward through our chain of command."

"Yes sir. You know, I wonder...I wonder if he's more concerned about this VC offensive than he lets on."

"Yeah. That's the bigger issue at the moment. Last year's truce at Tet was quiet, and I heard today that President Johnson has stood down any bombing of North Vietnam over Tet, so I don't really think anything significant will happen until after Tet."

"I hope you're right, sir," John said, getting to his feet. "But this might be a good time to review our contingency plan for an attack on this compound."

"Good point. I'll get Major Bradley working on it, and we'll make sure the district advisors are alerted. Thanks for keeping me advised, John. It's good to have you back on your feet."

When John got back to his bunk he saw a letter lying in the middle of the cot. When he picked it up he was surprised to see his mother's handwriting on the envelope. Usually his Dad typed their letters, and Mom added a few lines. He slit open the envelope with his pocketknife and began to read. After a minute he sat down and read the letter again. It was short; his mother usually didn't waste a lot of words on trivialities. The paragraph that riveted his attention read:

"Your father had a heart attack last week. He's home now and resting. It happened at the office, and we were lucky that a paramedic got there in a few minutes. Dr. McGregor says he shouldn't go back to work for at least a month, and then only part time. The business is not doing well, and most of our savings are tied up in it. I know we've talked about it before John, but I'd like you to think about taking over the business when you get back from Vietnam."

John fell back on his cot and closed his eyes. He prayed for his father's recovery, and then pondered what he should do.

Gisela took the Eastern Parkway exit from I-65 after leaving downtown Louisville. It was early afternoon, and before tackling the return drive to Fort Knox, she had an errand to run. She was glad to be off the expressway. It's three lanes of speeding drivers in light rain made her nervous, as if she wasn't already nervous enough behind the wheel of Fred's Porshe. At least the traffic on Eastern Parkway moved at a moderate rate, and there were traffic lights after several blocks to give a driver time to think.

"Where are we going, Mama?" Anna asked from the front seat.

"I'm just going to stop for a minute at Gail's house to leave a gift for the baby. I'm afraid we can't stay, because they are all sick." Anna began to fuss about wanting to play with Susie, but Gisela was firm. "I'm sorry, but they have caught some bad germs, and if you are near Susie, you could get sick too."

That prompted questions about what germs were and how children caught them, which Gisela explained as best she could, while looking at street signs for the place where she should turn. Since John left, Gisela had visited Gail three times, once with Fred, and twice by herself. She was becoming more confident about getting around in a large city, but she tried to time her shopping trips between the morning and afternoon rush hours.

"I should have called," she said out loud. "But I wasn't sure we would have time for this." Besides, she thought, if I wait much longer the baby will have outgrown the shirt and pants outfit that was in the gift box next to her. Better to just knock at the door and leave it. As she drove slowly along the tree-lined street, looking for the familiar house, the drizzle changed to a steady rain. She almost passed it, but caught a glimpse of the swing set John had erected in the back yard in time to pull into the driveway.

Gail was lying on the living room sofa when she heard the noise of a car in the driveway. She felt worse than yesterday, and upset that all doctors' offices were closed on Wednesday afternoon. The earliest appointment she could get was on Thursday afternoon. She was at the point of bundling all the kids into the car, and going to the Emergency Room of Baptist Hospital, but they had all laid down for naps without fussing. The rest was better, she hoped, than exposing them to the damp, cold weather. She raised up on an elbow and looked out the window. Oh no! It was Gisela. And she must look like one of the characters from *Night of the Living Dead*. Gail sat up on the sofa, and tried to fluff her hair into some decent arrangement. Then she heard a sound at the front door, and gave it up as a lost cause. She rose wearily to her feet, and moved to the door. For a moment she was afraid she was going to throw up. I wish she had called, she thought.

Gail opened the front door, to find a surprised Gisela trying to place a box inside the storm door.

"Gail, I'm so sorry to bother you. I was just going to leave this gift for the baby."

"Oh, that's all right." Gail pulled the collar of her robe together, and tried to sound enthusiastic. "I'm happy to see you. You and Anna, come on in out of the rain."

Gisela protested about not wanting to disturb them, but Gail insisted that they come inside while she opened the gift.

Gisela stepped aside, and guided Anna through the front door. She followed her daughter, and stepped into the living room just as Anna spoke up. "Mama, it smells bad."

Gail looked embarrassed, but Gisela reacted with alarm. "Quick. Open some windows. It's gas! We need to get the children out of here. It smells like it could blow up!

The next few minutes were a blur of frantic activity as the two women rushed into the bedrooms, threw open windows, and roused the listless children. Throwing coats and blankets around them, they hurried them outside into Gisela's warm car. Gail went back into the house to hastily pull on a pair of slacks and a sweater, and grab her purse and coat. Then she ran to the garage, and moved her car back to Gisela's, so she could transfer Matthew and the baby into her larger station wagon. Susie wanted to stay with Anna, and Gail willingly let Gisela take the girls. She led the way to the Baptist Hospital where they were checked by an Emergency Room Physician, and where she made phone calls to the gas company and her mother.

The fresh air and rush of adrenaline from the fright she had experienced, cleared Gail's head. Gisela and Anna left and Susie was getting whiny. She dropped the children off with her mother and drove back to the house to meet the man from the gas company. As she turned the corner to her street, she was shocked to see a fire truck, two LG&E trucks, and some neighbors outside her home. When she identified herself to one of the firemen, he said, "You're lucky the place didn't explode. Gas had built up in there somehow."

Without thinking she moved toward the house, but a man from the gas company stopped her. "We've got the gas line cut off, and fans inside to blow the gas out. It's going to be a few hours before it's safe to go inside. Do you have someplace you can go?"

Gail nodded dumbly, seeing the doors and windows wide open. For several minutes she stood watching, responding briefly to a few questions from neighbors. At last it dawned on her to ask a man from LG&E, "What happened? We just had the furnace checked. How did gas leak into the house?"

"I'm not sure, Ma'am. We didn't see any immediate signs of a leak. It might be something else. We'll check it carefully when it's a little safer."

A neighbor offered to watch the house for her, and Gail decided to return to her mother's. The LG&E foreman said he would call when it was okay to enter the house.

Three hours later the call came, but at that point she didn't object to her mother's insistence that they spend the night. According to the foreman, the problem was a cold air return that had been taped over, probably by the previous renters, and had caused a build up of gas fumes. Would it have caused an explosion? Possibly, though it was more likely that they would have been asphyxiated first. Gail shuddered at the thought, and considered what she would tell John. When she remembered his agitated letters about Matthew's bicycle accident, she knew she wasn't going to burden him with this news. When he got home would be soon enough.

Bang, bang, bang! Three shots rang out nearby, and John bolted upright under the mosquito netting. It was pitch dark outside, but he could hear the crackle of small arms fire that sounded like it came from the river. He rolled out of his bunk in the darkness, and slipped on his pants and jungle boots. He found his flack jacket and web gear where he had placed them, hanging on the back of a folding chair next to the bed. While he was still sitting on the floor, he grabbed his helmet off the chair, and reached for his M-16 under the bunk. He knew the three shots were from inside the compound, and he could hear voices yelling commands around him. Cautiously, he made his way outside, and trotted in a crouch to a spot along the compound wall.

Crump, Crump…Crump, Crump. He saw the flash and heard muffled explosions from heavy mortar rounds landing near the market square. Looking across the open square in front of the compound, he couldn't see anything moving; but to his right a stream of red tracer rounds erupted in the direction of the river. It must be the guards firing the .50 caliber machine gun from the water tower emplacement, he thought.

Turning to a figure lying next to him by the wall, he asked, "Where are they? Are we taking any fire?"

"I don't know." The high-pitched voice belonged to Scrap Ingram, the civil affairs advisor. "One of our guys on the back side was firing at something…haven't seen any movement out front."

Near the entrance of the compound, he heard a voice calling, "Captain Parker. Where are you? Command Group is moving to the TOC…Captain Parker?"

John got to his feet and moved toward the gate, just as two more mortar rounds hit outside in the middle of the soccer field. He dove to the ground beside a concrete pillar that held the gate, as shrapnel pinged off the fence behind him. Major Bradley was crouched on the other side of the pillar. When he saw John, he pointed in the direction of the Tactical Operations Center, and motioned for John to follow him. John saw two figures ahead of him, darting along the street between bursts of gunfire.

He and Bradley sprinted to the next building and took cover behind a wall. So far the only incoming fire John could detect was from mortars that were targeting the Province Chief's villa and the Advisor's Compound. As they ran the final two hundred meters to the sandbagged TOC, John caught a glimpse of figures moving on the other side of the barbed wire fortification behind Colonel Nhu's villa. He heard the low-pitched chatter of AK 47's, and realized the VC were close. There was answering fire from a South Vietnamese .30 caliber machine gun.

Just as John ducked inside the wall of the TOC, a loud explosion rocked the bunker's occupants. Dai Uy Thanh was already there, talking rapidly into a radio handset. The TOC was crowded with the Vietnamese Operations Staff and their American advisors. John looked at his watch. It was 0245 the morning of January 31st. Thanh had called it right on the money!

The day after his brutal interrogation of the VC prisoner, Thanh had come to him and insisted on a meeting between the senior advisor and the Province Chief. With John's assistance, he laid out a list of indicators, which pointed to a VC uprising throughout the south, during the Tet Holiday. From the prisoner and captured documents, Thanh knew the enemy had begun their Tet celebration early, on January 28th. Considering when their three days of festivity would be over, Thanh made a convincing case that the VC intended to mount an offensive in South Vietnam's major cities on January 31st.

Even for Colonel Nhu, who was reluctant to call back his own soldiers, that was enough. He sent Thanh's report through the Vietnamese chain of command with a strong recommendation that the Tet Truce be canceled and all leaves be curtailed. LTC Rogers pushed a similar recommendation through advisor channels, but in the end President Thieu would only agree to limit the cease-fire by one day. On January 31st many of the government troops were visiting their ancestral homes outside the province, although American soldiers of the Third Brigade, Ninth Infantry were located near the province capital.

John listened to a quick briefing the Vietnamese S-3 was giving to the Province Chief and LTC Rogers. Three of the seven district towns were under attack, as well as the Chieu Hoi Center for VC deserters north of Tan An. About thirty returnees, who had responded to the government's amnesty program, were at the center, protected by a small security force that was now in danger of being overrun. The ARVN Company responsible for providing security to the Tan An Bridge and key government buildings was being hard-pressed. A VC sapper (demolition) platoon was detected by the bridge, and driven off by alert guards and accurate fire from the supporting 50-caliber machine gun. But another group of VC had reached the near side of the river, and was heavily engaged with ARVN troops only a few hundred meters away.

When Major Nha, the S-3, requested support from US Aircraft mounting 20 millimeter gatling guns with illumination capability, the duty officer informed the group that both Tan San Nhut and Bien Hoa airfields were under heavy attack. For the time being, American air support was unavailable. The duty officer also reported that the US brigade headquarters was receiving small arms and mortar fire in their bivouac site south of the city. Nevertheless, LTC Rogers said that, with Colonel Nhu's concurrence, he would contact the commander of the American brigade and request a company of infantry be sent immediately to reinforce the ARVN soldiers defending the Province Headquarters. Colonel Nhu was anxiously nodding his agreement before Rogers finished his statement, and the senior advisor quickly grabbed a field telephone to make the request.

John and the S-3 Advisor, Captain Ted Gardner, took the places of the night duty personnel, who remained as their assistants, and continued to track the ongoing battles through radio and telephone communications. At one point John asked for Dai Uy Thanh, and another Vietnamese officer replied that he had gone outside to check on the enemy threat to the Province Headquarters. John started to follow after him, to stay in contact with his Vietnamese counterpart, but LTC Rogers vetoed the idea. All hands were needed in the TOC, and he wouldn't be much help wandering around in the dark in a firefight between opposing Vietnamese forces.

In less than an hour from Colonel Roger's call a company of the US Ninth Infantry Division arrived, and Captain Gardner went outside with the duty sergeant to guide them into a defensive perimeter. One of its platoons was sent across the river, escorted by the duty officer, to reinforce the ARVN troops at the Chieu Hoi Center. Another platoon, using fire and maneuver tactics, subdued the remaining hot spot along the river. By daybreak the VC attack was over, and the only gunfire to be heard came from pockets of VC who were trapped and couldn't escape. Shortly after dawn, Lieutenant Feltner relieved John, and he left the bunker to find his counterpart and assess the damage.

The first thing he noticed was smoke coming from the top floor of Colonel Nhu's villa where either a mortar round or tracer fire must have started a fire. Across the soccer field the Nhut Tan Restaurant, where he had eaten a week earlier with Thanh, was a shambles, as was the building next to it. The Advisor Compound looked intact.

He turned to walk toward the river, when he saw four Vietnamese soldiers carrying a stretcher toward an ambulance parked behind him. As he came closer, instinct told him the identity of the motionless body. When they came abreast, he forced himself to look down at the sightless eyes and bloodied body of Dai Uy Thanh.

He took off his helmet, feeling helpless, and walked beside the stretcher-bearers. Random images of his counterpart crowded his fatigued mind. He remembered meeting Thanh's family when the two captains had been visiting Ben Luc District where Thanh's ancestral home was located. His wife was a little older than Gail, and there were four children, all under ten. Those children had never known a land without war, and for most of Thanh's life, neither had he. As he stood looking at the dead officer, the intelligence platoon leader, Lieutenant Tuan, came up carrying Thanh's helmet and pistol. There was a bullet hole in the side of the helmet. Tuan explained that the captain had been trying to get the ARVN troops to follow him in a movement to cut off the VC when he was hit. The ARVN soldiers had stayed in place, allowing most of the VC to escape.

Tuan and the stretcher-bearers moved on, and John started toward the river in a daze. What if he had gone with Thanh? Would it have made any difference? Or would he have been a casualty himself? The sights and sounds of the battle's aftermath were still present. Buildings were pockmarked from bullets and shrapnel, a crater revealed where a VC satchel charge had blown a gaping hole in the barbed wire fortification around the Province Headquarters, and several bodies were strewn about with women wailing over them. Vietnamese and American soldiers rested near their positions, a few already drinking the coffee or tea they had managed to brew.

Near the crater John saw the body of a VC lying beside the barbed wire. A smaller figure knelt over the body, trying to move it. There was something familiar about them. Moving closer, John stopped abruptly several feet short of the wire. The face of a boy looked up at him, tears streaming down his face, as he tried to turn the man over. It was Ba, and the dead man in the black clothing of a VC was the barber, Mr. Troung. John stood transfixed, as a vision of another boy, across a barbed wire fence, seared his mind. A woman came up and helped turn the body over. John felt powerless to move. Finally he walked back toward the TOC, the wailing of the woman and the cries of Ba echoing in his mind.

Five months later John remembered that scene as he sat in the cargo hold of a C-141 on his way home, a month early on emergency leave orders. He had a lot of time to think. He was the only passenger, surrounded by sixteen caskets bearing the remains of soldiers killed like Cowan. When the Red Cross notification came that his father was in critical condition from another heart attack, John was working on an Intelligence Estimate with MSgt Gonzales. He bid his new counterpart a hasty farewell and left the following day on the first flight out of Tan Son Nhut Air Base.

He had come to Vietnam highly motivated and convinced his government's policy was right. Now he wasn't sure. US soldiers were carrying the brunt of what was essentially a civil war. True, it was a communist inspired insurgency against the Government of Vietnam. But the North Vietnamese and the Viet Cong seemed more willing to sacrifice for their cause than the South Vietnamese were for theirs. Except for a few dedicated officers like Dai Uy Thanh, he had seen too many military commanders who were more interested in lining their own pockets than fighting the enemy. Even his own government seemed unwilling to take the steps necessary to win the war.

What should he do now? He had risked his life and the welfare of his family in a questionable cause, and his father needed help with a business that was on the brink of ruin. The word on officer assignments was to expect another tour in Vietnam within two years. But the Army he loved was beginning to disintegrate before his eyes. Morale was declining, drug use by soldiers was affecting discipline; units outside Vietnam were short of personnel and equipment; and the core of solid non-commissioned officers was shrinking under the pressure of repeated tours to Vietnam. He faced all this in the uniform of a country grown hostile to the military.

Before the plane landed at Dover Air Force Base, John made up his mind. He would submit his resignation, and take over his Dad's business.

PART THREE

AUGUST 1989 – SEPTEMBER 1990

James Pocock

CHAPTER 12

The express train from Moscow picked up speed as it pulled away from Poznan's main station, the last stop in Poland, before its 10:00 a.m. arrival in Berlin. Except for two young men in dark suits and an older man, dozing in the corner seat with a cap pulled over his eyes, the first class compartment was empty. Three other passengers had departed into a drizzling August rain that amplified Poznan's morning gloom. Turning from the window where drab, antiquated industrial buildings slipped by, the shorter man glanced at the slumbering passenger, and addressed his companion in German.

"These factories look like they haven't had a coat of paint since the war. If their equipment is as bad as the buildings, it's a wonder that they produce anything."

"They don't, Klaus. At least not like we do." Dieter Burchert recalled recent photos of workers demonstrating in Poland's factories and shipyards. If those Polocks would spend as much time working as they do demonstrating, he thought, they might reach some of their production quotas. Then there were the men who just got off in Poznan, supposedly on their way to some sort of business meeting. "The way those guys were passing the vodka around before they left tells you something about the effort they put into work."

"Ja. Bestimmt. They'll probably be smashed by noon."

"They don't give a damn," Dieter snorted. "And there isn't any discipline among the workers either." He sat across from his smaller

137

companion, facing the rear of the train. His dark, wavy hair and good looks attracted attention, especially among women, who often took him for a film actor. Actually he was an officer in the Volksarmee. In fact, both men were captains. They were returning from a Warsaw Pact security conference where each had been honored as the outstanding junior officer from their respective services.

Klaus Mühlberger, 28, a nervous, chain smoker from Leipzig, was a rising star in the ranks of the State Secret Police. Dieter first met him five days earlier when they reported in at the conference registration desk in the Hotel Lenin. After receiving their awards from General Zeiskov, the Russian Deputy Chief for Internal Security, the two men were treated to a couple of days of sightseeing and concerts in Moscow before returning for discussions on the last day of the conference. There they heard DDR Security Chief, General Major Hans Kleimann, raise objections to the relaxation of controls advocated by the Russian leadership

"You know, Klaus, this Glasnost thing of Gorbachev's is just stirring up trouble. All the emphasis on openness the Russians are talking about is going to cause some real security headaches."

"You're right. University students in Dresden and Leipzig are already demanding more consumer goods and the right to travel to the West."

"That's bullshit!" Dieter slammed his fist on the arm of his seat. "Students can travel anywhere they wish in socialist countries around the world. More contact with the West will only undermine our socialist system."

Klaus lit another cigarette and quickly exhaled. "You and I know that, Dieter, but students are easily corrupted. The number of agitators who want to tear down our society is increasing every day."

Dieter looked out the window at flat stretches of farmland rolling by. He was glad to be going home. This conference was an eye opener, a chance to see how Germany compared to the rest of Eastern Europe. They passed by a rural village, and his eyes fastened momentarily on a small shrine along a dirt road leading out of town. He caught a glimpse of a statue of a man hanging from a cross. A crazy religious relic from the past, he thought. It was amazing that some people still believed in that nonsense. In his view it was a mark of the superiority of communism that the number of religious believers had dwindled in countries where the enlightened doctrines of Marx and Lenin prevailed. He was still lost in thought when he realized that Klaus was speaking to him.

"I think it's time we cracked down on those radical students, and it sounds like General Kleimann is ready to do that."

"Hm...*Oh Ja!* The sooner the better. I wish I could be part of it when I get to Leipzig."

"You must be pleased with your new assignment. Getting transferred to a division staff in a big city is a great opportunity."

"Well, I liked working with troops, but I'm looking forward to getting back to Leipzig. That's where I went to university, and I still have friends there."

Dieter thought momentarily about Renate, wondering what she was doing now. Once they had been lovers, and he still carried her picture in his wallet. In his last year of study she had moved in with him; and they had even discussed the idea of marriage, though she still had two more years of school remaining. Then he found out about her activity with the clandestine Lutheran organization. She and other students were part of an underground group that was smuggling dissidents to the west.

When he confronted her and demanded that she stop her underground action, they quarreled. She walked out, slamming the door in his face. As was his duty, he contacted the Stasi office and filled out a report on her activity; but he didn't know what came of it. He hadn't seen Renate since. Three months later he graduated and left immediately for officers training at the Ernst Thälmann Offizershochschule in Löbau. Yet sometimes he wondered if he should have handled things differently.

The train whistle jarred Dieter's mind back to the present. "At least I get a week of leave before I report. I'm going to stop in Berlin and visit my folks. My father has been out of the country for several months."

Klaus looked at his watch. "Another hour and we'll be there. Let's get some coffee."

As they got to their feet, the stranger stretched and pushed his cap back uncovering a face that exuded an impression of intelligence and strength. "I'm afraid you're mistaken," he said in fluent German.

Dieter and Klaus stopped in their tracks, staring in disbelief at the man whom, when he embarked in Warsaw, they had given one look and forgotten. "Huh…" was all Klaus could say in response.

"I said you young intellectuals are mistaken! We Poles can produce anything as well or better than you Germans. The system is the problem." He straightened up in his seat, and his penetrating eyes held them motionless. "When workers have low pay, and no way to have their grievances addressed, then there is no incentive to work hard. Cracking the skulls of demonstrators is not the answer. It's about time the proletariat had a real voice in the revolutionary process of reform. Otherwise, Communism in our countries is dead."

Klaus's face turned red, and his words burst out in the confines of the train compartment. "Listen, you…you *dummkopf!* That kind of talk could get you locked up."

Dieter started to add something, but thought better of it. He grabbed Klaus by the arm and pulled him toward the door. "Come on, Klaus. Let's leave it." When they were in the corridor, he said, "You can report him to the *Bahnhof Polizei* when we get to Berlin."

"So, a toast to the outstanding captain in the Volksarmee." General Erich Burchert raised his wine glass and touched it to his son's, as did Inge and their guests, Generalmajor and Frau Steiner.

"We're very proud of you, Dieter." Inge's face beamed with pleasure.

"You're looking at a future chief of the Volksarmee, my dear," Steiner said to his wife."

Dieter sipped his wine and smiled appreciatively. Although accustomed to praise from his parents, he didn't want to appear smug. "Thank you for saying so, *Herr General,* but there are many fine officers in the Volksarmee."

"Well said, young man. Still, you should be promoted soon, and with your spirit, I see future promotions coming rapidly."

Dieter thought General Steiner was overdoing the flattery, possibly in consideration of his host. Dieter's father had told him that he had something to do with Steiner's selection to head the foreign intelligence directorate of the Stasi. They were seated in the dining room of his parents spacious home in the Wandlitz compound outside Berlin. Closely guarded by Stasi forces, the compound consisted of several dozen villas, shops, and recreation facilities. This was an area populated by senior government officials and high ranking Stasi staff that enjoyed special privileges their proletarian neighbors could only dream about.

General Steiner turned toward Erich. "How was your excursion in the Middle East? Looks like you picked up a suntan."

"*Ja.* The sun is hot in Iraq. I did some walking for exercise. Otherwise it was all work, but very productive. The Iraqis pay well, and they want more of our equipment for their chemical weapons factory near Baghdad." Erich chuckled, as though he was reminded of a private joke. "You know, Fritz, these consulting jobs are not a bad way to spend one's retirement, especially if you can find a warm climate during the winter." When Inge shot him an irritated look, he hastily added. "But after a while, I miss my Inge, and I miss my German beer." That brought a round of laughter.

A maid, who brought in plates of Wiener schnitzel with asparagus and a dumpling covered with gravy, interrupted the conversation. Erich had mentioned earlier that Inge had spent much of the day in the kitchen supervising the cook's preparation of Dieter's favorite meal. Her face glowed when Dieter took a generous helping and said, "*Ah, Schnitzel und Spätzle; dass ist Wunderbar!*"

"Dieter, your mother tells me that you are going to be stationed in Leipzig," Frau Steiner said. "Do you know yet what you will be doing?"

"*Ja.* I called the adjutant of the 113th Panzer Grenadier Division yesterday. He told me I am to have a special assignment as liaison officer to the *Staatsicherheit.*" The two generals exchanged glances. It was Steiner who broke the silence.

"I think you will find that to be an important task, my boy. The Committee for State Security is about to pull in the reins on those provocateurs who are fomenting disturbances in the cities."

Dieter was pleased, and with good reason. It seemed he was to get his wish to be involved in the roundup of agitators Klaus had warned him about. And he would have an opportunity to work with Klaus whose ideals he shared.

"It's about time," Inge said. "They don't know how much better they have it than we did. And they don't seem to care about working together for the betterment of our society."

"Now, Inge," Erich interjected. "Let's not get off on a political tangent. This is a night to celebrate our son's success."

"*Ja. Entshuldigung.* No more politics, I promise." Inge beamed at Dieter and played the gracious hostess, guiding conversation to other topics throughout the rest of the meal. When it was time for dessert she rang a small bell, and a maid brought in a colorful plate of Bienenstich.

As Dieter was finishing his second slice of the honey-almond cake supplied by the compound bakery, Erich leaned toward his son and said,

"Dieter, I have two visits in mind for you that I believe would be professionally useful. I would like you to come with me tomorrow. I have to make a trip into the countryside to a location you should see. Then the next day General Steiner will give you a personal orientation on the mission of his ministry. You do have a Top Secret clearance, correct?"

"*Ja. Natürlich.* Where will we be going?"

Erich winked and said, "You'll see, but it's an all day trip by car, and you should wear casual clothes as if we were hiking in the Thüringer Wald, which in fact we may do."

General Steiner nodded his understanding and added, "A good idea, Erich. An understanding of both operations will be invaluable to Dieter."

The next day, after two hours of driving on the E61 autobahn southwest of Berlin, Erich made the turn onto the E40, heading west. It was cloudy and rain was forecast.

"This is quite a drive," Dieter exclaimed. "You weren't joking about going to the Thüringer Wald."

"I never joke about military matters." Erich was wearing gray *Kniebundhosen,* similar to golf knickers, a dark green foresters coat, thick stockings and hiking boots. Dieter was more contemporary in his dress: khaki slacks, light blue shirt, and comfortable walking shoes. He had a light rain jacket with him.

"How long before we get there?" Dieter asked, stifling a yawn. Although his father's Czech-made Skoda sedan could easily average 130 kilometers per hour, there were too many potholes and cracks in the autobahn surface to risk traveling at that speed.

"We should be there by noon. There is a nice restaurant nearby where we can have dinner."

Dieter was pleased to be alone with his father for the whole day. He couldn't remember when that had happened before. Erich had been a stern and imposing figure during his formative years, and Dieter's love for him was tempered with a respect for his authority. He was a tough old soldier, who had been demanding on his soldiers, as well as on Dieter. Yet his subordinates believed he never asked more of them than he would of himself. He was intelligent too, and Dieter knew that his own academic achievement was due in large measure to Erich's oversight. His father had stimulated his study of the communist movement with stories from the past, and had encouraged his active participation as a party member. He didn't spend much time on small talk, and his social graces were a little rough, but Dieter couldn't think of any man he admired more. He smiled at him and asked, "Since we are by ourselves, can't you tell me where we're going?"

"Well, I wanted it to be a surprise, but I'll give you an idea of what to expect. We are going to visit an underground bunker, which is the wartime headquarters of the Sixth Guards Army. I was involved with the design of the bunker for defense against chemical, nuclear, and biological warfare, and I still act as a consultant. There was a recent modification to the chemical warning system, and I was asked to inspect the work."

Erich turned off the autobahn and the car proceeded along the two-lane road between Bad Berka and Ilmenau.

"That does sound interesting. Like going on a field visit from the staff college."

"*Ja*. Except such visits are not allowed there. Everything about the place is highly classified."

"So that's why we are dressed like we're on vacation?"

"Correct. Even the locals don't know what's there. It isn't staffed except on field exercises, and then we take extraordinary precautions to keep the place secret."

"That must be difficult. Wouldn't all the vehicles and uniforms make it obvious that something important was there?"

"There is a large maintenance building on top of the bunker which is off limits to the local inhabitants. During field exercises, headquarters personnel arrive during darkness in unmarked vehicles. They enter the bunker through the maintenance building, so no one outside ever sees them."

Dieter whistled softly. "Clever. And it's a well-kept secret in the Volksarmee too. I've never heard anyone mention this until now."

Another half hour of driving brought them through Ilmenau, after which the Skoda climbed steadily along a twisting, narrow road toward the village of Frauenwald. It began to rain softly, and the windshield wipers made a scraping sound that interrupted their conversation. Two kilometers outside Frauenwald was a hill with an open meadow on one side and another slope of dense trees leading still higher. On the forward edge of the hill was a small hotel with a cafe. Erich pulled into the hotel parking lot, and they entered the cafe.

They were seated at a table by a window looking out over the hillside. A pretty waitress in a peasant costume took their drink order and was back in a few minutes with two tall glasses of beer.

"Prost," Erich said, touching his glass of Bockbier to Dieter's. Dieter took a drink and looked around the room. Most of the tables were full, and the occupants all appeared to be vacationers, many in hiking clothes. As they examined the menus, Erich said, "They're famous for their *Kartoffelsuppe.*" On such a nasty day, that sounded fine to Dieter, and they both ordered soup with their dinners.

When the waitress returned and set two steaming bowls in front of them, Erich waited only a few moments for his to cool and then dug in.

"You won't find any better potato soup in Thüringen," Erich said, slurping a spoonful.

"*Ja. Sehr gut,*" Dieter agreed. But he was more pleased with the *Berner Platte,* an entree of pork chops and sausages garnished with sauerkraut.

After lunch Erich suggested in a loud voice that they go for a hike in the woods behind the hotel. As they started up the dirt road, a chilling breeze rustled the trees. Dieter pulled up his hood against the drizzle and, off to his left, saw the maintenance building his father had described. Erich looked around, and seeing no one, motioned Dieter to follow.

He opened the maintenance shop door and they stepped into a small office with a metal door on the wall to their right. A burly man in coveralls stood behind the counter. Truck parts and vehicle manuals were on the shelves behind him.

"Can I help you?" he said.

Erich pulled an identification card from his wallet and handed it to the man. "I'm Generalmajor Burchert, and I'm here with my son, Captain Burchert, on an inspection visit for the Ministry of Defense. I believe you have been sent a message confirming our security clearances." Dieter produced his identity card and placed it on the counter. The man examined both cards and checked the photos carefully with their faces.

"*Jawohl, Herr General.* Let me summon a guide for you." Reaching under the counter, he pressed a button. "Someone will be here to assist you right away."

Two minutes later the steel door opened and a muscular man with short hair entered the room. He was also dressed in mechanic's coveralls. He came to a position of attention and said,

"Oberfeldwebel Epler at your service, gentlemen."

Erich explained his mission and the Oberfeldwebel led them through the door into a large bay where vehicles were repaired. They followed him across the room and descended a steep concrete stairway. At the bottom was another metal door with a padlock, which Epler opened with a key. The first room they entered was long and narrow with three shower fixtures and drains near the entrance.

"This is for chemical and biological decontamination," Erich explained. We know the imperialist armies have a vast supply of nuclear, biological, and chemical (NBC) weapons. That is why we emphasize NBC training in all our exercises."

"So does NATO, according to the reports I have read. But they claim their NBC training is for defensive purposes only. They've even signed an international treaty banning the use of chemical weapons."

"Dieter, we have been close to war more than once in the last thirty years. If they attack, we believe that they will use all the weapons at their disposal. They've learned from their Vietnam experience, and their strategy now is to strike with overwhelming force."

"That means nuclear weapons against our panzer divisions and reinforcements."

"No doubt about it. NATO intends to use nuclear weapons to overcome the superiority in tanks and infantry that we have. However, if the Americans initiate an attack with nuclear weapons, that presents a dilemma for us."

"We can retaliate with atomic bombs and cannons, but we don't want to turn our homeland into a nuclear wasteland."

"Precisely. But if we respond immediately with non-persistent chemical agents, we can disrupt the enemy's attack, and crush them with superior forces."

"So we need our chemical weapons to give us an edge."

"That's it exactly, Dieter. Of course, once nerve gas and other agents are introduced, NATO may retaliate with gas as well. That's why I want you to see how well protected and equipped the Army headquarters is. The ceiling and walls are made of reinforced concrete, and it's three meters thick over our heads."

"That should withstand all but a direct hit with a hydrogen bomb."

"*Ja, Bestimmt.* And the building is equipped with food and water, a self-contained ventilation system, and living quarters for fifty officers to function over two months without resupply."

"Fantastic. There's no way enemy air reconnaissance would ever find it."

Erich opened another heavy steel door. "Now, follow me. The equipment I need to inspect is in the next room."

Against the far wall was a large control panel with color coded knobs and buttons connected to an elaborate wiring diagram. The right side of the panel had switches and meters which Erich began examining.

"This is the instrumentation for the whole complex. The modifications will allow us to seal off any room which is penetrated by gas or radiation." He turned some switches, waited for a glowing path of indicators on the wiring diagram to light, and began checking his meters.

"Look here, Dieter. When I shut off these switches, I can simulate that the room shown in the diagram is contaminated. Then we have to isolate the area by locking the same colored switches on the control panel." He busied himself with the switches and measuring devices on the panel for several minutes. Finally he grunted with satisfaction, and said, "It functions like it should. For once the engineers did a good job."

Turning his attention back to Dieter, he said, "That turned out to be easier than I expected. Let's take a look at the rest of the building."

Dieter followed as his father led the way through a maze of rooms with map boards, telephones, and file cabinets. The Feldwebel brought up the rear. Dieter was amazed to see everything arranged in readiness for a command group to simply arrive and instantly be in business. Noticing a small room with a desk, red telephone and a painting of Lenin on the wall, Dieter asked, "If I picked up the phone, who would be on the other end?"

"That's the commander's office. The red phone connects him to the commander of the Russian Army outside Berlin. The other phone is a direct link to the defense minister."

"So this is the *Feldherrnhügel.*" Dieter referred to the term used in past centuries for the high ground on which the commanding general stood to direct the battle. He laughed and said, "Except in this case it's underground and well-planned. Yet there's more than enough comfort," he said, resting his hand on a small sofa in the commander's quarters.

"That's true, but keep in mind this headquarters may be a key factor in winning the first battle of the next war."

On the drive back to Berlin Dieter and Erich continued their discussion of chemical warfare tactics. It wasn't until many days later that Dieter realized the secret bunker might possibly be used to launch that first battle, supported by chemical and nuclear weapons, against NATO.

Early the next morning Dieter left the house in his father's car for the drive into the Lichtenberg district of East Berlin where the huge Stasi complex was located. As he neared Ruschestrasse he saw the dingy gray buildings that he sought standing like a fortress amid shabby apartment houses. He parked the car and hurried toward Building 3. Inside he showed his identification to a guard who checked his name on a list and gave him a pass showing he was an authorized visitor of the *Hauptverwaltung Aufklarung* (HVA or Main Administration for Foreign Intelligence). When he arrived at General Steiner's second floor office suite, he was pleased to see he had fifteen minutes to spare before his appointment. As he settled into a chair he couldn't help admiring the walnut paneling of the reception area. He was glad his father had suggested that he wear civilian clothes. Despite the proliferation of military titles in the Ministry of Security, no one in the building was wearing a uniform.

Promptly at 8:30 a secretary knocked on the inner office door and then addressed Dieter. "He'll see you now."

He entered the office and was awed by the lavish furnishings that included marble busts of Marx and Lenin. Fritz Steiner, rose from a gigantic desk and said, "Welcome, my boy, to the house of counter-intelligence. Please have a seat over here."

Dieter sat down in a comfortable easy chair next to the desk, and Steiner heaved his bulky frame into a matching chair across from him. After coffee was ordered and a brief inquiry about his trip the previous day, General Steiner got right to the point. "I'll give you an orientation here about our primary missions followed by a tour of our directorates, and then we'll return here to meet some visitors who should give you a feel for our foreign contacts."

During the next two hours Dieter learned that the HVA had over 4000 operatives engaged in espionage in other countries, surveillance of foreigners in East Germany, and in training foreign agents for support of national liberation movements. He discovered that their Soviet friends had assigned East Germany the lead in developing close cooperation with Middle Eastern intelligence services. On their walk through the building Dieter was surprised to hear that many foreigners working with the Stasi had been involved in terrorist operations against western governments or Israel. One of the officers in Directorate 5 confided that they had procured the weapons and explosives used by Libyans in the December 1986 attacks at the airports in Rome and Vienna. When they returned to the second floor reception area, two swarthy men with dark hair and mustaches were seated outside General Steiner's door. As Dieter and Steiner approached, they stood and smiled. Steiner went up to the older man and shook his hand. "Ali Mahmoud, it's good to see you again!"

"Likewise, Herr General," Mahmoud replied in fluent German. Gesturing toward his companion, he said, "Allow me to introduce my associate, Kemal Muhsin."

"*Sehr Angenehm*," Steiner grunted as he shook Muhsin's hand. Then he turned to Dieter. "Gentlemen, may I present Dieter Burchert, a Hauptmann in the Volksarmee who will be working closely with my department in his new assignment. Dieter, Herr Mahmoud and Herr Muhsin are from the intelligence section of the Iraqi embassy."

Dieter exchanged greetings with the Iraqis and then followed behind as the general led the way into his office and directed them to seats around a mahogany conference table. While they settled themselves, Dieter sized up the Iraqis. It was obvious that General Steiner and Ali Mahmoud had worked together before, and it soon became clear that the more polished Mahmoud was the resident chief. Muhsin was harder to figure out. A couple of centimeters taller than Dieter, with a husky build and pockmarked face, Muhsin looked like a bar room brawler. Whereas Mahmoud was almost jovial, Muhsin was deadly serious with suspicious looking eyes.

When the protocol formalities were out of the way Steiner got down to business. "Gentlemen, I wish to thank you for delaying action against your Kurdish dissidents in Europe until after the visit of the West German foreign minister. My government wants to avoid any negative propaganda directed toward us by the western press as we seek to improve our trade relations." Then he leaned closer. "But in no way does that mean we are less inclined to support your battle against the enemies of Saddam Hussein and their supporters. In fact we have the special explosives you have requested and the technical experts available to assist in the training of your cadres."

"Excellent, excellent," Ali said, rubbing his hands together. "We are anxious to expand our operations." A trace of a smile also creased Muhsin's face, making Dieter wonder about the morality of men who could find pleasure in a plan to blow up buses carrying women and children.

"Good," Steiner continued. "I'll have the head of Directorate 5 join us to work out the details." Steiner went to his desk and pushed a button on his intercom. "Tell Colonel Weber to come in." Then he nodded to Dieter who took his cue, and said goodbye to the Iraqis.

Steiner walked him to the door and put an arm around his shoulder, "I hope this has been a worthwhile visit for you. The Stasi is active in much more than our citizens will ever understand."

As Dieter left the building, he was buoyed by the strength of the organization he had seen, but troubled by its involvement with groups that might be considered terrorists in other parts of the world. Also troubling was the Iraqi called Muhsin. His face reflected no ideological conviction except malice.

CHAPTER 13

Gisela slept fitfully. The dream had come back as it often did when Fred was gone. A small boy who looked like Dieter stood crying by a grave. She was on the other side of the grave, and reached out to him. But he didn't see her, and she couldn't stretch far enough to touch him. As she tried to walk around the grave it kept getting longer, so she tried to jump across. The opening was too wide. She fell short, and was falling. Then she woke.

Sunlight streamed through the bedroom window and she knew without looking at the clock that it was late. Not that it mattered. She had nothing scheduled until the afternoon. The pill had helped her sleep, but as it wore off, her unconscious mind was bothered with troubling images. It seemed to be happening more frequently since they had left Germany.

She was in the master bedroom on the second floor of their brick quarters on "Colonels Row" at Fort Stewart, Georgia. They had moved into this big house a year ago, in June 1988, when they returned from Fifth Corps Headquarters, in Frankfurt, Germany. Ironic, she thought, to have this much space for just the two of them, after all the cramped places they had lived. Except for Anna's infrequent visits on leave from the Air Force, two of their bedrooms were usually vacant. A pang of remorse hit her as she thought of Fred's disappointment over their not having children. After many visits to Army doctors, an OB/GYN specialist finally concluded that her injuries and the trauma of the border crossing had something to do with her failure to conceive.

She pulled herself out of bed, determined to shake her gloomy mood. A slow walk brought her to the bathroom, where she was soon under the shower trying to revitalize herself through a brisk scrubbing. Minutes later, clad in a bathrobe, she was blow-drying her hair when the telephone rang. Returning to the bedroom she answered the phone.

A female voice said, "Mrs. Newman, this is Captain Baker from the Division AG office. I'm just calling to check with you about your participation in the Family Support Group meeting this afternoon. "

"Yes, Captain. I'm planning to be there. One o'clock at the NCO Club isn't it?"

"That's correct. And we have you scheduled to lead a panel discussion on family matters from 1400 to 1600 hours."

"Tell me again who's on the panel."

Captain Baker ticked off the names adding, "They have all worked with family support groups before."

"That sounds fine." It was reassuring that she had met two of the participants. "Are there any changes in the list of topics?"

"Yes. We want to address the subject of emotional problems, such as feeling isolated, not hearing from your spouse, depression, etc. That has come up in other meetings and is now being included in the latest Family Support Group plans."

How fitting, Gisela thought. I can relate to depression. But what can I say to help anyone else? She had wanted to beg off the invitation to be a speaker, but Fred persuaded her to accept, making it sound like it was a duty thing. That was usually the case, she thought regretfully. When it came to a conflict between her personal wishes and Army requirements, the Army always won.

"Okay. I believe the idea is to have the panel talk for about thirty minutes, and then take questions, isn't it?"

"Yes Ma'am. Since this is the first division conference in a long time, I'm sure there will be plenty of questions."

They finished their conversation and Gisela hung up. For a moment she stood looking out the window, considering the climbing temperature and humidity outside. God how she missed the cool breezes and the shade trees in the Erzgebirge! The thought that she might never again see the familiar scenery of her youth threatened to thrust her into another mood of melancholy.

With an effort she shook off her homesickness and returned to the bathroom. She stepped on the scales and saw it register 145 again. Frustrating, she thought. No matter how much I diet, I just can't seem to take the weight off. I'm going to have to find some exercise program that I can stay with.

She finished drying her hair and took a good look in the mirror. Her hair was still full and natural, no gray showing yet, thank God. Because of the Georgia heat she kept it short, cut just a little past the ears. Perhaps that helped it keep its luster and body, she thought. Her face, although a little fuller with the added weight, was without wrinkles, and didn't need much make-up. Altogether not bad, considering what a scrawny creature she was as a child.

It took a few minutes to decide what to wear. She didn't want to overdress, since most of the women would be wives of young soldiers. Fred taught her that she had a role to play as the wife of a senior officer, so she needed something presentable without being flashy. After looking at several dresses, she finally chose a pale red, Irish linen jacket and skirt outfit with a white short-sleeve blouse.

The thought of facing a large audience of women made her nervous and conscious of her accent. Still, she wouldn't be the only foreign born woman there, and an innate sense of who she was and what she had been through, helped overcome her apprehension.

It was nearly six o'clock in the evening when Gisela parked her station wagon in front of their quarters. She was surprised to see Fred's BMW in the driveway; he wasn't expected home for another day. Entering the front door, she called out, "Hi, Fred. Where are you?"

"I'm upstairs, honey, changing clothes."

Gisela climbed the stairs, and entered the bedroom where Fred was unlacing his combat boots. For a moment she stood looking at him. He didn't seem much different than when they first met, short cropped hair with some flecks of gray, and the same rugged body, although a little thicker at the waist. She walked toward him, and he stood to kiss her. Still holding her, he said, "Hey, you look great. Something special going on today?"

"Just the Family Support Conference at the NCO Club. Did I misunderstand? I thought you weren't coming back until tomorrow."

"No. The exercise finishes tomorrow, but the general wanted a few of us to come back early. He wants to get started on changes to our Mid-East contingency plan that we have to brief to Central Command next week." Fred was the 24th Mechanized Division Chief of Staff, responsible for coordinating the work of all staff sections.

Nuzzling Gisela's neck, he said slowly, "I'm not going back to the office until tomorrow, so why don't we have a quiet, romantic dinner at home?" Gently he peeled off her jacket and began unfastening the buttons of her blouse.

"Hmmm, that could be arranged." Gisela arched her neck and moved closer. "When do you want to eat?" she whispered.

"I'm not hungry for food right now," he said, pulling her toward the bed.

Later, sipping the remaining glass from a bottle of Merlot they had split with T-bone steaks, Fred asked, "So how was everything while I was gone?"

"Oh, fine, I guess." She looked away. "I ran errands, went to a luncheon at the Officers Club, and then I had that conference today."

Fred looked at her closely. "What's wrong, Gisela? Was that Family Support thing too much for you?"

"No," she sighed. "I suppose it was something I should do. I told the young wives about how little support we had when you were in Vietnam, and how difficult it was." She thought momentarily about Gail inviting her over so often, and how much that had meant to her. "I said that it was important to develop a network of friends who they could call on for help, or even if they were just lonely."

"Family Support has come a long way, thankfully. But why did it get you down?"

Gisela looked at her hands. "Yesterday was Dieter's birthday. He's 28 and I don't know where he is or even what he looks like," She looked up at Fred, her eyes glistening with tears. "I had another dream about him last night. The same one. Oh, Fred! What am I going to do?"

Fred reached over and took her hands in his. "I wish I had the answer, Honey." As Fred held her, Gisela thought of all their recent frustrations in trying to find some link to Dieter. Just the previous year they had spent two fruitless weeks in East Germany. Not surprisingly, the communist bureaucracy was uncooperative about providing information, and even more reluctant to trust Americans who spoke fluent German. In a last minute effort she had contacted a former neighbor, Claudia Schuman, hoping somehow she could help. Claudia's son had been a playmate of Dieter, and she was sympathetic. But she could suggest nothing they hadn't tried, and they left Berlin empty handed.

Nor had their German attorney, Herr Volker, been able to find any trace of Dieter's placement in an adoptive home. Her last letter to him brought only a short response that he had nothing new to report.

Fred looked like he was trying to think of something encouraging to say when the phone rang. He picked up the kitchen wall phone and said, "Anna, it's good to hear your voice. How's everything at Scott?"

Gisela was already moving toward the den to pick up on the other extension. The walls were filled with family pictures and mementos of military assignments. As she sat in the desk chair, she looked at Anna's picture as a cadet at the Air Force Academy, shortly before her graduation in '84. She was proud of Anna but concerned about her military service. That was Fred's doing, she thought. Lacking a son of his own, Fred had channeled his energies into making Anna an outstanding athlete and very competitive young woman. It bothered her too that Anna's interests seemed to follow Fred's more than hers. Still, even in uniform, Gisela couldn't deny Anna's resemblance to her. She looked trim and confident, as befitted a woman who was in the top ten per cent of her class academically and captain of the woman's track team. Nevertheless, Gisela wished Anna would forget about her military career, get married, and have children.

As she picked up the phone on the desk Anna was saying something about a party at the officers club, so Gisela asked, "Did I hear something about a boyfriend?"

She heard Anna sigh before answering, "No, Mom. I'm dating two or three guys, but there's no one special yet."

Fred interrupted the inquiry into Anna's social life. "So, what's the big news, Anna?"

"I've got orders, Dad. I'm going back to flying C130s in a squadron based in Little Rock, Arkansas." Currently Anna was a captain on the staff of the Military Airlift Command at Scott Air Force Base near St. Louis. But Fred had told Gisela that Anna, as one of the few women pilots, wasn't likely to spend any more time in staff jobs than she had to.

"That's wonderful, Anna," Gisela said. "You'll be closer to us won't you? Maybe you can come see us more often."

"I won't be that much closer, mother. Little Rock is about 300 miles directly south of Scott. But there will probably be some training flights to Air Force bases in the southeast. So, yeah, I'll surprise you sometime by dropping in out of the blue."

"When do you report to your squadron at Little Rock?" Fred asked.

"October 1st, which gives me time to finish a project I've been working on, and maybe take some leave."

"Anna, it would really help your mother if you could swing by here for a few days on your way to Little Rock." Fred's tone was serious.

"Sure, Dad. Is something wrong?"

"Oh, Fred. You shouldn't frighten her. No, Anna, nothing is wrong, and I don't want you to go to a lot of trouble just to come here for a day or two. I was just sad because yesterday was Dieter's birthday and we don't have any new information about him. But your call makes me feel better already."

"Mom, I know it's hard for you when you think about him. Listen, I was thinking about coming home on leave anyway. I just didn't want to mention it until I know how much time I will have. I'll call again when I know for sure."

"Well, if it is convenient, that would make me very happy. I do miss you, Anna."

"And, I miss you too, Mom. But I have some things to do to get ready for work tomorrow, so I've got to go. I'll call again soon. Love you, Bye."

"I love you too, Anna." Gisela hung up bothered by another regret. How much had her preoccupation with finding Dieter interfered with her relationship with Anna?

It was raining when dawn broke at Fort McCoy. It seemed like an axiom to John that whenever a field exercise was scheduled, the weather would be lousy. Last year it had been hot—unmercifully hot. Temperatures had stayed above 90 degrees for their two weeks, and his concerns then had been heat stroke and accidental injuries. Now it was unseasonably cold for June in central Wisconsin, and wet. It was unlikely that anyone would get frostbite, but you could never rule out the unlikely. Murphy's Law stated that if something could go wrong, it would. That was proven two nights earlier when a soldier in the 303d MP Company was hit by lightning, which struck a vehicle and traveled along a radio wire to make contact. He was recuperating in the civilian hospital in nearby Lacrosse.

John tried to avoid the mud near the entrance to a GP medium tent. A wooden sign with S-3 painted on it was driven into the ground next to the tent. He pushed aside the tent flap and stepped into the dimly lit interior. At the far end a large map board had been erected and next to it was an easel with several charts. Around the edges of the tent were some field tables with radios and telephones, more charts and a few wooden footlockers.

"Good morning, Colonel. Are you enjoying this fine weather?"

"Morning, Specialist Cooper. Yeah, it's going to be another beautiful day at McCoy, isn't it?" Specialist Fifth Class Sharon Cooper was seated on a folding chair, hunched over a VRC 46 radio, one hand holding the microphone, the other shoved into her field jacket pocket. Under a Kevlar helmet her brown hair was pulled back in a ponytail. She had looped the sling of her M-16 rifle over the back of the chair; and following standard field procedure, her gas mask was still strapped in its container to her left leg. Cooper, a junior at Eastern Michigan University, was one of those female soldiers who never ceased to amaze him. An ROTC cadet who earned extra money drilling with a Reserve unit, she was one of his sharpest soldiers, and a great role model for young women who enlisted directly in the Army Reserve.

A short, wiry major standing by the map board turned around at the sound of Parker's voice. "Colonel, we just got a report from the guard company. They cleared Checkpoint 4 and should be here by 0700."

"Good. They're right on schedule. Any problems with the transportation, Charlie?"

Charlie Thompson was operations officer, or S-3, of the 301st Prisoner of War Camp when John took command two years ago. A Vietnam veteran with a combat infantryman's badge, Major Thompson was on the promotion list for Lieutenant Colonel. That made him, in John's opinion, a prime candidate to command the next MP battalion that came open.

"No, sir. I told Captain O'Brian to send a sergeant and driver to the Transportation Company's command post at 0400 to make sure they were up and to guide them to the EPW holding area."

EPW, an army acronym for Enemy Prisoner of War, in this case referred to 150 Army Reservists from the 300th MP Command who were tasked to play the role of captured Warsaw Pact soldiers to realistically test the effectiveness of Parker's camp and guard companies in handling enemy prisoners of war.

"Nice going, Charlie." John noticed a well-built black officer with a Fourth Army shoulder patch on his field jacket watching Thompson. Lieutenant Colonel Wendell Wood had two strips of white tape encircling his fatigue cap that, together with a white armband, designated him the senior evaluator of this field exercise.

"I think you've done this a few times before," Wood observed.

"That's true, sir. But I learned that trick the hard way a few years back when a transportation company showed up late, and my company almost missed a scheduled parachute jump. Would either of you like some coffee?"

A studious young Specialist Fourth Class poured two mugs of coffee from a thermos and brought them to the officers. John took off his helmet with the darkened eagle insignia of a full colonel, and sat in a folding chair in front of the map board. They were beginning the second week of annual training, which brought together his 301st Military Police Enemy Prisoner of War (EPW) Camp headquarters, from Inkster, Michigan and subordinate companies from Michigan, Illinois and Iowa. Only half the units assigned for their wartime mission were present on this occasion, because the training budget didn't have sufficient funds to bring the rest from more distant states.

"Have the prisoners been fed, Charlie?" John asked.

"Yes, sir. Only coffee and MRE's for now, but they'll get a hot meal tonight."

"How are we handling the prisoners waiting to be processed?"

"We're going to process them in groups of fifty, so the waiting groups will be searched again and the officers segregated. They'll be moved into tents inside the enclosure and rotated through the processing as soon as one group is completed."

John nodded his approval. He didn't doubt Thompson's plan, but experience had taught him that unforeseen glitches often screwed up what actually took place. Rain spattering outside convinced him that he was right to insist on moving waiting prisoners into the enclosure where tents were available. The chugging of a five-ton truck penetrated the tent. John swallowed the last of his coffee and set the cup on a footlocker.

He looked at the evaluator and said, "Let's see how well this works."

As they walked toward the parking area on the edge of the camp, LTC Wood asked, "How long has your unit been organized for EPW operations?"

"Since the early sixties. You ever hear of Koje-do?"

"Hmm...wasn't that one of the battles in Korea?"

"You could say that. Actually it's where the Army operated a POW camp for over 100,000 Chinese and North Korean prisoners. The prisoners got out of control, staged demonstrations claiming inhumane treatment, and even took the camp commander hostage. Eighth Army had to send an infantry regiment with tanks to subdue them. Before it was over about 50 prisoners were dead, many wounded, and the camp commander and his deputy were facing charges of dereliction of duty."

Lieutenant Colonel Wood pulled out a pack of Marlboro cigarettes and offered one to Parker who shook his head. As Wood lit his cigarette, he asked, "I remember something about that. That was a major flap, wasn't it?"

"That's for sure! It got headlines around the world and prolonged the peace talks at Panmunjom. Afterward the Army created special military police units to handle enemy PW's, and that's when the 301st was formed."

They halted about thirty yards from the parking area. MPs in combat gear, armed with M-16 rifles, were herding the "acting prisoners" off the trucks and into marching groups.

After a few minutes of watching the activity, Wood said, "I don't think I've heard of any EPW units in the active army."

"That's right. They're all in the Army Reserve and National Guard. And one of our problems is continuity of training. The MP School writes the doctrine and provides some guidance, but few of our soldiers have been trained there. Most come to us with active duty experience in other skills, and we have to retrain them."

"I noticed some classes on the Geneva Conventions and the Rules of Land Warfare on the training schedule."

"Yes. We usually hold those at home station, but I wanted to give some background for this exercise." John smiled, adding, "And we worked in the lessons from Koje-do."

Wood changed the subject, "Have any of your units been deployed?"

"We didn't have much of a role in Vietnam, but in 1980 part of the 300th was mobilized to handle hundreds of unruly Cuban refugees here at McCoy."

"Oh, yeah," Wood said thoughtfully. "I'd forgotten about that operation."

John wasn't surprised at the evaluator's reaction. Most active duty officers had little contact with the Army Reserve or National Guard, and LTC Wood was a hard-charging infantry officer, without much experience with military police units.

"Looking back makes me realize how long I've been wearing a uniform." It didn't seem long, but earlier that week when filling out some personnel forms, John realized he was only a few years away from his mandatory military retirement. He had been coming to Fort McCoy and other posts for training since 1969, following his resignation. The Army Reserve turned out to be a pleasant surprise, made up, for the most part, of dedicated soldiers who had not remained in the full time Army.

Then his attention returned to the acting prisoners being lined up by the MP escort guards. John recognized his executive officer, LTC Bill Hacker, and Command Sergeant Major Jack Erickson standing among the columns of bedraggled soldiers with their arms up, hands clasped on top of their heads. No one was excused from the humiliation of being treated as a prisoner. They needed everybody they could get to make it realistic, and he made sure every soldier, including himself, was assigned to one of the two rotational groups of prisoners.

"Your role-players don't look too happy," LTC Wood said, motioning toward the columns of solemn faced soldiers trudging off in the rain with MPs yelling at them to keep quiet and keep their hands up. "I'm going to follow the first group and see how your guys process them."

"Fine. I'll catch up with you later." John watched as LTC Wood unobtrusively moved off with the first group. Having Wood around the last few days as Fourth Army's observer made him think again about the life he had left. Where would he be now if he had stayed on active duty? Perhaps in the Pentagon, or commanding a brigade somewhere, or on a headquarters staff like Fourth Army.

Instead he had picked up the pieces of his Dad's business, and after some difficult years brought it back to the thriving insurance office it once was. Now the business operated smoothly without his constant presence, and he found these training exercises a welcome diversion from the routine of contacting clients and processing claims.

John wrenched his mind back to the present. Three MP guards were marching off the last group of prisoners, so he followed at a distance where he could observe without interfering. The rain let up and a faint hint of sunshine was evident above the tops of dripping pine trees. When they reached the camp he watched as the soldiers were led in small groups, officers segregated from other ranks, through the double gates of the entrance to the enclosure. They were supposed to be capable of handling 12,000 EPWs, separated among three enclosures within the entire compound. But for this exercise only one enclosure was laid out with concertina wire around the perimeter with a few guard towers to add realism.

Except for that brief experience with Cuban detainees, they had never tried anything larger. Getting enough soldiers to act as prisoners was a problem that made it hard to know what his unit could really accomplish. Sure, he thought, they know the doctrine and procedures for handling prisoners. But when the call came, if it ever did, would their limited training opportunities measure up to the task of controlling thousands of hostile prisoners?

CHAPTER 14

Dieter sat quietly at the end of a long table in the second floor conference room of Stasi Headquarters on Nikolai Strasse. Since assuming his duties as liaison officer to the Stasi, he had attended many such meetings, providing some input on communications and logistical support from the Volksarmee, but mainly listening and taking notes to brief his commander.

Leipzig, where Dieter's new assignment placed him in September 1989, was the second largest city in East Germany, with a population of over a half million. Its location along major trading routes made it an important market for commerce and printing in the Middle Ages, and its prestige as a trading center had continued to the present. But since his student days, Dieter had taken greater pride in its international reputation as a city of culture from the literature of Goethe and Schiller, to the music of Johann Sebastian Bach, Richard Wagner, and the Gewandhaus Orchestra.

Oberst Werner Schwarz, a big round-shouldered man who wore a tight-fitting gray suit and dark-rimmed glasses, chaired the meeting. The Stasi colonel was gruff and direct in conversation, traits that carried over from his early days as a policeman. He was also notoriously short on patience for a long-winded speaker like the tall, young major who was briefing the group about an increase of escapees to the west.

"Get to the point, Major Röder. How did the students know they could cross the border from Hungary to Austria?"

Major Röder tugged at his chin with his left hand. "That's just it, *Herr Oberst,* they didn't know at first. A few students met some Hungarian border guards in a Gasthaus, and found out that the Hungarians had relaxed their controls. A handful of adventurers took advantage of the situation and fled that night. Some doubters stayed behind to see what happened, and they spread the word to others."

Pointing to a map on the wall behind him, he continued. "By the middle of August, hundreds of our young people on vacation were flocking to Schlagbaum and other towns to cross the border at night. Information came back to other students that there was an open route, and that the Austrians were bussing the refugees on to West Germany."

"Ja, ja. I know the rest. And Kohl's government promised them automatic citizenship and social welfare payments. Those damned capitalists will do anything to lure people away from us."

As the colonel continued ranting, it occurred to Dieter that he was expressing the concern of the Stasi, as well as other privileged members of the Communist Party, about the security and stability of the regime.

Schwarz raised his arms in a gesture of exasperation. "How many crossed last week?"

"We don't know exactly, Herr Oberst." Major Röder tugged at his chin again.

"What do you mean, you don't know? Don't we have anybody down there who can count?"

"Yes sir. We have agents in the area, but the Hungarians aren't keeping count, and the best we have are estimates."

Oberst Schwarz pulled a pack of cigarettes from his coat pocket and lit one with a gold plated lighter. "Well, are you going to share the estimates with us, Major, or do I have to keep interrogating you to get an answer?"

"No sir. I mean, yes sir. That is, about a thousand made it across to Austria last week."

"Very well. Sit down. I want to hear from Herr Kramer what our Foreign Office is doing about this collapse of security by our Warsaw Pact ally," he said bitterly.

Dieter thought about previous alliances his country had formed and wondered if the Warsaw Pact would really be effective if they became involved in a shooting war with NATO. Once before a great battle had been fought on the edge of this city when German and Russian armies together stopped Napoleon's invasion in 1813. His visits to the huge monument that commemorates 22,000 Russian soldiers, who fell in the battle, had helped solidify his belief in their Russian allies. But he had grave doubts about the Hungarians and other Eastern Block nations.

Rudolf Kramer, a slight balding bureaucrat of about fifty, was their liaison to the DDR Foreign Office in Berlin. Seated across the table from Dieter, he looked up from a tablet where he was making notes.

"*Herr Oberst*, both the Foreign Minister and Defense Minister sent strongly worded messages to the Hungarian Government demanding that our border security agreements be enforced. Then Chairman Honeker made direct contact with the Hungarian premier and reinforced our demands. We received a message this morning from the Foreign Office, that Hungary will restore border controls tomorrow."

Oberst Schwarz took a puff on his cigarette and ground it out in the ashtray in front of him. "Finally, some good news," he growled. "It's about time those zither playing idiots woke up to reality. I don't know what got into their heads to allow these crossings. Probably this Perestroika and Glasnost nonsense we keep hearing from Gorbachev."

"Sir, there's another development that may cause trouble here in Leipzig." Klaus Mühlberger, Dieter's companion from the Moscow conference, spoke hesitantly from the end of the table where he sat next to Dieter.

"And what is that, Muehlburger?" Oberst Schwarz's tone was patronizing. The young man might be a bright star in the future Stasi galaxy, but Schwarz didn't like sharing the spotlight with subordinates.

"There is word on the street that people will be gathering at Nikolai Church tonight for a peace vigil at five o'clock." Klaus shifted in his seat uneasily, trying to avoid Schwarz's glare.

"And how reliable is that word, Mühlberger?"

"Sir, I've gotten reports to that effect from three different informants. Their reports have always checked out before."

"Humph," the colonel snorted. "Ever since that meddling Kurt Mazur got those street musicians together, we've had nothing but trouble." Schwarz stood and began pacing across the front of the conference room, gesturing with his right hand to emphasize his words.

"Just because some riff-raff can play musical instruments, Mazur thinks they should be able to play and sing subversive songs on any street corner. And when they're arrested, what does he do? Herr 'Conductor' calls a meeting at the Gewandhaus with this street rabble and the city council. Now everybody wants to chant political slogans. Well, it's time we put a stop to this nonsense!"

All eyes were on the big colonel as he stopped pacing and placed his hands on the table. "In only a month the whole world will be watching as we celebrate the 40th anniversary of our German Democratic Republic. Gorbachev and the other East-bloc leaders will attend the festivities, and for damn sure we are going to have stability by then." He punctuated his last sentence by slamming his fist on the table.

Colonel Schwarz sat down, and in a calmer voice said, "Now, this is what we will do. Mühlberger, I want you to take a squad and infiltrate the rally at Nikolai Church. Of course you will monitor and report what goes on, but more importantly I want your agents to foment doubts about the leaders. Whenever there is direction on what to do, have one of your people voice disagreement and suggest getting approval from the city council."

Pointing a stubby finger at another member of his staff, he said, "Kemper, have the Psychology Section prepare a disinformation campaign against the church leaders. Develop some unsavory background story about their motives, and make sure it gets published in the newspapers."

Turning to the other side of the table where the lone woman sat nervously fingering her necklace, he smiled cunningly. "Marianne, have Public Affairs distribute an avalanche of patriotic stories about the accomplishments of our government as it marks its 40th anniversary.

The theme should be that it is every citizen's duty to support *Socialistiche Einheit* (Socialist Unity) and denounce troublemakers."

"Yes sir. We are already working on that. But I'll make sure that we highlight the point about denouncing troublemakers."

"Very well. That covers everything for now." Schwarz stood and then looked around the table. Keep me informed. Especially you, Mühlberger. I want to know what goes on at Nikolai Church, and I don't want to wait for a meeting to find out." He grabbed his notebook from the table and strode out of the room.

As the staff members gathered their papers and shuffled toward the door, Klaus looked across the table and said, "How about going to that peace rally with me tonight, Dieter? It should be interesting, and I could use your help."

"*Ja, Gewiss.* I'd like to see how many show up, and how your team handles the situation."

"Fine, I'll see you at the church. Dress like a student and don't give me away. I'll meet you afterward at Auerbach's, and we can talk over a beer."

Dieter took a bus to the city center and got off at the Augustusplatz Ring stop. He wore a polo shirt, jeans and sandals. Along Grimmaischer Strasse he noticed large numbers of students, as well as middle-aged people, heading in the same direction. With no previous religious experience, Dieter had done some research on the target of the Stasi's surveillance. He learned that St. Nikolai Church was Leipzig's oldest church, dedicated to the patron saint of travelers and merchants. Originally built in 1175 on a site near the city market, it was remodeled several times and contained elements of many architectural styles from Romanesque to Baroque.

Thinking about architecture reminded him of Renate's criticism of Leipzig's post-war building. World War II had brought devastation to Leipzig, especially the city center. After the war communist city planners shunned the Renaissance style to create architecture, which in the opinion of many, including Renate, distorted the perspective of the old city. Instead, Dieter thought, it was Leipzig's perspective that was being distorted by demands for reform from a vocal minority of malcontents.

Nearing the church, he fell in with a group of students and followed them inside. Ten minutes before five o'clock the church was almost full. Dieter was astonished. He had expected a couple of hundred students on the extremist fringe to show up, but there were several thousand people of all ages. The beauty of the church interior also struck him, particularly the white marble columns running down the center of the sanctuary.

Next to him a teen-age boy and girl were talking excitedly. "Look at the crowd," she said. "This is really something."

"People are fed up with being told what to think," her companion said. "We should be able to express our opinion about reforms, and this is a way to show it."

Stretching his neck, Dieter looked carefully around the large sanctuary for Klaus. He did see one man he knew to be a Stasi agent, but he couldn't find Klaus among all the people. He leaned across the girl next to him and addressed the boy.

"What do you mean about expressing opinions? I don't see that as much of a problem."

The boy was seventeen or eighteen with long, brown hair and the beginning of a mustache. He was wearing an earring in his left ear, and looked at Dieter suspiciously.

"I don't know where you're coming from, man, but if you request Rolling Stones music on the radio or in a record store, they say that's not allowed. Rock and roll music is supposed to be harmful, but that's just a bunch of crap from the higher ups."

"And if you complain about not being able to travel to Italy or England, the authorities tell you to shut up," his girlfriend chimed in. "One of my friends got three months in jail because he made a fuss about that stupid policy."

"But that's just it." Dieter tried to sound persuasive. "The western capitalists are just trying to subvert our form of socialism any way they can. There are plenty of places to visit in friendly countries, and Leipzig has some of the best music in the world."

The boy looked at Dieter like he was crazy. "Come off it, man. You sound just like Honeker." Glancing at Dieter's short haircut, his eyes narrowed. "Say, what are you doing here anyway, if you feel that way?"

"I'm here because I love my country, and I believe in peace," Dieter said forcefully. "I don't want to see anything harm the progress we've made." He wanted to say more, but the pastor entered the pulpit and a hush came over the sanctuary.

The pastor started to pray, and many people bowed their heads, surprising Dieter. This was the first religious ceremony Dieter had ever attended, and he watched the pastor's movements and the congregation's responses with curiosity. It was obvious that for most people, this was a first time experience also. Yet he could sense a genuine fervor. There seemed to be a shared belief in something; a feeling that together they could make a difference.

After a few minutes the prayer ended and the pastor looked out on the assemblage, and said in a strong voice,

"Blessed are the peacemakers, for they will be called sons of God.

Blessed are those who are persecuted because of righteousness, for theirs is the kingdom of heaven."

Continuing his discourse, the pastor told them that Jesus taught that people should not seek retaliation for wrongs that had been done to them. Rather, they should work for justice instead of revenge. He added that the Bible makes it clear that Christians should resist the forces of evil in society. When he stressed that resistance should be non-violent, Dieter remembered reading about Martin Luther King leading black protesters in America. Surely his fellow Germans couldn't believe that they needed to adopt the tactics of a group so badly oppressed as black Americans! It was frustrating that the people around him didn't appreciate that they were members of a classless society whose benefits were open to all.

Dieter's attention returned to the man in the pulpit, to hear him say that through prayer changes could occur. "When it seems that answers to prayer are slow in coming," he said, "Jesus urges us to keep on praying and not give up."

Finishing his sermon, the pastor made a sign of a cross with his hand, and mumbled a few words Dieter couldn't understand. Then he said, "I have been asked to urge you to come here again next Monday at the same time for another peace vigil to pray for political freedom."

An audible stirring swept through the church, followed by a spontaneous burst of applause and a clamor of excited conversation. Finally the pastor raised his arms to quiet the crowd, and offered a closing prayer. Dieter looked again for Klaus, and he noticed that many around him seemed to be earnestly praying. The service concluded with the hymn, *A Mighty Fortress Is Our God*, and then people began filing out the doors.

Dieter craned his neck, trying to spot Klaus, when he saw someone and gave a sharp intake of breath. It was Renate, in line to go out the side door. She looked lovely; her face aglow with enthusiasm, but her slim figure was pressed closely against a handsome man of about thirty. As the couple came to the exit door, she looked his way. For a moment their eyes met, and there was a spark of recognition. But she abruptly turned away and walked out the door. Dieter felt like someone had hit him in the stomach. At the first sight of her his hopes were raised, only to be dashed by her reaction.

Outside clusters of people were milling around in the streets adjoining the church. Dieter heard a man with a beard loudly suggesting a march to the new city hall.

"That's too far and nobody's there now," said a man wearing a student's cap who Dieter recognized as one of Klaus' team.

He moved on to another huddle that was discussing their demands and arguing about when to hold a peace march. Several groups moved off in the direction of Markt Platz, and he followed along. When they reached the market place in front of Old City Hall, the crowd had dwindled to a couple of hundred.

They hung around for nearly an hour alternately chanting slogans like, "We Are The People, Freedom Now, and Peace—Not Violence." Several cars of *Volkspolicei* arrived, and some of the demonstrators drifted away. Dieter spotted Klaus with a squad of policemen, hustling several protesters into a police van. After that the crowd's momentum seemed to wane, and within a few minutes people readily obeyed police orders to disperse.

Dieter watched the crowd break up, and then made his way past a large monument of Goethe, crossing the street to reach the portal to Mädler Passage. The open archway led to a magnificent enclosed mall with bright lighting and expensive shops. A few steps into the mall, Dieter paused by two sculptures illustrating the student scene of Goethe's day. What a change, he thought, between the carefree, partying students Goethe knew and the intense radicals of the present.

He walked down the steps, entered Auerbach's Cellar, and found a small table in a room called the Barrel Cellar after Goethe's story about Dr. Faust's barrel ride. A large wine barrel and a figure depicting Faust as the devil in one corner enhanced the atmosphere of the room. Dieter ordered a beer and waited for Klaus. Across the room several students were jammed around another table, engaged in an animated discussion. He couldn't hear everything being said, but from their gestures and the few words he could pick up, he judged that they had been at St. Nikolai Church.

One couple was holding hands and was obviously more interested in each other than in what was being discussed. They made him think of his time with Renate. What had gone wrong? He really did love her, and for a while he knew she loved him. But they had quarreled about politics, and even religion. Then came the confrontation over her activity with a Lutheran group smuggling people to the west, and the next thing he knew she was gone.

His reverie was interrupted by the arrival of Klaus. "Well, that was a big mess, wasn't it," Klaus said, sitting down heavily across from him.

"There were a hell of a lot more people there than I expected," Dieter replied. "If these protests aren't stopped soon, they're going to spread out of control."

"*Ja, Bestimmt.* It's getting worse. The problem's not just the students. I saw office workers, old women; even some factory workers were there." A waiter came to the table and Klaus ordered a beer.

"You arrested some people at the Marktplatz," Dieter noted.

"We needed to break up that demonstration before it got larger, and arresting them did the trick. Most were students, but one was a salesman in his thirties. They're being interrogated now at police headquarters." Klaus lit a cigarette and inhaled deeply.

Dieter slouched in his seat with a morose expression. "I'm worried about what happens next week at the church. I heard a lot of talk about bringing more people and having a peace march to city hall."

"I heard the same thing. I'm going to include that in my report to Schwarz. And I'm going to recommend that we meet them with enough force to stop this movement cold."

The two officers continued their conversation for several minutes. But when the waiter returned to ask about a refill, Klaus got up. "I'd better go down to police headquarters and check on those we arrested. I want to include anything they said in my report." Dieter left with him, but outside the Mädler Passage they went their separate ways.

As Dieter walked back to the Ring bus stop, his mind replayed images of the evening. There was something about the service in St. Nikolai Church that troubled him. The large cross behind the altar with a man hanging from it seemed to be a link to a distant memory. Although he knew it was just a symbol of an antiquated religion, he couldn't escape the feeling that the cross had some connection to him.

It wasn't until he returned to his comfortable apartment near the Landsberger Strasse Barracks that he recalled a hazy memory from his childhood. There was a chain that he used to sleep with—a chain made of some kind of beads. And that chain had a figure on a wooden cross fastened at the end!

The next few weeks saw an upsurge in protest activities throughout East Germany. Even at state sponsored anniversary parades there were shouts of "Glasnost and Perestroika" and "Gorbachev, help us." Such pleas for soviet-style liberalization were particularly galling to the communist hierarchy in the DDR, which had always portrayed itself as a blood brother of Russia. Scenes of increasingly violent confrontation took place in the streets of East Berlin, Dresden, Karl Marx Stadt, Plauen, Magdeburg, and Leipzig as security forces cracked down on demonstrators. Still, the crowds swelled at St. Nikolai's Monday peace rallies, until thousands spilled out onto nearby streets where police were waiting for them.

Dieter was on hand at one of those peace rallies in uniform, wearing the new shoulder boards of a major, when Volkspolicei and Stasi forces waded into the mass of protesters packed into Marktplatz with clubs and pepper spray. Hundreds were arrested, thrown into trucks and taken to police stations and temporary jails where they were photographed, fingerprinted, and interrogated. Dieter was standing by one of the trucks when a Volkspolicei squad in green uniforms dragged a man and woman from the crowd and came toward him. The man was nearly unconscious and bleeding profusely. The woman was shouting angrily and struggling with two guards to free herself.

"Let go of me, you stupid pigs," she said, while trying to kick the nearest guard. Despite her contorted features, bleeding lip, and disheveled hair, there was no mistaking that voice. It was Renate. Her back was toward him as the Vopos heaved her companion into the truck.

"Just a minute, Feldwebel," Dieter said to the sergeant in charge. "I want to talk to that woman." Motioning toward a military automobile, he said, "Put her in the back seat, and I'll take charge of her."

"We'd better put handcuffs on her, Herr Major. She's a mean one."

As if confirming the Feldwebel's assessment, Renate, seeing Dieter, spat out some blood, and said, "You! I might have known you would be with these goons."

"Never mind the cuffs. I can handle her. Just put her in the car and take care of the others."

Splat! A ripe tomato hit the side of the truck and pieces splashed on the Feldwebel's jacket. Turning toward two strapping Vopos holding Renate between them, he yelled, "You two do what the Major says, and then join me." He took the rest of his squad back into the melee, looking for the person who had thrown the tomato. The Vopos hustled Renate over to a police sedan and pushed her roughly into the back seat where she was locked in. Dieter dismissed them, opened the front passenger door, and positioned himself where he could look at her. Despite her defiance, he felt a longing to put his arms around her.

Renate sat up, pushed some strands of hair away from her eyes, and stared angrily at Dieter. He took off his high peaked cap, and returned her look with a mixture of concern and tenderness.

"Renate, what are you mixed up in now? You couldn't pick a worse time to be in the middle of a demonstration. Don't you know the State is going to use maximum force to stop these protests before the 40th Anniversary celebration?"

"I'm doing what every decent German wants to do. I'm demonstrating for freedom—something you're not capable of understanding."

Her words stung, and his resentment came out in a rush. "You and your friends! You're tearing the country apart. You talk about freedom and tell everyone how good it is in the West. And you encourage those fools out there to overthrow the government."

"We're tired of living in a police state where you get beat up and tossed in jail for expressing an opinion." She reached up and wiped some blood from her mouth, and continued in a derisive tone. "Have you looked around, Dieter, and seen just how screwed up this 'democratic republic' is? Buildings haven't been repaired in 40 years, highways are full of potholes, apartment housing is overcrowded, and factory pollution is slowly poisoning us."

"And you think capitalist democracy is better?" he said scornfully. "Our system may not be perfect, but I'm proud to be a communist. This is a good place to live. Everyone who wishes can work to retirement; and we have plenty to eat and good medical care. It's a hell of a lot better than a society of homeless people, dominated by drugs and crime."

Across from them Vopos were crowding more prisoners into the truck containing Renate's friend, and preparing to move out.

"I don't want to leave my country, and neither do they," she said pointing toward the crowd. "But we need a government that listens to people, instead of locking us up."

Dieter lowered his voice. "I'm not a politician, Renate—just a soldier. I don't want to argue with you." He paused, looked away for a moment, and then faced her sadly. "I still love you, Renate. I can't get you out of my mind."

"Oh, Dieter." Her voice softened, and she put her hand on the screen separating them. "If only you were more open-minded." She started to say something, but just then the police truck rumbled past them, interrupting her thought. Her eyes followed the departing truck and she asked, "What's going to happen to my friend?"

"I don't know. If he is one of the leaders, he'll be kept in jail until there is a trial. What's his name?"

"Stefan. Stefan Biederman."

He sensed that the moment for shared feelings had passed. But he couldn't let her go through any more punishment. "I'll check on him for you, and let you know what happens. Now, if you promise not to go back into the square with those rioters, I'll walk you to the edge of the crowd and let you go."

Renate sat silently, contemplating his offer. Finally, she sighed and said, "All right, I won't go back today." In a stronger tone she added, "But that doesn't mean I won't be here another day."

Shaking his head in disbelief at her determination, Dieter got out of the sedan and unlocked Renate's door. As they walked away from the uproar, he said, "I can't believe you want to risk arrest and jail to be part of this…this anarchy. I should warn you, Renate, that next time you may not be this lucky. The next riot will only bring more severe security measures."

Reaching one of the side streets leading away from the square, Renate stopped and faced Dieter. "I don't want to be thrown in jail, but I don't want to see this country turn into one big jail either. You and your Stasi friends should think carefully before harming anybody. Someday you may be held accountable." With that she turned abruptly and ran down the street.

Two hours later Dieter was at the main police station. The lock up area was packed with sullen people, many with cuts and bruises. A thick-set police sergeant carrying a clip board approached Dieter and asked. "*Herr Major*, aren't you the liaison officer to the Volksarmee?"

"That's right. What do you need?"

"More jail space is what we need. There are so many prisoners here we can hardly move. Do you think we could transfer a hundred or more to the Army Barracks?"

"Probably. I'll need to make a couple of phone calls. Where's your phone?"

"Just down the hall. Please follow me."

As Dieter followed the policeman, he saw a room off the hallway where men and women leaned against the wall, feet spread apart, while a police officer seated at a table took them one-at-a-time for finger prints and booking. Another Vopo kept the line in order through the liberal use of a truncheon.

"How long are you going to keep them?" he asked when they reached the office.

"Until they have each been interrogated and signed their interrogation statement. A couple of days for most, but longer for those with a record of provocation. They'll go in front of a judge and then to prison."

Dieter made a call to his regimental executive officer and another to the support battalion commander. It was arranged that the Volksarmee would transport and hold two hundred male prisoners until they could be interrogated. After the details were completed, Dieter said, "Now I have a request. Can you bring me a prisoner by the name of Stefan Biederman?"

The sergeant raised an eyebrow, but shrugged and consulted his clipboard. "He's here, awaiting interrogation. *Jawohl, Herr Major.* Let me get him."

A few minutes later a slender man with a torn shirt and broken glasses was standing in front of Dieter holding a blood-soaked rag to his head. With a wave of his hand, Dieter dismissed the policeman.

"What's your name?" Dieter barked at him.

"Stefan Biederman," he croaked through swollen lips.

Dieter led him through the remaining questions and completed the interrogation report. "Sign here," he ordered, pushing the form across the table at the sagging prisoner who feebly scrawled his signature. Then Dieter stood, squared his shoulders, and stepped forward until his face was only a few inches from Biederman's."

"Now listen to me, you stupid bastard. I'm going to have you released, only as a favor to a friend of mine. But I know you're one of the instigators. If you show your face at another demonstration, we'll be looking for you and put you away where you won't see anyone for a long time. Do you understand me?"

Stefan looked at Dieter cynically, but only said, "*Ja*, I understand."

As he left police headquarters, Dieter thought about the large number of protesters rounded up and jailed. The Volkspolicei and *Stasi* had done their best to root out the leaders, but others took their places. Why was the unrest spreading when they should be celebrating their nation's achievements?

CHAPTER 15

In the early evening of Monday, October 9th, a long column of T-62 tanks and BRP troop carriers was parked along Leipzig's outer ring. Soldiers in helmets and battle gear waited alongside their vehicles in nervous anticipation of what lay ahead. The usual joking that was a part of troop maneuvers faded once they were issued live ammunition. Honecker had issued a command for the "Maintenance of Order" which authorized security forces to shoot if necessary. Medical staffs in city hospitals were on alert, blood supplies prepared, and ambulance crews were standing by. The numbers attending Monday peace rallies had been growing exponentially week-by-week. That would change today, if the Stasi had their way.

Dieter stood next to Volksarmee battalion commander, Oberst Leutnant Strassman, consulting a map of the city, when Gefreiter (Private First Class) Hauser approached Dieter and saluted.

"*Herr Major*, there's an announcement on the radio about the protests that you should hear."

"Very well, Hauser. I'll be right there. Sir, you may want to hear this. It might affect our plans."

The two officers folded their map cases and walked across the street to where Hauser had parked Dieter's staff car. Hauser opened the rear door for the Oberst Leutnant. Dieter got into the front seat and turned up the volume on the broadcast band. They heard the speaker saying, "And so our committee reached an agreement. We insist that if the demonstration tonight remains peaceful, the Party will ensure that the military and police forces will not be aggressive. Isn't that your understanding, Herr Masur?"

"Yes, indeed." Kurt Masur, for 19 years conductor of the world famous Gewandhaus orchestra, was a celebrity in Leipzig. "The Cultural Affairs Department asked me to be on this committee because they know I believe in peaceful dissent. Therefore, I want to stress that protesters should be non-violent. If that is the case, the government has pledged that security forces will refrain from violent actions. In the interest of peaceful change and a brighter future, I implore all who are on the streets tonight to honor this agreement."

Dieter slapped his hand on the dashboard, and turned toward Strassman with a grim look on his face. "Peaceful or not, our orders are to break up this demonstration and restore order. General Lecker told us to be prepared to shoot if necessary."

Strassman took off his cap and wiped beads of perspiration from his forehead. "Do you really expect German soldiers to shoot down fellow citizens, Burchert? There are thousands of people out there, young and old. And they're unarmed. If we give the order to shoot, it would be a massacre, and the blame will flow downhill."

An hour later Dieter realized Strassman was right about one thing, when his staff car reached the city center. Packed into the Platz der Republic between the Hauptbahnhof (main rail station) and Gewandhaus Concert Hall was the largest crowd of demonstrators he had ever seen. People were chanting, "We are the people!" "Freedom, Equality, Liberty!" and "No Violence!" There were banners calling for "Glasnost (openness) in Church and State," and others demanding "Public inquiry into Stasi Crimes." People were even carrying posters of Gorbachev, who had become a symbol of progressive reform, despite the efforts of Honecker to separate East Germany's plan for communist utopia from that of the Soviets.

A heavy cordon of police and soldiers in riot gear protected the Hauptbahnhof and other city buildings. It was clear to Dieter that if the crowd became a mob bent on destruction, it would take tear gas, tanks, and even bullets to stop them. But other than chanting slogans, the protesters were surprisingly peaceful as they slowly moved forward.

Dieter was amazed to see men and women from all walks of life. Many had come from prayer meetings in nearby churches and carried candles as symbols of peace and hope.

Some students were talking with soldiers. And to Dieter's disgust, instead of keeping strict discipline, many of the young conscripts had relaxed and were carrying on conversations with their adversaries. Seeing girls place flowers in the gun barrels of nearby soldiers, he ignored the fact that he was not in their chain of command.

"You there," he shouted at the squad closest to him. "Take those damned flowers out of your weapons. Straighten up, and act like soldiers. You're here to provide security from these troublemakers, not to support them."

The soldiers did as ordered, but when Dieter moved off, they were again chatting and laughing with other young people in front of them. The crowd continued to march and chant slogans as they progressed around the inner city of Leipzig, until by eight o'clock they had returned to the Gewandhaus. Then, miraculously, they began to disperse peacefully. A concert was scheduled at that hour, and many, with joyous expressions, moved toward the large concert hall.

Others streamed past Dieter, leaving the inner city. Dieter noticed his Stasi friend, Klaus Muehlburger, standing in the shadow of the building housing the Bach Archives, and walked over to him. Klaus wore a brown leather coat and a crumpled hat. He lit a cigarette, and offered one to Dieter who gratefully took it.

"Did you see those signs about the Stasi, Klaus? It's outrageous."

"I don't know why we didn't break up that demonstration right at the start," Klaus said. "What are the people at the top afraid of?"

"I don't know either," Dieter replied. "A company of tanks moving toward them with some tear gas, would have sent those agitators running. Now we have a real threat to the government."

"It may be too late to regain control, Dieter." Klaus's face was pale, and his hand was shaking. "I'm afraid Honecker and the Central Committee have lost their nerve." He tossed his cigarette to the sidewalk and squashed it with his boot. "I'd better get back to the office and see what's going on there. *Wiedersehn.*" He walked slowly toward a parked car, his shoulders sagging.

Dieter waited a moment, not sure what to do. Next door the strains of music could be heard. He recognized Brahms's Second Symphony and, drawn by the music, walked up the steps of the magnificent concert hall. The lobby was packed with people listening fervently. An usher noticed his uniform and came over and whispered. "There's no room, *Herr Major*. The place is full."

"Never mind," Dieter said quietly. "I'll just stand here a moment." As he listened to the beautiful harmonies of the orchestra, his mood began to change. The tension slipped away, and he could imagine rippling streams and blue sky. The minutes passed unnoticed, as if he were in a trance. Suddenly, he was aware of people jostling him as they moved to the doors. He was carried along by the flow of the crowd and found himself outside in the darkness.

Next to him a middle-aged woman wiped her eyes with a handkerchief. A man who appeared to be her husband, said in a husky voice, "That was incredible. The audience just standing—no applause—standing in solidarity together." On his other side a young woman wearing a blue jean jacket said to her boyfriend, "Awesome. We made it through the day peacefully. I think there's hope for real freedom." Dieter knew then that something profound had changed in all their lives.

The next two days were surprisingly calm. People went about their business as usual, and the central government was uncharacteristically silent. Oberst Schwarz was called to Berlin for consultation, and Dieter sensed an uncertainty among Stasi leaders. On Wednesday he decided to call his father, but he was not home. Instead he spoke with his mother who was appalled at so many people being fooled by West German propaganda. When Erich called back, they talked about the government's timid response to the demonstrations.

"Why didn't the leaders carry out the attack orders?" Dieter asked.

"I don't know, Dieter. Maybe it was the size of the crowds, or the appeal by Masur's group that influenced them. But if Honecker had been himself, these disturbances would have been closed down long ago."

"What do you mean? What's wrong with the General Secretary?"

"He's sick, Dieter, and he's old. He's almost eighty, not the same man who shocked the west by building the wall overnight."

"What is happening to the country, Father? Is the government going to be overthrown?"

"Not if I have anything to say about it! I've been in touch with some friends on the Army General Staff and the Central Committee. It's time for Honecker to step down, and the government needs to make some reforms and build a stronger socialist system."

"But is there anyone strong enough to make a difference?"

"There are two or three men tough enough to control the situation: Egon Krenz, for one, or Gunter Mittag. Maybe even Joachim Hermann is up to the task."

"Well, I hope something changes soon, or the people in the street will take over."

Events moved rapidly in the weeks that followed. Demonstrations continued in Leipzig, growing in size; on 16 October 120,000, on 23 October 300,000, on 30 October almost half a million. People of all sorts—trade unionists, students, environmentalists, professors, feminists, and artists, even the handicapped—were taking part. As Erich predicted, Egon Krenz, a Honecker protégé, who immediately began talking about reforms, soon replaced Honecker. The new administration promoted an image of dialogue and town meetings between citizens and public officials. But the more the people were involved in addressing their grievances in public discussion, the more their appetite was whetted for demands the new regime was afraid to consider.

The media began to test the relaxation of government restraints, and to Dieter's dismay, the 30 October demonstration was reported live on DDR television. Previously forbidden topics like economic problems and political corruption were being discussed on television.

As a result, discontent was further aroused, and protests spread to smaller cities all over the country. The new leadership struggled to hold on to its control, but was afraid to use harsh measures. Lacking clear direction, security forces simply stood by and let people march and carry whatever banners they wanted.

Dieter was watching television in Leipzig's Stasi headquarters on November 4th with Klaus and several Stasi officers. A massive demonstration against the state was taking place in Berlin. As one speaker after another denounced the present system, Dieter erupted in exasperation.

"How do they do it, Klaus? Who's organizing these demonstrations and providing the leadership?"

Klaus took a drag from his cigarette, exhaling the smoke slowly while he considered his answer. "It's hard to say. We can't find any dominant leader or anyone seeking to exploit the situation to gain power for himself. The New Forum is just a loose organization that seems to operate through a large committee. Of course, the churches initially provided a spark through their peace rallies, but there doesn't seem to be any consistent plan."

A close-cropped, husky officer in his mid-thirties whom Dieter knew only as Rolf, pointed at the television set and said, "That guy is inciting a revolution."

The speaker at the microphone in Berlin's Alexanderplatz castigated the government for ruling through a corrupt elite that relied on spies and the illegal use of power. The only one who made an argument for the legality of the State and the need for security was Gregor Gysi, a prominent communist lawyer.

The news coverage went on for hours, and Dieter lost track of the number of speakers. Eventually he became convinced that Rolf was right. A revolution was occurring, yet it was a peaceful one. It was significant that no one was talking about reunification with the west. The overwhelming sentiment was for a more democratic form of socialism within their own country. The huge crowd was more festive than rebellious, and it dispersed peacefully in the early hours of the morning.

A few days later Dieter requested leave to go home. He wanted to see first hand what was going on there and he was curious about his father's activities. The Regimental Executive Officer agreed that a few days in Berlin might be more useful than remaining in Leipzig, and approved his travel. Dieter took the train, and arrived at his parents' home in time for dinner on November 9th.

Again Inge pampered him with a delicious meal of rolled beef and dumplings, a specialty of their cook. Between bites, Dieter said, "A fabulous meal, Mother. I haven't had *Rouladen mit Kartoffelklosse* like these since I left home." Later over coffee and ice cream, Dieter inquired about the current political situation in Berlin.

"It's terrible," Inge said. "Everything we've worked for is threatened. The people are deluded with visions of fancy cars and modern gadgets in every home. They don't realize how much poverty and misery exists in the West."

"Krenz and his ministers are too weak," Erich added. "They're too eager to promise reforms which only serve to weaken the party and encourage the opposition. They're rapidly losing control, and Kohl's "Wessies" are rubbing their hands in anticipation of taking over our country."

Dieter nodded at his father's derogatory reference to West Germany and its premier, Helmut Kohl. "Isn't there anything we can do to turn things around?"

"I don't know, Dieter. It may be too late." Leaning closer, Erich spoke in a low tone that couldn't be overheard by the servant in the kitchen. "I've been talking to some of the generals about taking over, but so far only two have said they would even consider it. The others are frightened of a blood bath and being held accountable. Unfortunately, we can't count on the Russians to support us; and, frankly, we're not sure if we can depend on our soldiers."

"It's a shame to say it, but that's what I saw in Leipzig. Most of the young soldiers are in sympathy with the people, and the sergeants and officers are reluctant to take responsibility for using force."

Dieter continued the discouraging conversation with his parents until it was time for the evening news broadcast. They moved to the living room and turned on the television just as Gunter Schabowski, Communist Party District Secretary for East Berlin was explaining some new reforms pertaining to travel.

"Does this mean that people will be free to travel across the border to the west?" asked one of the journalists.

Schabowski hesitated a moment and looked down at some notes he was carrying before he responded. "I believe so," he said slowly.

"Are you saying that you don't need to have border passes anymore?" another reporter asked. "That the border crossing points will be opened?"

Looking confused, Schabowski paused and licked his lips. "That's my understanding," he muttered.

There was an immediate buzz of conversation among the journalists and a clamor of voices simultaneously asking more questions. The district secretary quickly announced, "I'm sorry, that's all the time I have for questions," and backed away from the microphone. As the camera followed Schabowski's exit from the room, an announcer began summarizing the news conference.

"Ladies and gentlemen, in an interview filmed a few minutes ago on national television, District Secretary Gunter Schabowski disclosed that the interzonal border with West Germany has been opened."

"Is he crazy?" Dieter looked at his parents. "What good is the Wall, if people can come and go as they please?"

"He must be mistaken," Inge said. "Only a few weeks ago the government was saying the Wall would stay for a hundred years."

"If what he said is true, we'll be right back where we were thirty years ago," Erich said getting to his feet. "I'm going to call the Defense Ministry and find out what's going on."

Half an hour later Erich returned looking grim. "It was difficult to get through, and then no one seemed to know what's happening. I finally reached a colonel who had spoken with the defense minister. The defense minister believes Schabowski is misinformed, and he's trying to get confirmation. He was at the same meeting where the travel policy was discussed, but had to leave early."

"This could cause a hell of a mess," Dieter said. "What if people start flocking to the crossing points?" He thought for a minute and then jumped up. "I'm going into the city and see what's happening.

"Good idea." Erich said. "I'll try to reach the Chief of Staff or his deputy, and see if they can issue some clear orders to the border guards before it's too late. Let me know what you find out."

It was nearly midnight when Dieter got to the center of Berlin near the Brandenburg Gate. He parked Erich's Skoda on the broad, tree-lined Unter den Linden, and walked toward the gate on foot. Despite the hour there were hundreds of excited people on the street headed in the same direction. A young couple dressed in blue jeans rushed by him. "Do you think we can really cross into West Berlin?" the girl said to her male companion. "That's what they said on the radio, and look at the crowd! Something's going on."

As Dieter got within three blocks of the barrier, he could see more clearly the scene being illuminated by security floodlights at the crossing point. At first it appeared that people were just milling around and not able to move past the guards. But when he was able to push further through the crowd, Dieter's fear was realized. A single file of people was moving slowly in both directions through the barrier, and he could even see several young men celebrating on top of the wall.

With a sinking feeling in his stomach, Dieter continued to shove his way forward until he reached one of the guards. Taking his military identification card from his wallet, he held it in front of the dazed guard and said, "I'm Major Burchert. Who gave you permission to open the barrier?"

"I'm not sure, *Herr Major*. People starting showing up here a couple of hours ago saying that it was announced on television that the border was opened. When we called for instructions, the officer of the guard checked, and then told us that it must be so because all the news broadcasts were reporting it. The other checkpoints have also opened."

Dieter started to say something when an exuberant fellow wearing an expensive leather jacket jostled him trying to hand him a bottle of champagne.

"Have a drink, my friend. Isn't this great! Let's celebrate. At long last we Germans are together again." A woman behind him coming from the west shouted at the guard, "I'm going to visit my aunt and wake her up. She's been waiting a long time for this day. I don't want her to miss it."

Dieter handed the bottle of champagne to a face in the crowd, and stepped into the guard shack. "I need to use your phone," he announced to another bewildered guard. He dialed the number, and after two rings his father was on the line.

"It's worse than we expected," he shouted above the noise. "There's complete chaos here. The guards are just standing aside and letting people pass through in both directions." He looked out the window and continued. "People are flocking here from east and west, and the guards say it's like this at other crossing points."

"Then I don't know what more we can do," Erich said in a tired voice. "I'm afraid we've lost the struggle. You better come home."

"I will, but it will take awhile to get through the streets. It's beginning to look like a big party here."

CHAPTER 16

Fred and Gisela watched television coverage of the incredible events unfolding in Germany with a sense of awe. It was November 10, 1989, the day after the Berlin Wall fell, and they were tuned to CNN's report of East Germans spilling into West Berlin and other border towns. Gisela's pent-up excitement made it difficult for her to sit still, and she repeatedly interrupted reporter comments.

"This is wonderful! Oh, thank God! I was afraid I would never see such a sight. Fred, look at the welcome they're giving the East Germans!" Her eyes started to well up, and she reached for a box of tissues.

"They're certainly being generous. Giving each visitor 50 marks must cost a bundle. I wonder if the two countries will reunify."

"I hope so, Fred. I think that is what West Germany wants. But I'm just happy to see that terrible wall being torn down."

The phone rang, and Gisela jumped up to answer it. She wasn't surprised to hear Gail Parker's voice. Although separated by many miles, they managed to have a long talk every few weeks.

"Are you watching the news from Germany on television?"

"Gail, I've been glued to the TV set for two days. Isn't it fantastic?"

"It certainly is. When we were stationed in Fulda, I thought the only way the wall would come down would be through a war."

"Me too. Fred and I were just talking about that."

"This may be the break you've been looking for. When are you going back?"

Gisela frowned and turned her back to Fred. "I've been thinking about that a lot. I want to go right away, but Fred says it may be too soon for policies to change. And he can't get away from work now."

Gail thought a few moments, and then said, "Well, I understand the East Germany government is in turmoil, but I know how much this means to you, Gisela. Hasn't the window opened a little? Maybe you should take advantage of the opportunity before it closes."

Gisela made a decision. "You're right, Gail. I'm going to leave as soon as possible, with or without Fred." Their conversation moved on to the latest activities of Anna and the Parker children. Fifteen minutes later, Gisela thanked Gail for calling and said good-bye.

As she returned to her seat in front of the TV, Gisela said, "That was Gail Parker. She thinks I shouldn't wait to go to Germany."

Fred put down the newspaper he was holding. "You know I'd like to go with you dear, but I just can't take leave right now. We're in the middle of revising our war plans for the Middle East and the old man has made it clear that none of the key staff is doing anything else until Central Command gives its approval." He continued in a more contentious tone. "Besides, you know how regulation-bound the East Germans are. Until someone issues different instructions, they're not going to tell you any more than we learned two years ago. Which was nothing!"

It's always one thing or another with the Army, Gisela thought. This could go on for months. Aloud she said brusquely, "I told Gail I want to go now, and that's what I'm going to do."

Fred looked irritated, but said nothing. Gisela continued to stare at the celebrating images on television, but her mind began making a list of the things she needed to do to get ready. First, she would make airline reservations, and see about a car rental. Her passport was still current, but she would need traveler's checks. Despite the winter weather, she resolved to pack light in a rolling suitcase she could manage herself. She had a doctor's appointment next week that she would cancel. And the mammogram could certainly wait until she returned. If there was time, she wanted to get her hair cut and styled.

Fred interrupted her thoughts. "If you would wait, Gisela, until after the holidays, I could probably get away for two or three weeks at least by February."

"No, Fred," she said firmly. "My mind's made up. The sooner I go, the better I'll feel. And it won't be so expensive if I go alone. I know how costly this search has been to the savings account."

He dismissed her concern with a wave of his hand. "Don't worry about the money," he said, but in a tone that Gisela knew indicated his growing resentment of the cost of her obsession. "It's just that I think you stand a better chance of getting information after things get sorted out over there. I don't want you to have your hopes dashed again."

Gisela gestured toward the TV. "There's a new spirit sweeping through East Germany, Fred. You can see it. The people have hope now and so do I." She got to her feet. "I'm going to make a call to the airlines."

United Flight 410 was three hours out of Atlanta on its night route to Frankfurt, Germany. Although it was late, Gisela was wide-awake. A glass of Chardonnay with the airline dinner of Chicken Kiev had helped her relax, but she couldn't concentrate on the movie being shown. Her mind kept returning to the details of a plan that she was formulating to find some trace of Dieter. After landing in Frankfurt, she would call Attorney Volker's office to see if he had any new information. If not, she would rent a car and drive into East Germany to make inquiries at government offices administering the region that included Geisa, the town from which she and Walter embarked on their fateful flight twenty-five years before.

Thinking of the night that had changed their lives forever, Gisela reached into her handbag and pulled out two worn, black and white photographs. The first was taken in a studio a few weeks before their escape attempt. It showed Gisela, with Anna on her lap, Walter seated next to her, and Dieter standing between them. Except for Anna, who was at least looking directly at the camera, everyone was smiling. It was an image of a young family with every right to expect a happy life together. The other photo was taken on Dieter's third birthday. It was a close-up just before he blew out the candles on his birthday cake. She looked at both photos for a long time before placing them again in her handbag. So much time has passed, she thought. Am I focused too much on the past, and ignoring Fred's feelings? She closed her eyes and drifted into a fitful sleep, frequented by phantoms that resembled Walter and Dieter.

"We'll be landing at Frankfurt Airport in about an hour. The cabin crew will begin serving coffee and a breakfast snack momentarily."

The loudspeaker announcement jarred Gisela awake, and sent her scurrying to the lavatory ahead of the stewardess's serving cart. She was still feeling groggy as the DC 10 started its final approach to the airport.

Debarking from the aircraft, Gisela could see that it was a damp and windy day in Germany. It was a long walk through the narrow Rhine-Main terminal to the baggage claim area. As she waited by the conveyer console for her luggage, she realized that the loss of sleep was catching up with her. After retrieving her luggage, she hailed a taxi.

"Please take me to the American hotel on the other side of the airport," she told the driver in German.

"That's for military and dependents only," he growled.

"Yes, I know. My husband's an officer in the American Army, and I need some rest from this jet lag."

"*Jawohl.*" His tone was more conciliatory. "Most tourists are in too big a hurry to see the sights."

Twenty minutes later, Gisela was in a modest room on the third floor of the Air Base transient hotel, sitting on a double bed with her shoes off. After consulting a printed page of telephone instructions, she reached an outside line and made a local call.

When her call was answered she said, "This is Gisela Newman. I wish to speak to Herr Volker please." The receptionist asked her to wait, and in a few minutes, a booming voice came on the line.

"*Guten Morgen, Frau Newman. Wie geht es Ihnen?*"

"I'm fine, Herr Volker, but tired." It seemed natural to be speaking in German. Despite her years in America, it was always more comfortable to use her native language. "I've just arrived in Frankfurt from the

States. Now that the wall has come down, I'm going to start another search for my son."

"*Ja.* This is a tumultuous time for Germany, isn't it? So many exciting changes, coming so fast."

Always a smooth one, that Volker, Gisela thought. Despite his reputation for extraordinary contacts with East German officials, he didn't have much to show for the money they had paid him. She put it to him directly. "Have you picked up anything new about Dieter?"

"*Leider nicht.* Nothing specific concerning your son. However, I hear that New Forum and other dissident groups in the east are demanding that government offices open their records to the public. I'm sure it's just a question of time before we find something. Where will you be staying?"

"I'll be at the American Air Force Hotel at Rhine Main until tomorrow." She gave him the phone number, and in view of his unpromising report, took a moment to consider her next move. The first destination she had in mind was the hospital where Dieter was taken. All she could tell him was, "Then I intend to rent a car and drive into the East Zone, probably to Bad Salzungen. I'll call again when I find a hotel."

After she hung up the phone, Gisela set the clock-radio alarm for four in the afternoon, and placed a "Do Not Disturb" sign on the door. She took off her pantsuit, hung it in the closet, and slipped into bed in her underwear.

"Protests continue in Prague," a cultured voice was saying. "An estimated 200,000 demonstrators crowded into Wenceslas Square and clashed with police. There are reports of protests spreading to other cities in Czechoslovakia. In other news…"

Gisela reached over and switched off the radio alarm. It took several minutes to get her bearings before she got out of bed and headed into the bathroom. After showering, she dressed in a wool skirt and sweater, and then hunted through her purse for the car rental information. Her reservation was through Avis, and the clerk told her that she could pick up a Volkswagen Polo with automatic transmission in the morning.

Having last eaten on the airplane, Gisela was hungry; but the idea of going to the Officers Club alone didn't appeal to her. She decided to treat herself and asked the hotel clerk about a restaurant Fred had taken her to before they were married. She took a cab to the *Altes Zollhaus*, and was pleased when she recognized the ancient half-timbered house with the large garden where they had eaten that long ago summer. An unhurried dinner of roast pork with mushrooms in apple-wine sauce, accompanied by a carafe of Gewürztraminer left her in a pensive mood. As she swirled the remaining wine in her glass, she wondered if her search for Dieter was hurting her marriage. Did Fred really believe there was a chance of finding a son whose identity had been hidden for so many years? Did she?

Back in her room, she placed a long distance call home, but there was no answer. A glance at her wristwatch reminded her that it was six hours earlier in Georgia. Fred was probably at work. Still, she missed him, so she tried his office number, only to find that he had left that afternoon for a meeting at Fort Bragg, NC.

Bothered by her concerns and the time adjustment, Gisela found it hard to sleep that night. Yet she awoke feeling refreshed shortly after seven as daylight brightened her room. A good breakfast in the cafeteria followed by a short walk to pick up the rental car, lifted her spirits. By the time she checked out of the hotel and loaded her baggage, her confidence had returned.

Gisela decided to follow the Avis clerk's advice and take Autobahn E40 to Bad Hersfeld, where, she was assured, it was now possible to cross into East Germany. The autobahn continued across the country to Poland, but she would take the first exit past the border and follow a zigzag of state and county roads to Bad Salzungen. With no traffic problems, she should reach her destination by early afternoon. A shorter route went through Fulda, Hünfeld, and Geisa; but that would have taken her close to the site of her traumatic escape, and she didn't feel emotionally ready to face those memories.

The weather was partly cloudy and cold, although not cold enough yet for snow. Gisela was glad she brought a winter raincoat with liner and gloves. Some of her driving would be in the *Rhön* Mountains, and at the higher altitudes snow was a distinct possibility. The Volkswagen was a two-door hatchback, which cruised comfortably at 110 kilometers per hour. Twenty minutes after she left the Frankfurt interchanges, she was startled by flashing headlights in the rear view mirror, and barely got out of the way of a red Mercedes that must have been going at least 150. After that she stayed in the right lane, except to pass slow moving trucks, usually going uphill.

An hour of driving brought her past Alsfeld, and the expressway began to climb toward the northern edge of the Rhön Mountain Range. A misting rain interfered with visibility, so she slowed down; but it annoyed her that most cars and even trucks sped past. Nearing the Bad Hersfeld exit, she decided to pull off the autobahn at a Gaststäte for some coffee and a rest stop.

Forty minutes later Gisela was back on the autobahn approaching the border-crossing point to East Germany. Traffic slowed to a crawl and she joined a two-lane file waiting to be checked by border guards. The waiting made her nervous, so she rehearsed in her mind the responses she would soon have to make. That process caused her to look again in her purse to make sure that her passport and military dependent ID card were still there. When she saw her rosary, she took the beads in her hands and began reciting the familiar prayers softly.

Rolling down the window as her turn approached, Gisela felt the perspiration forming on her palms. "There's nothing to fear," she told herself, but her sub-conscious mind was unconvinced. "Let me see your documents," an unsmiling border policeman said. He was in his early twenties, wearing a Russian style fur hat and green field jacket. A holstered pistol was at his side.

"What's the destination and purpose of your trip?" he demanded.

"I'm going to visit friends in Bad Salzungen, Geisa, and maybe Berlin," she said in a hesitating voice.

"Are you American or German?" he sneered, knowing the answer.

She looked right at him and said defiantly, "As you can see from my passport, I am an American citizen. I was born in Germany, and I am coming back to look for," she hesitated, "…a relative I haven't seen since the wall went up."

"Well, well, how nice you could come," he said in a mocking tone, waving her forward. "Your dollars are welcome, *Gnädige Frau.*"

Boiling with anger at what this barrier and its guards had meant to her, she missed her planned exit and drove almost to Eisenach before she found another exit. She pulled over to check the map and saw that the county road at this exit would connect to another two-lane road leading to Bad Salzungen. It was past one o'clock when she finally reached the government seat of Wartburg County.

Better known for its curative baths, Bad Salzungen lay in the Werra River valley between the green foliage of the Thüringer Wald and the imposing mountains of the Rhön. Driving past the train depot where her family had embarked on their fateful mission into the restricted zone, her mind was flooded with images from the past. She pulled over and stopped the car for a minute in an effort to regain her composure. The sight of a bank on the corner reminded her of her present purpose, and she decided that the first order of business was to change some money into East German Marks. When she returned to the car, she realized she was hungry and began looking for a place to eat lunch. She took a side street, which brought her to the old town square where she saw a Ratskeller that looked warm and inviting.

While she enjoyed a steaming bowl of oxtail soup, with fresh *Brötchen*, Gisela thought about where she would go next. When she and Fred were there before seeking information, the hospital administrator bluntly denied having any record of Walter or Dieter in 1964. Yet both the Bundesgrenzschutz and Attorney Vogel reported that they were taken there. I'll start at the hospital and try to find someone more sympathetic this time, she decided. An hour later Gisela was sitting in the admissions office of the Bad Salzungen Hospital talking with a friendly secretary.

"I've looked through all the files we have for 1964, and I can't find any under Hurwitz," the secretary said, returning to her desk. "But there was a note that two files from 1964 are in the suppressed section which concerns political dissidents. I'm sorry, but I don't have access to that section."

"Who can I see to check if those files refer to my family?"

"Herr Ebert, the chief administrator, keeps them in his office. He is the only one who handles the suppressed files."

Gisela groaned, recognizing the name of the man who rebuffed her before. She was mulling over some approach that might crack his negative disposition when the secretary offered a suggestion. "There's another possibility. Frau Münzer was a nurse here at that time. She still works part time at the hospital. Maybe she could remember something to help you."

Gisela's expression changed to show the gratitude she felt. "When could I see her?"

The secretary reached in her drawer for a schedule. "She works tomorrow from seven to three in the afternoon. Why don't you come at half past eleven? You could talk during her lunch break."

"Thank you. I'll do that. Would you please let her know I'm coming?"

"Of course." The secretary seemed to take pleasure in helping Gisela circumvent the rigid regulations of the system.

"You have been very kind. Thank you so much." Gisela left the hospital with a glow of hope that energized her. She drove to the Salzunger Hof, the city's best hotel and reserved a room for two days with a tentative hold for the rest of the week, if necessary.

The next day she was back at the hospital admissions office at eleven thirty. The helpful secretary was there and willingly escorted Gisela to the staff dining room and introduced her to Nurse Münzer. Ursula Münzer was a big-boned, tall woman in her late fifties. She had the face of a farmer's wife, yet her eyes shown with the pride and assurance of a professional person. Her long fair hair, tinged with gray, lay in a braid around her head, and she wore no make-up. Although Gisela was wearing a fashionable green plaid dress, she couldn't help admiring the simple elegance of Frau Münzer in her crisp nurse's uniform.

The nurse was seated alone at a table and invited Gisela to join her. While she continued eating her dinner, Gisela sipped a cup of coffee and explained the purpose of her visit. When she finished, Frau

Münzer said, "My poor dear. What a dreadful burden you carry." A far-away look came into her eyes, and she was silent for a minute. At last she said slowly, "Yes, I remember a man and his son being brought to our hospital that summer. The man died soon after he arrived, but the child had only minor injuries. I can't recall the names. Yet Dieter sounds familiar."

Gisela's heart was racing. "Do you know what happened to the boy? To Dieter?"

"I've been thinking about this since the secretary told me you were coming. It was so sad. The little boy was traumatized, and would scarcely respond to any of us. I found a little stuffed bear in his father's back pack and gave it to him, and he held on to it all the time he was here."

Gisela gasped. "Did the bear have a blue jacket with Berlin written on it?"

"*Ja.* I believe it did."

The image of her lost son, separated from his parents, and in a strange place was tearing Gisela up inside, but she willed herself to stay in control. "Do you know where he went when he left the hospital?"

"After about a week a young couple came and took him. I don't remember their names, and they weren't from around here. I'm sure they were adopting him, but I don't know where they lived."

Gisela's heart sank. "Can you tell me anything more about them that would help me find them?"

Frau Münzer thought a minute and said, "They were educated people, and well- dressed. In fact, the man was wearing a uniform—Grenztruppen, I think. But I don't know where they went. They just got in a car and drove off."

The two women continued talking for another fifteen minutes. Gisela desperately sought more details, but Frau Münzer had exhausted her recollection of the events so long ago. She did suggest that Gisela try the local office of social welfare for information concerning adopted children, and provided directions on how to find the office.

"I don't know what their regulations allow, but it's worth a try," she offered.

"Thank you. I'll do that. You have been very considerate. Your assistance means so much to me…" her voice trailed off.

"I'm pleased to help. This division of our country has caused much grief. I hope the changes that are going on now will make life happier for all of us. Good luck to you."

Gisela waited until mid-afternoon to call at the social welfare office. After several inquiries, she was directed to a small office on the third floor where a thin woman of about forty was in charge. As she listened to Gisela's plea for information concerning her lost son, her face hardened. She pushed her dark-rimmed glasses back from her nose and said, "All information concerning adopted children is confidential. For the protection of the children from unwanted contacts, we don't release any information about their new families. Anyway, your son would now be a grown man, and would have no memory of you."

Gisela's face flushed and she felt the anger and frustration boiling within her. "It's your damned protective system that has kept my son and me apart. He remembers! I know he does! And when I find him, he'll know about the lies that your 'system' has fed him." She glared at the officious clerk for a minute, and then turned on her heel and marched out of the office, slamming the door behind her.

She was still breathing hard when she reached her car. She opened the door and sat for a few minutes trying to collect her thoughts. Ahead of her on the corner was a kiosk with a man selling newspapers and magazines. That gave her an idea. She got out of the car and walked over to the kiosk where she bought a copy of the *Eisenacher Zeitung*. Ten minutes later she was back in her hotel. She entered the dining room, ordered coffee and *Küchen*, and opened the newspaper to the classified advertisements. When she finished her coffee and cake, she went to her room and made a telephone call to the newspaper office.

"I'm interested in placing an advertisement, but I would like to know if your circulation covers Geisa and the former border region?"

"Yes, certainly," was the answer.

"Then I would like to place the following advertisement in the personal section. Lost Son. A mother offers reward for information about her three-year-old son, Dieter Hurwitz, adopted in July 1964, in Bad Salzungen by a military family. Contact Frau Newman at Salzunger Hof, telephone, 03695-6720. What will that cost for a week?" She made arrangements to pay and was told that the ad would begin in the next day's edition.

That night Gisela waited until almost midnight and called Fred. It was six in the evening in Georgia; and when Fred answered, she felt sorry for leaving him alone.

"Gisela, it's great to hear your voice. I got the message you arrived safely, but I didn't know where to reach you."

"I know. I wanted to call as soon as I knew where I would be staying for awhile."

She gave Fred her telephone number and briefly summarized her activities and what she had learned.

"Where are you going next?"

"I'm going to stay close to my hotel for a few days to see if anyone responds to the newspaper ad. But I'm wondering, Fred, if there would be any way to trace Dieter's adoptive parents through the military?"

"I don't know, Gisela. They probably won't be very open with information, if they even keep that sort of thing. Do you know where to go to contact a military headquarters?"

"No. Not really. The nurse said she thought he was in the Grenztruppen, but she wasn't sure. It could be Volksarmee or something else."

"All right. I'll see what I can do." His tone of voice implied that this was a waste of time. "There's a German Liaison Officer at Fort Knox. Maybe he can help"

They chatted a few more minutes. Fred had no recent news from Anna. He was working hard, including weekends, to finish his project for the general; and he missed her. When she hung up she realized how much Fred meant to her, and she began to have doubts about what she was doing.

The next morning she was even less sure that trying to contact the military would be worthwhile. Nevertheless, she went to the post office building and asked about locations of military headquarters in the region. The inquiry brought some suspicious looks, but eventually she learned that there was a tank regiment stationed in Gotha, and other Volksarmee units in Erfurt.

Fred called back just before she went to supper. "I spoke to the German Liaison Officer at Knox. He had some order of battle information that was recently declassified. I think your best bet would be Grenztruppen Southern Command in Erfurt. That's only forty or fifty miles from you. But I should tell you that he thought it very unlikely that they would have records going back that far."

"I know Fred. But I've got to try. Someone here must know who took him."

After two more days of waiting for an answer to her newspaper ad, Gisela was becoming frustrated. She had been to every public office seeking information, and she had resorted to asking anyone of sufficient age if they had knowledge about Dieter's adoption. Most were reluctant to get involved, and those who wanted to help had nothing further to offer.

So, after telling the desk clerk that she would be gone most of the day and reminding him that she was expecting calls in answer to her ad, she left in mid-morning on a drive to the Thüringen state capital, Erfurt. For late November, it was a beautiful day, clear and crisp with bright sunshine. Feeling a need for some pleasure in her mission, Gisela avoided the Autobahn and took a more scenic route through the wooded hills and the romantic cities of Eisenach and Gotha. More than one doctor had told her she needed to find ways to reduce the stress this separation caused in her life. Perhaps a visit to some of the tourist attractions of Erfurt would help, if she could fit it in.

After a leisurely drive, Gisela reached Erfurt shortly after noon, and began looking for a restaurant. Turning on to Marstall Strasse, she noticed a sign on a large building advertising a combination restaurant and cabaret called Dasdie. Since there were a number of cars in the parking lot, she decided it must be a decent place. Besides, she needed a rest room quickly and didn't want to spend any more time trying to select the perfect place to eat.

When she was seated, she observed from the menu that there were several hearty dinners at reasonable prices. Declining the waitress's recommendation of wild boar, Gisela remained conscious of her diet, and chose vegetable soup, a salad and a glass of Mosel wine. As the noontime group of diners finished eating, Gisela had an opportunity to chat with her waitress who advised her to be sure to visit the antique shops along Krämerbrücke and gave her directions to the Grenztruppen Headquarters.

Gisela decided to get the harder task out of the way first, and, following the directions she was given, arrived at *Grenztruppen Kommando Süd*. The reception office was just inside the main entrance of a World War II Wehrmacht barracks. She waited several minutes while the only soldier in the office continued working at his desk. When she asked if he could help her, he grudgingly pushed his paper aside and walked nonchalantly to the counter. He was in his early twenties and dressed in a rumpled green uniform. Gisela wasn't familiar with East German insignia, and didn't know his rank. When she explained what she was seeking, his attitude was one of weary disdain. The impression he gave was that she shouldn't be bothering his office with such a trivial and hopeless request.

"*Nein*. We don't keep records of adoptions by Grenztruppen personnel. You should go to the county municipal office."

Twenty-three years of marriage to an army officer had taught Gisela a thing or two about dealing with overbearing clerks. In a loud voice she said, "I want to know your name and your rank, young man."

"I am *Stabsunteroffizier Johann Felber*."

Realizing that she was dealing with the equivalent of an E-5 buck sergeant, Gisela's eyes narrowed and she slapped her hand on the counter. "Listen here, Felber. I want to see your commanding officer, right now. I didn't come all this way to be brushed off by a paper-pusher."

The young man's back stiffened and he flushed at the rebuke. Before he could say anything Gisela continued, "Tell him that Oberst Newman's wife wants to speak with him."

"Very well, Ma'am. Please have a seat."

Five minutes later she was shown into the spacious office of Oberst Gerhard Reiman, a pleasant looking colonel in his mid fifties. He stood up when she entered the room, and beckoned her to be seated in an armchair near his desk. After introductions he settled into an adjoining chair and regarded her with a bemused expression.

"Ah, Frau Newman. I'm sorry if we upset you, especially an attractive wife of a fellow officer. However, I don't believe I know your husband. Of course, my clerk wasn't very clear about where you were from."

"My husband is a colonel in the American Army, presently stationed near Atlanta, Georgia. We were married when he was assigned to the 14th Armored Cavalry Regiment in Fulda on the other side of the border. But I am here seeking information about my son, and your clerk was treating me like I was some tourist who had wandered into the wrong building."

"I apologize for my young staff. I'm afraid they don't get enough training in dealing with the public. How can I help you?"

"My son, Dieter, was three when we were separated, crossing the border to the West in 1964. His father stepped on a mine and was killed, but I know that Dieter was taken to the Bad Salzungen hospital. An officer believed to be in the Grenstruppen and his wife later adopted him. Can you please help me identify that officer so I can find my son?" She bit her lip to keep from crying. "He has been lost to me for twenty-five years."

Oberst Reiman sat up suddenly. "Were you escaping across the border near Geise?"

Gisela looked up. "Why, yes. How did you know?"

Reiman stared at her like she was a ghost from the past. "Because I commanded a border company in that region in 1967 . They were still talking about the incident in the regiment." His expression had hardened, but it didn't deter Gisela.

"Then what happened to my son?" she demanded. "That wall has kept us apart. Now I must find him."

Reiman didn't answer immediately, causing Gisela to wonder what he was thinking. Was he one of those stubborn functionaries who regarded her as an enemy, or did he recognize that times had changed?

Then his face softened. "I have a son about the same age as your son. How terrible it must have been for you—to have your child taken away. Frau Newman, I don't know where your son went, but I can tell you something. What I heard was that he was adopted by a major and his wife who lived somewhere in the area. The major was in the Grenztruppen, but I understand he was transferred later to the Volksarmee. I'm sorry, I don't know who they were. It all happened before my time in the regiment.

"Aren't there records here that would give their names?"

"*Nein.* We only keep personnel records here for five years after someone leaves."

Gisela swallowed hard, and thought a minute. "Maybe the Volksarmee Headquarters can tell me. Where is it located?"

Oberst Reiman shrugged. "I doubt if they will be very cooperative, but you can try. Go to the *Ministerium fur Nationale Verteidigung* in Strausberg, outside Berlin."

He stood, signaling an end to the meeting.

Gisela held out her hand, and after a moment's hesitation, he took it and walked her to the door.

"Thank you for being open with me. Maybe someone there will be so kind."

Reiman relaxed and smiled. "I wish you good luck, Frau Newman. But please don't tell anyone at the Ministerium that I directed you there."

Gisela left the building in a better mood, even flashing a charming smile at Stabsunteroffizer Felber on her way out. When she reached her car it was still mid-afternoon. She needed to relax, and the prospect of seeing the sights of Erfurt before returning to Bad Salzungen seemed like an enjoyable diversion.

When she was a young girl helping plant a garden, her mother told her about Erfurt being one of Europe's largest flower and vegetable seed producers. She wanted to see the flower market and the restored

Renaissance Bridge the waitress had mentioned. If there was time she would visit the Fourteenth Century cathedral, reputed to have the largest bell in the world.

By the time she reached her hotel, it was almost dark. Stopping at the reception desk for her key, she was given a message. She unfolded the note and read, "Franz Weber, telephon 6653-2768, responding to your advertisement." Her heart beat faster as she rushed to her room and dialed the number. After four rings a man answered.

"Herr Weber, bitte."

"Ja, Ich bin Weber."

"This is Frau Newman. I am returning your call about the advertisement concerning my lost son."

"Ja. I was in the hospital that summer for appendicitis. I remember the boy, and I was there when he was taken away." Weber's voice sounded hesitant about volunteering anything more. "Why haven't you tried to find him before now?"

Gisela wanted to cry with frustration. Instead she said slowly, "I have, Herr Weber. Believe me, I have. Please, could I meet with you and explain what happened and find out what you know?"

There was a pause, and Gisela could hear some whispering in the background. Finally, Herr Weber said, *"Ja, shön.* Can you come to Kieselbach? I work in the only butcher shop in town."

Gisela asked directions, and when she realized that it was a small village only 20 kilometers away, arranged to meet with him at 10:30 the following morning.

Kieselbach is a rural community about ten kilometers east of the border, one of several bottlenecks along Highway 84 that meanders northeast to Eisenach. Gisela had no trouble finding the butcher shop among the few buildings that made up the village. Franz Weber was a stocky man of about fifty with a ruddy complexion. He greeted her somewhat cautiously, but took off his apron and accepted her invitation to go next door to a cafe for coffee. After ordering, Gisela explained her situation in detail, even showing him her Military Dependent's ID Card. Herr Weber listened politely, sipping his coffee slowly.

When she finished, he nodded and said, "I'm sorry if I seem mistrustful to you, but here one never knows whether someone is working for the Stasi. I understand now. In fact, as a young man I even thought about fleeing to the West, but I could never persuade my wife to go."

"It looks like those days are changing, Herr Weber. I hope so, anyway. If the border hadn't opened, I wouldn't have learned what I have." She set down her cup, and looked at him anxiously. "What can you tell me about Dieter and the couple who took him?"

"Well, as I said, I was working on a farm near here when I had this terrible pain in my stomach. They took me to Bad Salzungen Hospital and took out my appendix. While I was recovering, they put this little boy in the same room. At first I didn't know what was wrong with him. He had some cuts and bruises and he cried for his mother and father. I never could get him to smile or talk. Then I heard that his father was trying to cross the border with him and was killed by a mine."

Gisela left her coffee untouched and listened breathlessly.

"Anyway, after four or five days the nurses came and dressed him in some new clothes. An officer and his wife picked him up and took him away."

"Can you remember their names or anything about them?"

"Not the names. I don't think I ever heard them. The man was in uniform—the Grenztruppen. He was of medium build and wore glasses. The woman was blonde, nice looking, and a little taller than the man."

"Is that all? Isn't there anything that will help me identify them?

Weber frowned and thought a minute. "*Ja,*" he said slowly. "The officer had a limp. It looked like it was a birth defect or from a permanent injury. I remember now that I was surprised he was in the military."

Gisela's disappointment showed. Her hopes had been high that she would learn the names of Dieter's adoptive parents. Instead all she had was a possible clue to the father's identification. She reached for her purse and took out a couple of hundred mark notes. "I promised a reward," she said, offering the money to Weber.

"*Nein, nein,*" he protested. "I don't want any money. I just wish I could be of more help."

On the way back to her hotel, she decided that she would wait three more days for any other replies to her ad. In the meantime, she would try to reach her former neighbor in Berlin, Claudia Schuman, to see if she had any suggestions. That evening she was lying on her bed before dinner watching the evening news on television when the phone rang.

"Hello, Gisela. How's everything going?"

"Oh, Fred. I'm so glad you called. I was going to wait up and call you tonight."

"Well, I thought it would be easier for me to come home for lunch and call you from here. I miss you." There was a pause as if he wanted to say something more. "Are you having any luck?"

"Oh, I miss you too, Fred. At times I feel so alone, that it's almost frightening. And I wonder if this isn't hopeless. Even if I find him, he's a grown man, maybe with his own family. Will I just be an unwelcome intrusion?"

"Listen, I know it's difficult, but you can come home, and we can try again in the spring when I can get away."

At the thought of another delay she swung her legs over the side of the bed and sat up. "I'm not ready to give up yet, Fred." She told him what she had learned. "If I don't get any more answers to my ad by Saturday, I'm going to Berlin, and try to get something out of the Ministry of Defense in Strausberg."

"Okay, I understand. But remember Christmas is only a few weeks away. I talked to Anna yesterday, and she wants to come home then. Her squadron is being liberal with passes and leaves over the holidays."

"Oh, dear. I'm so wrapped up with what I am doing, that I've almost forgotten about Christmas. Yes, of course, I want to be there for Anna. I'll arrange a return flight around the 20th, and come back here if I must."

A few days later Gisela was driving east out of Berlin on Highway Five looking for the county road that connected to Strausberg. Traffic was slow owing to freezing rain that made the roadways slippery. Because of the weather and her unfamiliarity with the area, it took her over two hours to reach the complex of buildings that made up the Ministerium für Nationale Verteidigung (National Defense Ministry). By the time she found a parking space, the weather had changed to a mixture of sleet and snow that was falling heavily. She wrapped a scarf around her head and got out.

Gisela saw a sidewalk leading into a wooded area shielding some buildings, and began walking in that direction. Icy snow was stinging her face, and she had difficulty making out direction signs. Coming down the walkway from the other direction was a tall, young man in uniform. As he drew near, Gisela stopped him.

Major Dieter Burchert's mind was still on the meeting he had just left. At his father's urging, he had arranged an appointment with the Volksarmee personnel office to discuss possible future assignments. The meeting was discouraging, and he was dejected as he left the building. Everything was in a state of flux, and big cuts in military personnel were forecast when reunification occurred. The nasty weather only worsened his mood, and he turned up the collar of his overcoat.

"Excuse me. Could you please direct me to the reception office?"

Dieter stopped abruptly, focusing his attention on the middle-aged woman who was holding tightly to a scarf to keep the blowing snow from whipping it off.

"*Ja, doch.* Follow this sidewalk straight ahead, and it's the first building on your right."

She stared at him, wiping wet snowflakes out of her eyes, but not saying anything.

"Is something wrong, ma'am?"

"Oh, no. I'm sorry. I thought…that is, the snow makes it hard to see." She mumbled, "*Danke Shön*," as he touched the tip of his cap with his gloved hand. She hesitated another moment before a shiver made her hurry on.

As Dieter strode toward the parking lot, he thought momentarily about the odd look the woman had given him. What was it, he thought. Perhaps he reminded her of someone, but he was sure he had never seen her before. In a few minutes she was forgotten as he cleaned the snow from his car and waited impatiently for the engine to warm up.

Gisela slowed her pace as she neared the building. That officer had resembled Walter, but she was reluctant to make the mistake again that had so often embarrassed her by asking if he was Dieter. Still, she thought, what have I got to lose? She turned abruptly, and quickly retraced her steps. However, when she reached the parking lot, all she could see was a small car going out the gate.

The rest of her visit to the Defense Ministry turned out to be just as futile. After some waiting she was able to meet with a polite Oberst Leutnant who explained that there was no way to search the personnel records of the Volksarmee for an officer who adopted a child in 1964. Moreover, he said that when dependents were added to the military pay records, it wouldn't show whether someone was adopted. She asked if she could put a notice in a newsletter that might be distributed to all officers. He indicated that anything with that sort of distribution was limited to official business, and regretfully concluded that there was nothing he could do to help her.

That evening she sat in Claudia Schuman's apartment, and reviewed the efforts she had made. Claudia poured them each a glass of wine, and Gisela was making an effort to overcome her discouragement. In the background the television was carrying a live broadcast from Dresden of West German Chancellor Kohl making a speech in front of the Frauenkirche. As they sipped their wine and talked, Gisela heard a reference to "one nation", and the women interrupted their conversation to listen. "My aim remains, if history allows," the Chancellor was saying, "to achieve the unity of our nation." Helmut Kohl concluded his speech by stressing that "in the future Germany must be a source of peace."

"Imagine, Claudia, East and West together as one Germany. Wouldn't that be wonderful?"

"I don't know, Gisela. Many people in the East want us to remain a separate country with a more responsive government."

But Claudia, I read that a lot of people are demanding reunification, and Kohl's party is going all out to make that happen."

"I'm not sure what would be best. It's just been decided that we will have elections next May. Things are moving so fast it makes my head spin."

"I don't see how East Germany could remain separate with its own economic system and keep people from moving to the West. As long as the communists are still in power, the young ones will leave. And now, thank God, they don't have to risk their lives to do it."

"No, not any more. Oh, Gisela, I wish you had stayed. I know the government controlled everything, but life wasn't that bad. Dieter and Hans could have grown up together, and we could have celebrated some good times with you and Walter."

"You can't imagine how many times I have wished the same thing." She sipped her wine in silence for a minute. They had paid a terrible price, but she knew Walter would never have been happy. He probably would have been arrested sooner or later for his activism, and it would have affected Dieter and Anna. They probably would have been ostracized from most activities and not allowed to go to a university.

Aloud she said, "Anyway, it's too late to think about that. Now I would be happy if I could just find Dieter, but it seems that I've reached a dead end."

"I have an idea. Why don't you offer that hospital administrator some money to see those suppressed files?"

"I already tried that," Gisela said in a tired voice. "Before I left Bad Salzungen, I went back to the hospital and spoke with Herr Ebert. He was offended by my offer of money, and claimed that any suppressed files he may have had were sent to Erfurt for consolidation at the State Office of Social Services. I called that office and was told that under penalty of law, no information concerning adoptive parents could be released. So there's nothing to do now but go home to Fred and Anna. Maybe I'll try again in a few months."

"Don't give up, Gisela. Changes are happening here every day. I even heard that people are being allowed to see their Stasi files. If that is true, I'm going to go see if there is one on me."

In a fleeting thought Gisela suggested, "If you do, Claudia, see if there is anything about my family. Maybe there will be some connection to Dieter."

The next day on her flight back to the United States, Gisela thought about her conversation with Claudia. The Stasi might still have something in their archives about her or Walter, but there would be no way to locate Dieter unless one knew his last name.

CHAPTER 17

1990 at Fort Stewart started badly for Gisela. She had put off her doctor's appointment until a self-examination revealed a problem. Then a call from a nurse informed her that the mammogram confirmed her suspicion, and a biopsy was needed. On a rainy day in March Gisela's mood matched the weather. The report from the doctor was worse than she expected. The biopsy of the lump in her left breast indicated the presence of a malignant cancer.

Neither she nor Fred slept much that night. Until recently Gisela paid little attention to discussions of breast cancer that occasionally came up in conversations with other women. Now the realization that she had cancer was making an impact that she was trying to come to grips with.

She sat in the kitchen watching it rain outside, wondering who she might call for advice. It was mid-morning, and Fred had left for work. Since coming to Fort Stewart, she had only heard of one woman who had breast cancer, and she didn't know her personally. At length she decided it would be more comforting to talk to an old friend before getting into all the details of treatment. She picked up the phone and dialed the number in Michigan.

Gail's cheerful response turned somber as Gisela sadly explained what had happened.

"I don't know why this had to happen now," Gisela said in a choked voice. "I mean…" Suddenly her control gave way, and she began crying.

After a minute she heard Gail say, "I'm so sorry that you have to go through this, Gisela, but there are many women who have been treated successfully. Have you seen a cancer specialist yet?"

Gisela found a tissue, and wiped her eyes, making an effort to speak. "I have an appointment next Monday to see one in Savannah, but that's not what worries me most. I asked the Army doctor about traveling to Germany, and he strongly advised against doing anything to delay treatment. Fred and I were going next month, and now I'm not sure when I'll be able to travel." She was finding it difficult to keep from crying again.

"I know that is a big disappointment, Gisela, but you need to think about yourself. You have to overcome this cancer and get well. You have a lot to live for, and your first priority now is to care for yourself."

Gisela sighed as she acknowledged her friend's advice. "I suppose so. But with everything changing in Germany, I feel like I am close…so close to finding out something about Dieter."

"Listen, Gisela, even if you went to Germany again soon, you may come up against a blank wall. Or if you don't go, something might happen anyway that will lead you to Dieter. Either way, I think you have to deal with your cancer first, and trust God to find Dieter for you."

"Oh, Gail, I have prayed so much for God's help in finding Dieter. And every time I think a prayer has been answered, something happens that sets me back."

"I understand. But you have a spiritual strength that I have always admired. And tearing down the wall was truly an answer, not only to your prayers but for millions of others."

There was a short silence before Gisela responded in a more positive tone. "Yes, you're right. I'm not the only one who has suffered. Thank you for reminding me."

"You know, Gisela, John and I have been talking about a trip to Europe this summer. We want to see Fulda again and see what was on the other side of the border ourselves. Maybe we could be of some assistance, if you're not able to travel."

Gisela was grateful for her friend's offer, but she still hoped to be the one to find her son. "Thank you, Gail. Right now I'm not sure what you could do, but if I think of something, I'll call you."

Just talking with her made Gisela feel better. She thanked Gail for her encouragement and hung up. For a moment she thought about how her life and Fred's had been intertwined with the Parkers over the years. They had been an answer to her prayers before. Perhaps they would be again.

Another telephone conversation about faith was taking place about the same time in East Germany, although it concerned political—not spiritual—faith. Dieter decided to call home to see how his parents were weathering the storm of political change sweeping through the country.

"I read in the Leipziger Zeitung that Egon Krenz and fifteen other leaders have been excluded from the party," he said to his father.

"That's right." Erich's voice sounded tired and discouraged. "And even worse, they changed the name of the party to Party of Democratic Socialism. Everything is going to hell. Honecker and Mielke are under house arrest, and a mob stormed the Stasi headquarters in Berlin and broke into the files."

"*Ja,* that created quite a shock here in Leipzig." His Stasi colleagues had been burning documents for days. Other Stasi staff officers were so discouraged and uneasy about their association with the Secret Police that they stopped going to work. "My friends in the Volksarmee are wondering what's going to become of them. I heard West Germany's Chancellor interviewed on television, and he sounds convinced that East and West Germany will be unified."

"Well, that's supposed to be decided by this election," his father said. "But if you ask me, Kohl has rigged everything. They've moved the election up from May to March, and Prime Minister Modrow sounds like he's singing the same tune as Kohl about reunification."

"It does seem like things are moving too smoothly in Kohl's direction," Dieter said thoughtfully.

"*Ja*. And it wouldn't surprise me that some organization in West Germany is secretly supporting New Forum and some of the other dissidents in our country."

"That may be, but the protesters I saw seemed to genuinely want a change."

"*Ja*, but it only takes a few dedicated agitators to motivate others. A small cadre of provocateurs can influence thousands. We were on guard against overt attack from the west. Somehow they fooled us and managed to take control of people's minds."

Dieter doubted that a group of plotters could have swayed public opinion to the extent he witnessed in the demonstrations. Still, his father might be right. Hadn't Lenin managed to do something similar in Russia in 1917? "I believe our people will vote to remain a separate socialist state." At least that's what he hoped would happen. Otherwise, their institutions, including the Volksarmee, would be swept away.

"I don't have much confidence in these elections, Dieter. The West will pour money into skillful propaganda that will overwhelm the people. They'll vote for reunification, thinking they will soon be rich and able to do anything they want. They are in for a big shock when they find themselves unemployed and unable to afford their luxuries."

"Most of my friends in the Volksarmee are planning to vote for the Socialist Unity Party. We believe the SED will keep East Germany separate and maintain a strong Volksarmee."

"Then you have more faith in elections than I do, Dieter."

The March sky was gray and a few snowflakes were falling as John Parker hurried down the steps of Fourth Army's headquarters building. Their Oldsmobile 98 was parked across the street, and Gail was sitting in the front seat. It was late Sunday afternoon, and the Fourth Army Commander's Conference had just concluded. If the weather held and there were no unusual delays on the expressway, they should get back to East Lansing by ten o'clock that evening. Of course, he could have flown to Chicago and rented a car for the hour drive north of O'Hare Airport to Fort Sheridan. But the weather in mid-March made air travel uncertain, and he preferred to drive, especially if Gail would accompany him and do some of the driving. The five-hour trip gave them an uninterrupted time to talk, and allowed him an opportunity to review the accumulation of Army correspondence.

He opened the rear door, tossed his briefcase and army raincoat on the back seat, and got in the driver's seat. "Hi. Been waiting long?"

"About thirty minutes. I did some shopping in Lake Forest and got here about three. How did the meeting go?"

"Not too bad, at least for me. My unit was recognized for having the best retention rate in Fourth Army. But General Thompson and his staff went through a stack of performance indicators, and the 300th wasn't doing so great in some of those." Thinking about his boss, the commander of the 300th Military Police Command, John added, "General Ralston is really feeling the pressure." John returned the salute of the MP at the gate as they left the small Army post, and headed toward I-94.

"Of course Ralston is not the only commander feeling the heat. Tony Lawson said the 425th Transportation Command was in hot water over their latest IG inspection. And Joe Roberts in the 123d ARCOM told me that the Fourth Army maintenance inspectors had come down hard on two of their subordinate commands. General Thompson has really been raising hell since he took over Fourth Army."

"That's easy for him." Gail scoffed. "He only has to work at one job. Doesn't he realize that reservists just have weekends and a few weeks of summer training to meet those standards?"

"Of course he does. He commands 150,000 soldiers, and most of them are in the Army Reserve or National Guard. He expects a lot. But I give him credit for not sitting back and coasting in a job that usually is the last stop before retirement."

"Well, he should take into consideration that many of you are working seventy hours a week to keep up with your civilian and military jobs."

"Hand me some change, dear." They were approaching the first of many tollbooths that made driving around Chicago so aggravating.

After tossing some coins into the receptacle, John decided it was time to switch the subject. "How was your day? Any trouble checking out of the hotel?"

"I couldn't get back to sleep after you left, so I got up and wrote some letters. Then I got dressed and had some breakfast. Since there was time, I decided to go to church at the post chapel."

"See anyone you know?"

"No. There wasn't a very large crowd, but the chaplain delivered a good message." Then she smiled and said, "It made me think of our early days in Fulda."

"I'm glad you went. Chaplain Jones is a good man. He's held some services at our conferences."

"After that I had lunch, and killed the rest of the afternoon shopping."

As they cleared another toll, John asked. "Where do you want to eat dinner?"

"How about that little cafe by the river near the winery? Is that too far?"

John glanced at his watch. "We could be there in a couple of hours. Sounds fine to me."

The cafe was in Paw Paw, Michigan, roughly the midpoint of their journey; and they reached it about seven-thirty, after crossing into the Eastern Time Zone. They had discovered the charming restaurant, with its patio overlooking the Paw Paw River, on one of their first trips to Fort Sheridan. It was cold and dark outside, so a table near the fireplace was inviting. Enjoying a nice meal in a comfortable restaurant was one of the ways John tried to compensate Gail for putting up with his frequent trips on Army business.

Waiting for their dinners, they sipped a glass of fine Chablis from the winery across the street and relaxed.

"John, I think we should talk about this trip to Europe and get it on our calendar. The kids are doing fine now on their own. Couldn't we plan on three weeks in July or August?"

"Let's see…our annual training is scheduled for the first two weeks of July. Then we have a Capstone Conference in August.

"Can't someone else go to this Capstone thing in your place?"

"Well, yes, in an emergency. But it only takes place once every three years. Representatives of all the 300th's subordinate units are meeting to coordinate mobilization plans. Commanders of my guard companies from different parts of the country are coming. I've never met some of them, so I really need to be there."

Gail frowned, but didn't comment. Instead she pulled a pocket calendar from her purse and said. "Well what about late August or early September?"

"That's fine, but let me check the dates on that conference. Maybe we can work the trip in earlier. Besides Fulda, where do you want to go?"

Gail smiled. "Oh, Paris, Rome, Berlin, Prague, London, Vienna, Copenhagen, and…"

He started to protest, but her chuckle stopped him. "Just kidding, John. I know we only have three weeks. I'll call a travel agent tomorrow, and see what we can work out."

Savannah in March can be beautiful. The weather is warm, the fragrance of spring flowers exhilarating, and the ocean breeze is invigorating. But Gisela took little note of their surroundings as she and Fred entered the office of Dr. Diane Williams, an oncologist at the Savannah Breast Cancer Center. Since her cancer was first diagnosed, Gisela had been through a variety of procedures including ultrasound evaluation and cell cycle analysis to determine the size, type and stage of the tumor. Dr. Williams, a sympathetic woman in her late forties, was the primary oncologist among a team of specialists who were working together on a plan of treatment.

Because the size of the tumor was relatively small, with no evidence of spread to nearby lymph nodes, Gisela's cancer was classified as a Stage I on a scale of I to IV.

"The standard treatment," Dr. Williams was saying, "is to remove the tumor and a portion of the surrounding tissue while conserving the major portion of the breast. I also recommend the use of radiation therapy to attack any microscopic cancer cells remaining in the breast. Otherwise those cells are undetectable."

"What are the chances of the cancer spreading?" Fred asked.

Dr. Williams smiled confidently. "Patients who have had this treatment generally have a good prognosis, with only about one chance in four of further tumor spread."

Gisela was quiet during the doctor's explanation. One out of four chances of further cancer were not comforting odds. However, instead of pursuing the worst-case scenario, Gisela simply asked, "How long will the treatment take?"

"We'll schedule the surgery as soon as possible, probably within ten days. Radiotherapy would begin within four to six weeks of surgery. The radiation is given five days a week for about six weeks."

"Are there any side effects? Doesn't radiation make you feel sick?"

"Not usually. Nausea and vomiting may occur in radiation of the abdomen, but it's rare for radiation to the chest area. The most common side effect is fatigue, although more so for patients receiving treatments to large areas. Some people may have skin reactions which appear as a redness called erythema. This is similar to sunburn, and will usually go away within a week."

Gisela asked a few more questions concerning the surgery, and Dr. Williams patiently reassured her. Then she looked at Fred. "I think I should do what she says."

Fred took her hand, gave it a squeeze and said, "I agree." She could see the concern in his eyes even as he tried to sound confident. "I know you'll be fine."

As spring turned into summer, Gisela was too busy with her treatment to think much about traveling to Germany. Moreover, the radiation left her tired and depressed. Nevertheless, Dr. Williams was satisfied that the surgery was successful, and remained confident that the radiotherapy would work as planned.

By summer people in both Germanys knew reunification was on its way. Free elections were held in the German Democratic Republic

(GDR) for the first time with Helmut Kohl's coalition of Christian Democratic Unity and Democratic Awakening parties winning with 48% of the vote. The SED/PDS party of former communists received only 16%, effectively ending their forty-one year reign of totalitarian control. CDU leaders in East Germany agreed to monetary, economic and social union with West Germany that went into effect in July. With CDU in control of both defense ministries, it was readily determined that a united Germany should remain in NATO but without extending its power to GDR territory. Surprisingly, in talks among the four victorious powers of the Second World War in Berlin, it was Soviet Foreign Minister Shevardnadze who proposed that Germany should have combined forces of no more that 250,000.

These swiftly developing changes had a demoralizing effect on loyal party members, dedicated communists, and faithful military leaders in the east. Dieter often imagined that he was in a bad dream that summer, expecting each day when he awakened that life had returned to the secure days under Erich Honecker. Some of his comrades gave up hope in the Volksarmee and moved to Frankfurt, Hamburg, or Munich in search of new careers.

Dieter, however, clung to the belief that the unified army would need his talents. But his reaction to the lack of mission and uncertainty surrounding the military was a mixture of anger and frustration that manifested itself in an uncharacteristic fashion. He began frequenting the bars of Leipzig and became involved with women he normally wouldn't have given a second glance. One morning in July he woke with a headache in the apartment of his latest girlfriend, Margrit Kuhn, a flighty young beauty of no serious intellect. She was propped up in bed reading a copy of *Der Stern*, a West German magazine she had picked up in the beauty shop where she worked.

"Dieter, *Schätze*, let's take a trip to the West. Everybody's been going to West Berlin, Hamburg, and other cities. I haven't been anywhere," she pouted.

Dieter raised up on an elbow and looked at the picture on the page she had shoved in his face. An attractive saleswoman was showing off the latest in swimsuits to a group of women from East Berlin. The caption under the picture boasted that Western fashion was making a big splash with the Ossies, a slang term for East Germans.

"Why does everyone think they have to have something made in the West?" Dieter groaned. In his mind their society was based on materialism that had no lasting values. He let his head fall back on the pillow and closed his eyes.

Margrit stroked his neck and squirmed next to him. "Listen Dieter, I have a cousin in Fulda who invited me to come visit her whenever I wish, and I want you to come with me." Her hand moved down his chest. "I know we would have a good time."

Dieter's body was awakening faster than his mind. As he turned closer to Margrit, he thought, what the hell. Why not go? He had to admit to a degree of curiosity about the West. He put his arm around her waist and said, "All right. If you promise a good time, I'll go along." Margrit squealed with delight and kissed him.

The following week Dieter and Margrit took the train from Leipzig to Fulda. It wasn't difficult for them to get away. Margrit already had planned a week's vacation, and the Volksarmee maneuvers that Dieter had expected to occupy his time were canceled. They left early from the large and imposing Central Railway Station and had breakfast on the train. It was a long journey, across a historic route of conquering armies, and through cities which had endured many changes in rulers: Weimar, Erfurt, Gotha, and Eisenach. As the train passed slowly through Herleshausen, the last town before crossing the former border, Dieter leaned across Margrit who was sitting by the window and pointed.

"That's something I never thought I would see," he said.

"What is it?" A border guard was standing near the end of the station. Hanging on the wall next to him were some uniform jackets, hats and insignia.

"They're for sale," Dieter said with disgust. "I heard that soldiers were selling uniform items, but I didn't believe it. They're trying to get the new marks, and they're willing to sell what the state gives them to make a little money." He shook his head and leaned back in his seat. "What have we become?" he muttered.

Margrit ignored Dieter's dismay. She was eagerly looking at the changing scenery as they crossed into West Germany. Soon they had passed through several small towns and the bustling city of Hünfeld. In places the train paralleled the two-lane highway.

"Dieter, look at all the cars on the road! And they're bigger! I thought only rich people had such cars."

He hadn't expected to see so many cars in the countryside either. "Maybe they are from Fulda or Bad Hersfeld, coming to some event in Hünfeld."

"Have you noticed the buildings and the roads? Everything seems modern and well kept up—not like Leipzig."

What he had seen so far was impressive, Dieter had to admit. But wouldn't that be the case along the major route into West Germany from the East, he reasoned? This area probably got the priority for goods and services.

Margrit continued her chatter as their train pulled into the Fulda Hauptbahnhof. Inside the depot a well-dressed couple was waiting for them. Dieter hung back as Margrit rushed forward to embrace her cousin, a small, blonde woman in her mid-forties. That was followed by a somewhat reserved hug by her cousin's husband, a bald man of about fifty. Then Margrit turned around and pulled Dieter over to introduce him to Thomas and Charlotte Frey.

"Please call me Lotte, everyone does," she said, giving Dieter a quick appraisal. Apparently satisfied, she turned back to Margrit. "Oh Margrit, you are much prettier than your picture. It's such a pleasure to meet you face to face. How are your parents?" Taking Margrit's arm in hers, she propelled Margrit toward the exit. Thomas took Margrit's duffel bag and led the way out of the station to the parking lot. Dieter fell in step with him.

"So, Dieter is this your first visit to the West? Margrit hasn't told us much about you."

Dieter resented Thomas's patronizing tone, but tried not to let it show. "*Ja*, it's my first visit. Margit and I haven't known each other very long."

Thomas shot him a sharp look, but said nothing as they came to a dark blue Opel, which he unlocked with his remote key control. The bags were stowed in the trunk while the ladies, still talking about family, climbed into the back seat. Dieter joined Thomas in the front, and they pulled out of the parking area on to Kurfursten Strasse.

"We thought we would drive around for a few minutes and show you some of the sights of Fulda," Lotte said. Then we'll stop for coffee before we take you back to our house. How does that sound?"

Dieter shrugged, and Margrit said, "That sounds fine, Lotte. I hope we can find time for some shopping tomorrow."

"Of course. Thomas and I are both on vacation now, so we have all day to show you around. Just let us know if there is something in particular you would like to see." Dieter remembered Margrit saying that her cousin was a teacher of English in the Gymnasium, a high school for university-bound students, and that Thomas taught a construction class in Fulda's technical high school.

They drove past the shopping district with Lotte pointing out the Kaufhaus Department store, and other specialty stores. Margrit seemed enthralled with the displays in store windows, and asked one question after another about shopping. Dieter was curious too about one thing. As Margrit chatted with Lotte in the back seat, he asked Thomas, "How long did you have to wait to buy this car?'

Thomas looked puzzled for a moment. "I didn't have to wait. Once I decided what model I wanted, I just used my old car as a down payment, and drove away in this car the same day."

Dieter was speechless. He had waited five years to take delivery of his Wartburg, and he had to pay half the cost up front and the remainder before he could get the car. His mind tried to reconcile the economic system that granted him a small four-cylinder car whose top speed was barely 90 kilometers per hour, with this comfortable Opal that could cruise the Autobahn at 120.

A few minutes later they drove slowly past the cathedral and parked across the street so that they could walk through a gate to Castle Park and sit on the terrace of the Orangerie. Erected in 1736 as part of the Prince Bishop's palace complex, the Orangerie has beautiful reception halls with ornate ceiling murals. Sitting at an umbrella table, Lotte ordered coffee and a slice of *Kirsch Torte* for each of them.

"We thought you would enjoy the scenery and view from this terrace," Lotte said, gesturing toward the flight of stairs leading across a well-kept lawn to the palace. A statue of a goddess holding a flower in her hand dominated the stairs leading to the terrace.

"What does she represent?" Dieter inquired, looking at the statue.

"That's the *Floravase*. It's one of the finest pieces of baroque sculpture in the world," Thomas explained. "It honors Prince-Abbot Adolf von Dalberg, whose emblem is the lily being held by the goddess Flora."

Dieter was unimpressed. "Does the prince's family still own this property?"

Thomas smiled. "No. Not any more. The city owns these buildings. The palace is the city hall, and the grounds are a city park."

Dieter nodded in agreement. "That's the way our socialist government has dealt with the aristocracy. Their fine buildings and castles are now used for the benefit of all citizens."

"Well," Thomas said after a pause, "There are still some homes and castles owned privately by descendants of the nobility. But they pay heavy taxes on their property, so they are gradually being turned over to the public."

"What about the Dom?" Dieter had noticed many people in the Dom Plaza, some taking pictures. "It looks like quite a tourist attraction."

"That's right." Thomas said. "Thousands come from all over the world to see the birthplace of Christian religion in Germany." In a professorial tone Thomas began to lecture. "On the spot where the Dom now stands, the abbot Sturmius founded a Benedictine Cloister called Fulda in 744 A.D. St. Boniface used Fulda as his base for missionary work throughout Germany, and is buried there." Then Lotte cleared her throat, and he realized that he was boring their guests. He hurriedly concluded. "Anyway, each year German bishops come here for their annual conference."

"So the church owns the property, but the city and state profit from all the travelers who come to see these historic buildings," Lotte added. "Would you like to take a tour of the cathedral and St. Michael's?"

Dieter looked at Margrit, and said, "I'm not that interested, but if Margrit wishes..."

"Oh, perhaps later. If we have time."

Thomas and Lotte lived in a new section of houses on the northern edge of Fulda. Their house was spacious and charming, decorated with Lotte's paintings and Thomas's woodcarvings. Dieter deposited their bags in a guest bedroom, and joined Margrit for a tour of the home. Both were clearly impressed with the size and comfort the Frey's enjoyed. Later they ate dinner on a porch opening to a sizable yard, accented by a beautiful garden. The evening was warm and still, and after a couple of bottles of wine, everyone was feeling mellow.

Margrit admired her cousin's collection of spoons from different countries. "Lotte," she asked. "How did you manage to get all those spoons? You didn't really go to all those countries, did you?"

"No, not to all. Two or three were gifts from friends, but the rest I picked up as souvenirs on different vacations we took."

Margrit looked surprised. "You have traveled all over the world? I didn't realize you were so well off."

"Oh, we're not rich, if that's what you mean," Lotte laughed. "We both work, and we've raised three children, but we're just middle class people."

Dieter looked at his hosts curiously. "You have a beautiful home, but I was just wondering where the working class lives. I didn't see many apartment buildings when we drove around the city."

"We have some apartment buildings, but they are not so large, four or five floors usually," Thomas said. "Younger people who are just getting started in life, or temporary workers from other countries live there. But most people our age live in their own homes."

"Even the factory workers?" Dieter persisted.

"Listen, Dieter," Thomas said impatiently. "You saw the home across the street. The husband is an accountant and his wife works in a bank. Next to them is a couple who both work in the Fulda Tire Factory. You don't have to be rich to own a home along this street."

Dieter stared at him blankly, trying to comprehend what Thomas said. After a moment he said, "There are not many houses like this in the East, but then everyone has a job. No one lives in poverty."

"There is very little poverty here also. We do have some unemployment. But the government pays unemployment compensation until they get back to work."

That night in the room where they shared a bed, an arrangement that brought some awkward glances, Dieter was perplexed.

"I just don't think everything is as fantastic as they make it sound. Two teachers living in a home as nice as my parents! They must have inherited some money."

"I don't know, Dieter. There certainly are a lot of houses, and none of the big apartment buildings like we have in Leipzig. Anyway, it's time you relaxed and enjoyed yourself. Come over here and let me give you a massage."

The next day after breakfast Thomas drove them back to the city center and parked near Markt Strasse. Dieter tried not to show his surprise at the quantity of goods displayed in the shops, particularly in the Kaufhaus department store. He was also shocked at the prices. Even with a currency conversion that put East Germans on a par with the Deutsch Mark, prices were much higher than he expected. Nevertheless, Margrit had accumulated a sum of money and was determined to buy as much as possible.

After awhile, Dieter tired of looking at all the consumer goods, and he suggested to Thomas that they leave the women and return to a bookstore they passed earlier. There he found a number of books on West Germany's government. He perused several, and finally purchased one about the application of democracy in the Bundesrepublic.

When they were back outside, Thomas must have realized he was not interested in visiting more stores. "Dieter there's an American *Kaserne* here. Would you like to drive by while the women are shopping?"

"Do you think we could get inside?"

"Not without a pass. But we can drive along Haimbacher Strasse, and sometimes tanks and other vehicles can be seen from the road. The airfield is a little further, and usually you are able to see some helicopters there."

Ten minutes later they were driving slowly alongside Downs Barracks, and Dieter could see a few American soldiers walking across the parade ground. When they came to a space between buildings where they could catch a glimpse of vehicles in the motor pool, Thomas stopped the car.

"That looks like one of the new American tanks," Dieter said, pointing toward a large tracked vehicle with a long gun tube.

"*Ja*. It takes up even more room on the road than their old tanks. It has a big gun too."

"Not any bigger than our T-72," Dieter boasted, although he remembered reading some intelligence reports that made him doubtful.

"An American major told me they can shoot on the move and hit targets as far away as the old tanks could standing still."

"Shoot on the move," Dieter scoffed. "*Ja*, anybody can shoot the gun while the tank is moving, but anything they hit is probably an accident." But his companion had touched a nerve. Is it possible the Americans could really hit distant targets without stopping to aim and fire?

Thomas put the car in gear and drove past the remaining buildings on the west side of the *Kaserne* toward the distant airfield. In a few minutes Dieter could see 20 to 30 helicopters. About one-third were light, observation helicopters; the rest were bigger and more menacing. They were Apaches, Dieter knew, capable of carrying tank-killing missiles.

"Didn't the sign back there say this was an armored cavalry regiment?" he asked.

"*Ja*. That's right. And this is the airfield for the regiment."

Dieter looked at Thomas in disbelief. "But this many helicopters must be for a division or larger!"

"Nein, I'm quite sure that all these pilots belong to the Fulda Regiment," Thomas answered. "The airfield's been here for a long time."

Dieter was stunned. There was more aviation support here for a regiment than East Germany had for two divisions. And the Russians were not much better equipped. They watched silently a few minutes. A couple of choppers took off, and another landed. They could see a few mechanics working on other helicopters. Finally Thomas turned the car around, and they headed back to town.

Something Thomas said had been nagging Dieter. "Do you have much contact with Americans?"

"Lotte belongs to a German-American Friendship Club for women, and I have met different Americans at military displays and at Fasching Parties. We also know a couple who rent a house near us."

Don't their soldiers cause a lot of trouble?

"Occasionally some of the younger soldiers get drunk and unruly, but the Americans and our police do a fairly good job of keeping those incidents under control. For the most part, the problems are relatively minor."

"Well, Russian soldiers keep close to their barracks. You almost never hear of a Russian getting drunk in a Gasthaus or mistreating civilians."

"Really?" Thomas said with a hint of sarcasm. "It must be reassuring for those of you in the East to have such a large Russian Army stationed nearby. But from my viewpoint, I will be happier when they move back to Russia."

"And wouldn't you feel better also if the Americans left?"

"The honest answer is yes and no. I will be happier when our country is reunified, and we don't need foreign soldiers stationed anywhere in Germany. But personally I will be sorry to see the Americans leave Fulda. Besides providing security as part of NATO, they help our economy."

Dieter was doubtful. "But is your opinion typical of other West Germans?"

"Ja. There is not much anti-American sentiment that I know of, if that's what you're getting at."

On the way back to pick up the women, Dieter thought about the contrast in attitudes. He had espoused the official position concerning their Russian allies. Yet he knew most East Germans resented the Russians and had no interest in learning their language. What Thomas was saying flew in the face of all he had been taught. Why is that, he wondered?

The next day on the train ride home, Dieter was subdued. The first part of the trip he was lost in study of the book he bought in Fulda. Margrit, on the other hand, was her usual cheerful and carefree self.

"Come on, Dieter. Don't be so serious. What's the matter? Didn't you have a good time?"

Her breezy indifference to political events had also been irritating, but that wasn't what was bothering him. "*Ja*, sure, with you. But you know, Margrit, I'm beginning to think that we've been lied to by our government." He turned away and looked out the window. In his mind he wondered if he hadn't been lied to all his life.

CHAPTER 18

After four days of mounting pressure following Iraq's sudden invasion of Kuwait, the call had come at 2100 hours on August 6th from XVIIIth Airborne Corps to execute their wartime deployment. As Fred made his way to division headquarters he saw soldiers carrying rucksacks and duffel bags to assembly areas. Despite the steady rainfall, tearful wives and sweethearts had gathered in clusters around the brightly lit barracks at Fort Stewart, S.C. to say goodbye. Nothing was certain. Yet as Fred hurried past he could sense their fear that they would be separated from husbands or lovers a long time, for some perhaps forever.

By 2300 every brigade and battalion commander was assembled at the Victory Division headquarters for a briefing by the Division Staff. Fred felt the tension as he took a seat in the conference room of the 24th Infantry Division (Mechanized). The usual banter and light-hearted joking was missing, replaced by serious expressions among those about to go to war, some for the first time.

Major General Barry McCaffree, the 50 year-old division commander, emphasized in his preliminary remarks that the threat to the airhead, which the 82d Airborne Division would initially establish in Saudi Arabia, was severe. Because of that, he was ordered to have one brigade at the Savannah port within 18 hours ready for immediate loading on Navy transport ships. He set the tone for the staff officers who followed by saying, "Saddam's tanks are already near the Saudi border. We're in a deadly race to get to Saudi Arabia with enough tank-killing weapons to stop him."

Together with elements of two Marine divisions, the 24th Mechanized Division, with four battalions of M1 Abrams tanks, made up the heavy ground forces of General Schwarzkopf's Central Command. The airmobile elements of the 82d Airborne Division, 101st Air Assault Division, and the Ninth Air Force were already alerted, and would be flown by Air Force C141 transports to Saudi Arabia over the next few days.

As Chief of Staff, Fred supervised the work of the principal staff sections of the division and oversaw their support of the subordinate brigades and attached forces. On this day he was grateful that his key assistants, the G1 (Personnel), G2 (Intelligence), G3 (Operations), and G4 (Logistics), were experienced professionals.

Fred called on the G2 to open the staff briefing with the latest information concerning the enemy situation. As he expanded on the enemy threat, the G2 pointed on a large map of the Middle East to a number of red symbols along Kuwait's southern border.

"The same three Republican Guard divisions that led the attack into Kuwait are moving tanks and artillery to this area bordering Saudi Arabia. It's an indication that they may intend to continue their attack south to gain control of Saudi Arabia's oil fields. If so, they can reinforce their attack with three other heavy divisions."

There was a murmur of voices among the grim-faced commanders. Fred overheard one of the battalion commanders mutter, "If they do attack, the 82d will just be a speed bump in their way."

The G3 followed, and immediately tackled the problem of the 48th Brigade of the Georgia National Guard. The 48th was the *Round Out Brigade* attached to the 24th as part of a plan to bring active duty divisions to full strength by aligning National Guard and Reserve units with them for training and mobilization.

"Gentlemen, the Chief of Staff of the Army has made a decision that the 48th Brigade will be replaced by the 197th Brigade from Fort Benning."

Surprised looks and a murmur of comments greeted his announcement. The 48th and 197th Commanders, already counseled by General McCaffree, said nothing. The Division Commander rose abruptly from his chair and faced the room.

"I want it understood that this decision is in no way a reflection on the capability of the 48th or the professionalism of its soldiers. Their Mob Plan requires them to have several weeks of post-mobilization training, which means they should be a late-deploying unit." Fred knew from several high level conference calls over the past twenty-four hours that General Vuono, the Army Chief of Staff, was determined not to repeat the mistake of sending unprepared reservists into the initial battles. "Nevertheless," McCaffree continued, "General Schwarzkopf faces an acute shortage of combat power, and so the 197th will bring us up to normal strength of three brigades."

He took his seat and the G3 began an explanation of the division's mission.

He reviewed the concept for airborne forces to seize a piece of key terrain; and hold it against the larger Republican Guard Corps, until the Marines and heavy armor of the 24th arrived to secure the lodgment. The plan was familiar. They had rehearsed it in numerous exercises and simulated battles. He noted that 2d Brigade, already alerted that they would be first to move, had an advance group from the brigade at the railhead preparing to load their armored and wheeled vehicles. When the Operations Officer finished answering questions, Fred called on the G4.

"Gentlemen, the first priority is to get the division's combat forces to the Theater of Operations in the correct sequence with everything they need to fight if they have to go directly into combat. The transportation plan has been distributed, and I want to call your attention to the changes that pertain to the 48th and 197th Brigades. The transportation officer will go into detail about loading plans and sequencing when I finish. We're not sure which of the Navy's fast sealift ships will be available first, but whatever the case, we will transport all vehicles combat-loaded. The initial combat load of ammunition, fuel, spare parts and rations has already been completed. Upon arrival at the Dhahran Port, 22d Support Command will provide necessary logistical support until the rest of the division arrives." He covered several other changes in the logistical plan, and then answered a few questions concerning replacement of deadlined equipment.

Shortly after midnight the briefing ended, and the commanders hurried back to their units to implement their part of the operation. After dealing with several issues brought up by individual commanders, Fred returned to his office to tackle a growing list of problems his staff was confronting. Moving a mechanized division of 16,000 soldiers, 5,100 vehicles, and 90 helicopters is a monstrous task. The days ahead were going to be long and difficult.

It was late the following night before Fred got home. The headquarters was operating 24 hours a day, and he had directed the staff sections to set up 12 hour shifts to sustain the operation. Although Fred was dead tired, it was the first opportunity that he and Gisela had to talk about the crisis.

Gisela was lying in bed watching television when Fred came into the bedroom. She switched off the set as he crossed the room and sat next to her on the bed.

"Fred, you look terrible. When are you going to rest?"

"As soon as I can get into bed. We've started working in shifts. Barring another emergency, I won't go back until tomorrow morning." He reached over and took her hand. "More importantly, how are you feeling?"

"All right. I don't get as tired as I used to, now that the radiation is over. The doctor was pleased with the mammogram, and said I should regain my energy in a few weeks."

He squeezed her hand gently. "That's great. I've been worried about leaving if you were still sick. The trouble is that the burden for this initial phase of transporting our men and equipment to the Gulf, falls on the staff; and, short of an emergency, I can't duck that responsibility."

Gisela made an effort to sit up a little, and he moved a pillow to support her better. "You don't have to worry about my health. The doctor says I'm recovering nicely." Despite her words, concern showed in her eyes. "When are you leaving?"

He kicked off his boots. "I'm supposed to fly out with the Forward Command Post in six days."

"Oh, Fred, I wish you didn't have to go." There was a plaintive note in her voice. "Sick or not, I miss you when you're gone, and this time it's a war." She put her hand on his arm. "I don't know when you'll be back."

"It's not a war yet, Gisela." He tried to sound hopeful, but the fatigue made his words sound flat. "It's a show of force. If Saddam pulls back, it may end quickly."

Tears were welling up in her eyes. "Anna called and she's been alerted too. I'm so frightened. I can't bear the thought of losing either of you."

Fred pulled her to him and wrapped his arms around her, feeling her tears on his cheek. "It's okay, honey. We'll get through this. Neither Anna nor I are in combat positions. We'll be all right." He held her close a long time and then laid her back against the pillow before easing himself down on the bed next to her.

"Gisela, when you've been afraid before, you've turned to God for help." She nodded in agreement and brushed aside her tears. While he held her hand she began to say the Lord's Prayer. Before she finished, his grip relaxed and he was sound asleep.

Two weeks later President Bush signed the authorization order to call up the reserves. His order allowed the activation of up to 200,000 Reserve and National Guard troops for six months. The announcement sent a strong signal that the United States was committed to this military action. The news also sent a strong signal to members of America's Ready Reserves that they were needed.

John Parker got the word at the Reserve Center in the Detroit suburb of Inkster when Sergeant Ferguson interrupted a staff meeting to tell them about the President's announcement. He had made the 90-mile drive with Sam Wheeler to attend their regular Wednesday night administrative drill. No pay or retirement points. It was just another long day to ensure their reserve unit was keeping up with the demands of the Army.

John was excited at the news, but not surprised. He had known for a long time that if the United States became involved in a major conflict, Reserve and Guard units would have to be mobilized. Correcting one of the errors of Vietnam, the Army, in the intervening years, had developed what was called the Total Force Concept. Applying that concept to this crisis meant active duty forces would perform most of the combat and infantry missions; while soldiers of the Army Reserve and National Guard would be called quickly to handle combat support functions and train up for combat reinforcement.

After the staff meeting broke up a full-time technician came into John's office with a list of units that Fort Sheridan had identified as the first to be mobilized in Fourth Army. As they reviewed the list John could see that the initial units included logisticians as well as engineers, truck drivers, and medical personnel. The 327th MP Battalion outside Chicago was designated, but not John's headquarters.

It was past eleven o'clock when John turned off I-96 at the Okemos Exit to drop off Sam Wheeler at the commuter lot, before driving on to his home in East Lansing.

Gail must have heard the garage door opener and rushed to meet him. When John opened the back door he was startled to see Gail coming toward him with a stricken look on her face. Before she said a word, he knew what was wrong.

"John, did you hear? The President is calling up the reserves. Does that mean you'll be going again?" She was holding a dishtowel from a stack of laundry she had been folding. From the den John could hear the sound of a television set. Dan Rather's sonorous voice was describing the seriousness of the situation.

"I don't know, Gail. They've only mobilized 25,000 so far, which doesn't include us; but one of the 300th's MP battalions has been alerted for the next increment."

There was a tremor in her voice. "I never expected you to be sent into combat again. You did your time in Vietnam." Her hands were unconsciously twisting the dishtowel. "I don't want you to leave."

John set his briefcase on the kitchen counter and took her hands in his. "I don't want to leave either, Gail. They may not need us, but if they do, I'll have to go. That's what we've been training for all these years."

"That's what you've been doing because you wanted to." There were tears in her eyes. "It's not what I wanted."

For a few moments they were silent. John was afraid to say anything that would lead down the path of old arguments. From the den they could hear the voice of a TV reporter describing images of soldiers in combat gear climbing aboard transport planes. Instinctively he pulled her to him. "I love you, Gail, and I need your support."

After a few moments Gail reached for a tissue and dabbed at her eyes. Gradually her composure returned. Still holding onto John's arm, she looked into his face. "I'm sorry, John. I was just getting used to the kids being on their own, and there being only the two of us again. I was really feeling happy. This mobilization thing has just burst my bubble."

James Pocock

PART FOUR

JANUARY 1991- AUGUST 1991

James Pocock

CHAPTER 19

The *Thump, Thump, Thump* of an approaching helicopter made John squint eastward into the bright sunlight. The familiar sound and midday heat momentarily carried him back to Vietnam, as if he were waiting for a string of Hueys to touch down and load the Province Reconnaissance Unit for an operation against the VC in Long An. When he lowered his gaze to the shimmering sand, the figure of Command Sergeant Major (CSM) Erickson next to him in desert battle dress returned his mind to reality. John was feeling the stress of eighteen-hour workdays, desert climate, and a mountain of problems that engulfed his command in its effort to construct and organize a prisoner of war camp. The message informing him that Major General Carter's helicopter would be landing shortly at his location hadn't improved his frame of mind.

They were located on the edge of the Saudi town of Hafar al Batin, about 25 miles south of the Iraqi border and over 250 miles from their parent headquarters, the 800th MP Command, located in the Khobar Towers complex outside Dhahran. Since arriving at Hafar al Batin in early January 1991, it had been a race to assemble his guard companies and support personnel, as well as coordinating all the construction needed to support an operation the size of a small city. Unfortunately, preliminary coordination between the 800th MP Command and the staff of Central Command had overlooked several key factors, which could affect the success of his mission.

John's chief concern was getting the camp built and functioning properly in time to handle an influx of prisoners. As Coalition Air Forces pounded Iraqi divisions along the border, dozens of deserters had already straggled across front lines. No doubt their will to fight had been affected by the sight of T-72 tanks being blown apart by laser-guided bombs. John's MPs had to confine them even while the EPW camp was still under construction. But General Carter was chaffing over John's reluctance to release the engineers for what the general saw as more important priorities.

Parker and Erickson waited beside their vehicle, an Army version of the Chevrolet Blazer, until the blades of the general's helicopter slowed enough to keep the sand from blowing. A tall officer with two black stars on his helmet jumped out of the chopper and walked toward them. They saluted and John said, "Welcome to the 301st EPW Camp, General."

"Colonel Parker, right? Good to see you." General Carter returned the salute and shook hands with both men. Behind him, carrying the general's camouflage-covered briefcase was a lanky captain. As they strode toward the truck, General Carter asked about their mobilization and deployment experience.

"Well, sir, like many Fourth Army units, we went to McCoy for five days of weapons firing and pre-mob qualification. Of course that was the beginning of January, and with several inches of snow on the ground, it was a little difficult to make the connection to this theater."

The general grunted and said, "That's for sure." Like Parker he was a reservist with many annual training experiences at Fort McCoy under his belt. In civilian life he was an executive in an engineering company in Chicago. "They should have sent you to Fort Chaffee (Arkansas) or some other place in the south. Most of my troops were out of there before it got cold."

If they hadn't waited so late to mobilize us, John thought, I wouldn't have half the problems, and you wouldn't be on my back. He opened the door for the general who, instead of climbing in, stood facing him.

"Now, Colonel what's all this confusion about? My staff tells me you've got our engineers doing all kinds of work that wasn't in the plan coordinated with the MP Command. I'm here to tell you, that's got to stop."

"Yes, sir. That's true. But I can explain better, if we drive through part of the camp so I can show you what we're doing."

With the sergeant major at the wheel, they slowly skirted a berm of sand, pushed up to a height of seven feet by engineer bulldozers, which marked the camp's outside perimeter. The size of the camp was impressive, about a half-mile wide by one mile long, making it appear from the air as a southern extension of Hafar al Batin. They turned into the camp on a hard-packed sand road that led to a swath of open space about two football fields wide, separating the barbed wire enclosures from the administrative and logistics areas.

"General, on your right is the first of three enclosures for prisoners. The other two are still under construction. Each enclosure has eight compounds surrounded with triple-strand barbed wire, with 100 yards of open space between compounds. As you can see, there are guard towers covering the open spaces."

General Carter looked at the long rows of tents in each cluster and said, "There wasn't anything in the master plan about having all these compounds. What are you trying to prove, Colonel?"

John was tired and the weight of his helmet was aggravating a lingering headache. He paused a moment to keep his temper in check. "Sir, I'm responsible for housing, feeding, and controlling 24,000 prisoners in this camp under humane conditions. That means separating officers, females, refugees, and various ethnic and religious factions that might stir up trouble. We had planned on 500 prisoners per compound, but now we've been told to put up to 1000 in each one. It's going to make it tough for our guard force."

"That's another thing," the general complained. "My project officer tells me you insisted on moving the location we already constructed for your guard companies, and demanded that we build another site."

"Yes, sir. I did. We need the guard personnel as close as possible in case of a riot or disturbance where we have to reinforce the guards in the enclosure. The first location was too far away, and, for that matter, too close to Hafar al Batin. There have been intelligence reports of terrorists there who may target Americans."

General Carter was silent as they completed the drive-by of the enclosures and turned back up the row of logistics and administrative facilities. CSM Erickson brought the blazer to a stop outside two GP tents that sheltered the 301st Headquarters, and the men dismounted. Parker led the way toward the field table and folding chairs that served as his office. As the general sat down, a soldier brought a pitcher of lemonade and poured drinks for them. Leaving the two commanders in semi-privacy, CSM Erickson showed the aide to the nearest phones so he could coordinate the general's next stop.

General Carter drained his cup and set it back on the tray. Like a bulldog, he returned to the bone he was chewing. "Look, Colonel Parker, I understand you have a big task here, but there are other engineer requirements in this theater. I want this construction finished, so I can move my people to another mission. Frankly, I see no reason why we need to do anything more than what was agreed to in the master plan."

"Well, general, let me be frank also. I don't know who put together this master plan, but nobody consulted with this headquarters. I know what Army doctrine requires in the construction of an enemy prisoner of war camp, and that's what I intend to see done. If we have prisoner riots like those in the Korean War, it's my head that'll be in the chopping block, not yours. So I'm not going to release your platoon until I have this camp built right."

General Carter stood, his face flushed. John thought he was about to get a two star chewing out. Instead Carter said disgustedly, "I can see there's no point in talking with you further. I'll take this matter to General McGinty, and you'll be hearing from him."

"Yes, sir." General Carter stomped out of the tent with John trailing him. Having discussed these issues two days earlier at a meeting with General McGinty, commander of the 800th MP Command, John felt relatively confident that he would prevail. If not, they would get as much done as possible before the engineers were pulled out, and improvise the rest.

At the helipad, the general strode directly to the waiting chopper without shaking hands and barely acknowledging John's farewell salute. Despite the rebuke, John could empathize with him. With responsibility for all engineer support to CENTCOM, Carter had a big job. But so did he; and he was getting tired of the 301st getting shorted, even if it meant blowing away a chance of being considered for a star on any future promotion board that Carter sat on.

When he returned from seeing the general off, a short, slim officer was waiting for him. "Sir, you wanted to see me about the water situation?"

"That's right, Bill. I need you to contact Support Command and see what you can work out on getting connected to the Saudi water line. You and I both know we can't rely on bottled water when the camp starts filling with prisoners."

"Roger that, Colonel. The line extends to Hafr Al Batin, so I don't see why we can't plug into it." As Lieutenant Colonel Bill Hacker left, John mentally crossed the water problem off his list of concerns. Hacker, the camp executive officer, was proving invaluable by solving some of the larger problems encountered by the staff. Then John walked across the tent to find out what his S-4 had accomplished in answer to a problem brought up at the morning staff meeting.

"Colonel, I just got a call from Support Command. They said they're going to loan us a five ton truck and driver for a few days, as long as we provide at least two people to help with the ration distribution."

"Good. Now maybe we'll be able to provide at least one hot meal a day." Major Herb Jones, the Camp S-4, worked in parts management for General Motors in his civilian life. His experience and managerial skill were paying off, but the workload that fell on his section was pushing them to the maximum. "Herb, get hold of the S-1 and have him get those extra people for you."

Within a week the camp was 90% complete, and John felt comfortable about releasing the attached engineer unit. Neither General McGinty nor anyone else in his chain of command contacted him about his confrontation with General Carter, and John forgot about it. He had plenty of other worries to occupy his mind.

For one thing, the number of Iraqi deserters was growing, and there were now several hundred prisoners in camp. But as John and his soldiers learned, many deserters were not soldiers, but civilian refugees and shouldn't be kept in a prisoner of war camp. Of course, John realized, it wasn't always clear to GIs in combat units which stragglers were soldiers and which were not. So for now the best he could do was to keep the refugees in a separate compound.

Another problem was lack of interpreters. Fortunately, Staff Sergeant Habib in his processing unit was a second generation Arab American from Dearborn, and spoke Arabic. But the difficulties in processing these first prisoners made it clear that they would need more interpreters than were available. When it became apparent that the 301st would have to pick up the load of another EPW Camp that wasn't going to arrive before the ground war began, John began to feel like he was in a no-win situation.

Then there were the Scuds, the Iraqi ballistic missiles that Saddam was launching in retaliation for the Coalition air strikes. With only a primitive guidance system, they were not very accurate. But even their hip-shot precision could occasionally be effective. John had heard about the devastating casualties suffered by a reserve unit from Pennsylvania while they were bivouacked in a large building on the outskirts of Dhahran. He didn't care if his troops thought he was an SOB; he continued to be relentless in his push for protective bunkers and the wearing of helmets at all times.

Late one afternoon he walked out of the Camp Command Post to take another look at the processing area, when two soldiers came running from a nearby tent, which had a TV set, used for both classroom training and recreation.

"Scud Alert. Scud Alert," they shouted. "CNN just reported a Scud firing in this direction."

John raced back to his CP, and yelled to his S-3, "Charley, sound the alarm for Scud attack." Heads looked up around him. "Get moving," he shouted. "Get to the bunkers." Major Charley Thompson and two of the operations sergeants quickly sent the alert message out over radio and telephone nets to distant areas of the camp. Truck horns could be heard giving the three long honks that meant take immediate cover.

Satisfied that the alarm was spread throughout the camp, Parker ran out of the tent right behind Thompson and jumped into the nearest bunker. Scooped from sand with a backhoe, the bunker was little more than a section of steel culvert material covered with sand bags. Yet it would survive all but a direct hit by a Scud, and those inside were well protected from flying debris.

"Did the prisoners get alerted?" Parker asked CSM Erickson, who was sitting cross-legged on the floor next to him.

"Yes, sir. I saw them running toward the trench." Erickson was referring to a long ditch that John had dug by bulldozers in each compound to shelter prisoners from attack.

"Well, I guess we finally convinced them that they weren't going to be lined up, shot, and buried." Bizarre as that seemed, it was exactly what the first group of prisoners feared when they were led into their compound and caught sight of the trench in the open area at the rear.

"They've calmed down, after they figured out that Saddam has been bullshitting them about the Evil Americans," Erickson said. CSM Jack Erickson, whose usual job was on a GM assembly line, pulled his gas mask carrier out from under his leg where he could better reach it. "Old Sadam must be one brutal bastard."

It became quiet in the bunker as they waited for something to happen. After another minute, a loud explosion could be heard in the direction of the town.

"Was that a Scud or our artillery?" one of the sergeants asked.

"It was closer than our artillery," Major Thompson said. "I think it was a Scud, but we'd better wait a little longer."

Another ten minutes went by, and John decided to poke his head outside. About three miles away, a pillar of black smoke was rising out of Hafar al Batin. Apparently the town was the target. If so, this Scud was unusually accurate. John returned to the command post where the "All Clear" was being disseminated. Later his headquarters received a damage assessment report indicating that three buildings were destroyed, and eight Saudis were killed in the attack.

Two weeks later John was driving back from a meeting at the 22d Support Command Headquarters with CSM Erickson. The temperature was beginning to fall, but it was still hot in their truck where the windows were only partially open. By now he and his companions were acclimated to the climate. John was not concerned with the weather. Instead his mind was focused on what they had learned at the meeting.

"So, tomorrow's the day," Erickson said from the back seat.

"That's right. VII Corps has completed its movement into forward assembly areas, and the ground war kicks off at 0400."

At the wheel Pfc. Richardson gave his commander a surprised look, and exclaimed "Hoaah," GI slang for "All Right."

"You happy to see the show get on the road, Richardson?"

"Yes, sir. The sooner we clobber them, the sooner we can go home."

John turned toward Erickson. "I've already called Major Thompson and set up a briefing for 1900 hours. If the attack goes according to plan, we should see a bunch of prisoners by this time tomorrow."

"We're ready, sir," Erickson said. "It's really something to see how things have come together. Six months ago when we were practicing this stuff at McCoy, I didn't think we'd ever see a camp this size."

Their vehicle was behind a five-ton supply truck going around a bend; and when the road straightened Richardson accelerated to pass the truck and escape a cloud of sand that followed it. As he did the camp came into view. Despite his fatigue, Parker felt exhilarated. Scanning the large camp spread before him, John marveled at how smoothly the mobilization of Reserves had actually worked. Past mobilization problems, which he thought were never resolved, had somehow been overcome. Nearly half of American forces in the Gulf were from the Reserve or National Guard, men and women who left jobs and families on short notice to perform critical combat support missions.

He picked up on Erickson's comment. "I know what you mean, Sergeant-Major. We have fifteen hundred soldiers here from all over the country. Until a few weeks ago most of them had never worked together. Now it looks like we've got a team that can get the job done."

Twenty-four hours later that job was testing their resources. The sudden onslaught of the Coalition Army produced thousands of prisoners who were being delivered to the 301st EPW Camp as fast as they could be moved. John stood outside Enclosure Two with Major Thompson as guards herded several hundred Iraqis into one of the few vacant compounds inside the enclosure. A steady rain was falling. Not unusual for the winter, but it was already causing health problems among the prisoners.

"What a sorry looking bunch!" Thompson observed. Many were clad only in remnants of uniforms, and some were without shoes. All were wet and very hungry. The Iraqi supply system had broken down under relentless air strikes and their front line soldiers had been without rations for days.

"The Saudis say this is the most rain they've had in years," John grumbled as he brushed water off the notebook in his hand. "How many prisoners are being treated for hypothermia?"

"About thirty so far, eight are serious. The doc says a couple may not make it."

"Yeah; and it's going to be another cold one tonight. I want to check something," John muttered as he walked toward the cluster of guards at the enclosure entrance. "Where's the enclosure commander?"

A sergeant pointed toward an imposing black officer, with his back to them, who was supervising the distribution of food and blankets.

"You gonna have enough blankets, Captain?"

"What? The officer turned at the sound of John's voice. "Oh. Sorry, Colonel. I was concentrating on the prisoners. Blankets? Yes, sir. We've got enough so far." John had confidence in Captain Rodney Bell. He was a deputy sheriff who worked at the Wayne County Jail in Detroit and was used to handling prisoners. "How many we gonna get tonight?"

"It's hard to tell. We've had thirty-eight semis full of prisoners brought in by our escort guards, but six trucks arrived straight from VII Corps with no warning and no guards, other than the drivers.

That's almost 7000 today! Your group is gonna have to wait a couple of days to complete processing."

"Yes, sir. No problem. All they want is something to eat and a warm bed."

The two officers watched in silence for a few minutes as bedraggled Iraqis filed into the enclosure.

"What're you feeding them, Rod?"

"Cans of tuna fish and crackers for now. They're supposed to get MREs for tomorrow. They're damned happy to have anything right now."

The GI mocking reference to Meals, Ready to Eat, the modern version of C Rations, flitted through his mind. Those who had been subsisting on them for months said the acronym meant Meals Rejected by Ethiopians. John moved on to another concern. "How about water?"

"Should be in good shape, sir. Lister bags are full in all the compounds."

"Look's like you're on top of things, as usual. I'm gonna head back to the CP." John returned the captain's salute and moved off with Major Thompson as the Camp lights came on to illuminate the enclosures from approaching nightfall.

When they reached the Command Post, Parker ducked through the tent flaps and headed toward his office space. Part way there, Major Beachum, the Camp S2, stopped him.

"Excuse me, Sir. One of the 'intel' guys came up with something you should know about."

"What's that, Dave?"

"An Iraqi in the group they processed today mentioned a chemical factory in the desert that he says is producing nerve gas. He told the interrogator that the East Germans helped Sadam's guys develop a more lethal nerve gas, called Tabun, which they've been putting in artillery shells. He even gave them a location, a place called Al Hakam." Major Beachum consulted his notebook. "His name's Khadduri. Ahmad Khadduri."

"CENTCOM may want to target that place. Has the factory location been sent up through intelligence channels?"

"Yes, sir. We've already had a reply. They want to see Mr. Khadduri in person. They're sending a chopper to get him, first thing in the morning."

John was awakened in the middle of the night by the ringing of the field phone next to his cot.

"Colonel Parker, he mumbled."

"Captain Scott, sir, OD. There's a fight in Enclosure One. I've sent the reaction force. The SOP says to call you."

John sat up and switched on the generator-powered light. A glance at his watch showed 0240. He'd only slept a couple of hours, and it took an effort to concentrate. "What's that? I thought they'd had enough fighting. How bad is it?"

"The guard said two groups of prisoners in Compound Eight got into it. Maybe twenty prisoners involved."

"Okay," he said wearily. "Alert the back-up company, and call me if they're needed." Before hanging up he added, "Remind the commander that no loaded weapons are to go into the compound."

John sat on the side of his cot wondering if he should let his subordinates take care of what was probably a minor problem. Then he tried to remember which group of prisoners was in Compound Eight. Had they been properly segregated? After ten more minutes of worrying about different possibilities, John realized he wasn't going to get back to sleep until he found out for himself. He was pulling on his boots when the phone rang. It was the duty officer again.

"Captain Scott, Sir. I got another call from Enclosure One. The fight has spread to the rest of the compound, and they wanted the back-up company. The 1137th is on their way."

"All Right. Get another Guard Company alerted to stand-by. I'll be at the CP in a couple of minutes." He hung up and finished lacing his boots. Across the tent Bill Hacker raised his head from a sleeping bag.

"You want me to handle it, sir?"

"Naw, I'm already up. Go back to sleep. One of us needs to be alert tomorrow." Parker knew his XO, like most camp personnel, had been getting by each day on only a few hours of sleep. John slipped his web gear over the desert parka, strapped on a gas mask, and grabbed his helmet as he raced out of the tent.

By the time he reached the road separating the bivouac site from the camp, John could hear the loudspeaker in Enclosure One rattling off a string of Arabic phrases, mixed with a few words of English, the gist of which was to disperse at once. From the illumination of the perimeter lights, he could make out a formation of soldiers in combat gear moving into the enclosure.

There was a palpable sense of pressure in the CP. Fortunately the senior officer of the night shift, Captain Scott, was mature and calm. A teacher of special education in civilian life, Bob Scott didn't rattle easily. He was talking on a field phone when John approached.

"Okay. Roger that. The Colonel's here now. I'll tell him."

"What is it, Bob?"

Captain Scott pushed back his chair and stood facing Parker across a table covered with several sheets of taped instructions.

"Sir, that was Captain Foster. He says the 1137th is in the compound. They might have to use tear gas."

"No tear gas," John snapped. "We're not going to risk any news stories about gassing prisoners. Which company is on alert now?"

"The 705th, from Florida."

"Good. They're a sharp outfit, but let's hope they won't be needed. I'm going over to the enclosure and have a look."

The guard at the enclosure gate recognized Parker and swung it open. Inside the triple strand concertina wire were ten compounds, each about 250 by 500 yards, also surrounded by barbed wire. The compounds were filled with Iraqis, some shouting while most stood silently watching the action in Compound Eight.

"Where's Captain Foster?"

"Over there, sir. Next to the Enclosure CP."

John saw a couple of figures standing next to the General Purpose Tent that served as the Enclosure Headquarters. Their attention was directed toward the middle compound on their left. In the center of Compound Eight a large mob was slowly giving way before a V shaped formation of soldiers holding rifles across their bodies. At random intervals, the formation opened to allow a separate squad of soldiers to rush out and drag one or two instigators out of the crowd and back within the formation where they were subdued. Several bodies lay on the ground that the soldiers had passed over. From the guard tower a Saudi interpreter used a portable loudspeaker to relay orders for the prisoners to return to their tents.

As John approached the tent, a sergeant came out and yelled, "The medics are coming now, Captain."

Foster turned and gave a Thumbs Up gesture. Then, seeing Parker, he saluted. "What's the situation?" John asked.

"Sir, about thirty minutes ago, the tower guard reported a scuffle in Compound Eight. When the reaction platoon got here it had grown into a full-scale fight. The alert company is trying to separate them now. It looks like they're getting it under control. Some prisoners are down, but I don't know the extent of injuries yet."

"Yeah. I heard the medics are on the way. Any idea what started it?"

"Sergeant Habib thinks we've got some Sunnis mixed in with Shiites, and they started squabbling over something."

Sunnis were members of the larger of two great divisions of Islam. However, in Iraq the majority of population, particularly in the south, were members of the Shiite faith. Another source of friction between the sects in Iraq was that most of Saddam's subordinates in positions of power were Sunnis, whereas three-quarters of the lower ranks of the army were composed of Shiites.

"Damn. That's the problem with not having enough time for proper screening. A few fanatics can whip up a lot of trouble, if they're not stopped."

The two officers stood watching for several minutes. John folded his arms across his chest to keep his hands warm. The desert air was cold, only a few degrees above freezing, but it aided the guard company in restoring order. Once their exertions ended, the Iraqis were content to retreat to the warmth of their tents. Five minutes later the fracas was over. One prisoner was carried out of the compound on a stretcher, followed by two others, hobbling with the support of medics. Several bloodied prisoners, surrounded by guards from the reaction force, were also led out of the compound.

The latter group stopped near the enclosure CP, and an MP captain walked over to where Foster was standing. "These guys are the troublemakers; especially that big one in back. Where do you want me to put them?"

"What caused the fight, Captain?" John asked, moving closer.

"Don' know, sir." Captain Jerry Bennett drawled, saluting the colonel. "This bunch was leading the attack on the others. And that big mother would'a killed one of 'em, the one on the stretcher, if we hadn't ah grabbed him."

John took a closer look at the hulking figure that loomed above the other prisoners. The man's attitude was one of contempt, and he stared at John defiantly. As the guards led them away, the tall one turned in John's direction and yelled, "Death to Americans." His face was contorted with rage, and John wondered how many Iraqis shared his hatred.

The next morning John learned that there was more involved. The injured prisoner was the Shiite who provided information about the chemical factory. His assailant was a Sunni whose efforts to strangle him resulted in a severe concussion and a badly bruised larynx. The camp doctor treated him, but it was another week before he was well enough to be sent to CENTCOM. By then the war was over and interest in a potential chemical factory had abated.

The next few months went by routinely and rapidly as the 301st prepared to turn the camp, and its remaining prisoners, over to Saudi Army Military Police. John wondered briefly what they would do with the troublemakers and other Iraqis who had pillaged their Muslim neighbors. Yet in the flurry of packing and anticipation of their return home, John shoved aside any further thoughts about them.

CHAPTER 20

Gisela stood talking with a slender Air Force captain whose short brown hair was tucked into her blue flight cap. They were standing on the tarmac of Hunter Army Air Field amid a crowd of civilians and men and women in uniform.

"What time did they say the next plane is due, Anna?"

"It should be about five minutes, Mother. Don't worry. I checked with Base Operations. They're on schedule, and Dad is with the headquarters group on that plane."

Gisela turned toward her daughter and raised a hand to push into place a strand of hair displaced by the gentle breeze. She wore a blue paisley print dress with short sleeves. Even on a partly cloudy May afternoon, Georgia's temperature had reached the eighties, and Gisela was beginning to feel wilted.

"How do I look, dear?"

"You look wonderful, Mother." Anna's response was automatic, and sounded reassuring. After a moment, she touched her mother's arm, and said, "Really, Mom, you look great. No one would ever guess that you've been sick."

Gisela knew that outwardly she appeared healthy, but she couldn't hide from herself the constant feeling of being tired.

"There's a plane," a nearby voice said. Heads lifted around them, and Anna pointed to a rapidly moving speck between two clouds. Looking up, Gisela could sense a pulse of excitement around them.

In the distance the gray shape of a transport plane with sloping wings and a high tail section could be seen descending toward them. Out on the tarmac an Army Band began playing *The Stars and Stripes Forever.* Minutes later a huge C141 Starlifter came out of a cloud, and touched down at the far end of the runway.

The music shifted to a medley of Army songs, as wheeled stairs were moved into place at the fore and aft exits of the C141. Soon tanned soldiers in light brown BDUs and desert boots were charging down the steps and into the arms of loved ones. Gisela watched Anna push forward, dodge around embracing couples, and shout to a familiar figure, "Dad, Dad. Over here."

Fred Newman looked over his shoulder, turned and ran several steps to his stepdaughter, wrapping his arms around her in a very non-regulation hug. He held her for a few moments, and then stepped back. Gisela couldn't hear what they were saying but she saw him looking around for her. Anna grabbed his arm and steered a path through a mass of excited families toward Gisela. The moment their eyes met Fred rushed through the crowd and swept her into his arms.

"Gisela! I've missed you so much."

"Oh, Fred. Thank God you're home safe."

For a few minutes they simply held each other tightly while Anna watched a few steps behind them. Fred relaxed his hold and took a good look at Gisela.

"Gisela, I swear you're more beautiful than the first day I saw you in the Fulda PX. And your dress reminds me of the one you wore on our first date."

Gisela smiled and some color came into her face. "You're the one who hasn't changed, Fred. And you're so tanned." They kissed again, a long, tender kiss. When they parted, there was a mixture of tears and perspiration on Gisela's face.

A look of concern came over Fred's face. "How are you feeling, darling?"

"I'm fine, Fred. Just fine." Gisela brushed aside her tears. "My prayers have been answered. I'm so happy to have you and Anna back home." Although she had already informed Anna that the cancer had returned, she would wait until later to tell him. There was no need to spoil his homecoming.

"I promised that we would both come back safely, didn't I?"

Anna joined them, and Gisela smiled as she linked arms with her husband and daughter. "Yes, Fred. You did. You were right, as usual." She laughed, and nudged him playfully. Walking arm in arm toward the parked car and talking rapidly, Gisela momentarily forgot her fatigue.

Sunlight warmed the formation of soldiers, dressed in desert BDUs, and waiting on a June morning for the signal to begin marching down Michigan Avenue. A light breeze blew across Lake Michigan and rustled the flags along Chicago's parade route.

Sergeant Major Erickson walked up to the front of the formation. "We ran short of MP armbands, Sir. But everyone on the front and back ranks and outside files has one."

"That'll work," John said. I want people to know we're military police, and it will be easier for our families to spot us."

They had only been back in the United States for three weeks, and they were still trying to readjust to civilian life. The 301st was one of the last Army Reserve units to leave Saudi Arabia. When the war ended, prisoners were still being delivered to their camp, and it took awhile to determine what would happen to the mass of Iraqi soldiers. In the end they simply turned over the camp to the Saudi Arabian Army, packed their equipment, and flew back to Fort McCoy for demobilization.

John looked at his soldiers standing at ease, laughing and joking as soldiers do when morale is high. He felt a surge of pride mingled with relief. They had accomplished a difficult mission, and suffered no casualties.

As if sensing his thoughts, Erickson said, "Quite a change from the return home after Vietnam, isn't it?"

"That's for sure. There weren't any parades in '68."

"By 1970 you were lucky if no one spit on your uniform," Erickson added ruefully.

Gesturing toward the throng of people gathered along the street, John said, "It looks like the country's making up for it now."

Further up Michigan Avenue Gail sat in the bleachers erected adjacent to the reviewing stand. Gail wore a new navy dress that complimented her trim figure. Around her neck was a red, white, and blue scarf. Next to her Diana Hacker, the wife of John's executive officer, was watching the activity on the reviewing stand.

"Look over there, Gail. Isn't that Colin Powell?" A limousine had stopped in front of a flag-decked stand, and an erect figure in a green uniform was walking up the stairs followed by an aide and two men in civilian clothes. Gail caught a glint of sunlight from four stars on his shoulder, and recognized America's chief military officer.

"Yes. It's him. He's the Parade Marshall."

As if confirming her observation, a man stepped up to a microphone and introduced General Powell, and other distinguished members of the reviewing party. Then the drumbeat of a band could be heard, and the first unit of desert-camouflage clad soldiers came into view behind a row of police motorcycles with flashing lights. Formations of Army, Navy, Marine, and Air Force troops, intermixed with color guards and more bands, followed. It was a stirring sight, made more so by the enthusiastic response of the spectators. All along the parade route people were waving little American flags and applauding loudly.

Gail looked at the people packed into the bleachers and lined ten deep along Michigan Avenue as far as she could see. Viewing a stream of yellow ribbons on street lamps, parade bunting and cheering spectators, the women were caught up in the excitement. "There must be over a hundred thousand here," Diana said. "I've been to parades before, but never anything like this."

"What a grand homecoming," Gail shouted to make herself heard. It's about time our Armed Forces got some recognition, she thought. For a moment she visualized a parade at Fort Knox when she first met John. He was handsome and bursting with pride in his uniform, and she had been swept up then with the romance and excitement of the military.

"Here they come, Gail. There's the 301st." Diana was on her feet, pointing down the street.

Over the heads in front of her Gail could see the green and yellow military police colors carried by the color guard in front of a formation of soldiers with MP armbands on their sleeves. As they drew closer, she saw John several steps in front of the first rank of officers with a guidon bearer beside him. Damn, he looks confident, she thought. He loves this, and he's good at it. She felt a pang of regret that he had not remained on active duty. Then she remembered the long duty hours and family separations. Before she could sort out her mixed feelings, the unit was in front of them, and her thoughts were scattered by the sound of John's voice.

"Eyes...Right!" At his command, the guidon snapped down, heads turned right, and the front rank saluted General Powell. Everyone around them was applauding. "Don't they look sharp?" Diana shouted enthusiastically.

"Yes. They look wonderful." Tears were running down Gail's cheeks. She was crying, but didn't know why.

The parade continued, and Gail knew it would be at least another hour before John joined her. They were planning to have lunch later with some of the other husbands and wives from the 301st.

Following the military contingents, a number of patriotic organizations were also marching. Having seen what they came for, Gail and Diana were chatting when Gail's attention was attracted to a group of middle-aged men in an assortment of jungle fatigues moving down the street. Many were bearded and some wore their hair in ponytails, but their combat medals were proudly pinned to the relics of their uniforms. They had their own color guard, which included a black MIA/POW flag and a Vietnam Veterans Emblem. As they came closer, people began to stand, applauding, and the veterans acknowledged the response by smiling and waving to the crowd.

Gail stopped talking and a lump formed in her throat. She could sense the spirit around her. At last these men were receiving some long overdue recognition for what they had been through. Most had been drafted and didn't want to go. The unpopularity of their war made it even harder for them, but they deserved the thanks of their country too. Perhaps if that had come earlier there would have been fewer traumas in their adjustment to civilian life. She felt an urge to rush out and hug them. As they marched past and saluted the reviewing officials, a man behind her wearing a VFW cap said in a husky voice, "At last—a welcome home from Vietnam."

Late in the day, Gail was at the wheel as they drove east on I-94 toward Michigan. Gail looked across the front seat at John, who was sorting through a stack of military correspondence.

"I was proud of you today, John."

"What's that?" John looked up from his paperwork. "Thanks, dear. I'm proud of you too."

"I'm serious, John. I don't know that I've ever told you, but I'm proud of your Army career and that you stayed in the Reserve." John's eyes looked puzzled. "I know," she sighed. "I've complained when you missed birthdays and family activities, but today it all seemed worthwhile."

John was silent a moment. Then he reached over and put his hand on her arm. "Thank you for saying that. It makes this homecoming complete." After a few moments, he moved his hand and set the papers aside. "You know, I've been thinking about that vacation we had to postpone. I think we should go as soon as possible."

"You mean the trip to Europe?"

"Yes. I want to make it up to you, at least in part, for being separated again. The business got along fine without me for six months. I suppose the office manager can handle it again for a few weeks."

"Oh, John. That would be wonderful. It's been on my mind, but I didn't want to bring it up so soon after your return."

"Well, let's start planning. You check with the travel agent, and I'll start organizing my work and reserve duty schedules. Don't arrange too much in the way of tours. We deserve some time together, just the two of us."

They drove on in the gathering dusk talking about the different places they wanted to see in Europe and how much they could fit in the time available. "Let's plan at least an overnight stay in Fulda, Gail. That was our first home together, and we've never been back. I'd like to drive around and see what it's like on the other side of the old border. By the way, have you heard anything recently from Gisela? I know the 24th Division has returned, so Fred must be home."

"I talked to her a few weeks ago—just before Fred was due to arrive. She was excited and sounded in good spirits." Gail paused and then said soberly, "She has another tumor. I didn't write you about it because I didn't want to trouble you with bad news. With both you and Fred gone we talked almost every day." She gave a little laugh. "I'm afraid we ran up quite a phone bill." In a more serious tone she continued, "She's had a hard time—worrying about Fred and Anna, not to mention Dieter. And now this!" As the shadows lengthened Gail filled John in on what she knew about Gisela's condition.

Spring was giving way to summer in Georgia and Gisela felt the effects of hot weather more than ever. The chemotherapy left her tired and listless, and her lovely hair was falling out in clumps. She found it especially hard to get out of bed the morning after her treatment, as was the case this morning. She didn't hear Fred get up and leave for work, and it bothered her that this was no longer unusual. Fred's first weeks home were wonderful, almost like a honeymoon. He was compassionate and encouraging about her therapy, and his support had sustained her. But he was as busy as ever, as the division replaced equipment losses, and tried to maintain its level of training.

She heard the telephone ringing but moved too slowly to answer it. When the answering machine picked up, she sank back on the pillow.

"Halloo, Gisela. Are you there? This is Claudia calling from Berlin. I have some news about Dieter."

It took a moment to register, but the change in Gisela was electrifying. A burst of adrenaline propelled her to the phone. In her rush she knocked the receiver off the table, but managed to answer while Claudia was leaving her phone number for the machine's message.

"Claudia, *Entshuldigung*. I'm sorry to be so slow in answering. What about Dieter?"

"Gisela. I'm so glad to reach you. My telephone is out of order, and I'm calling from a neighbor's. You remember that I was going to look at Stasi files and see if they had anything on me?"

"Yes. I remember."

"Well, there wasn't anything about me, but I found a file on my uncle. He was a professor at Humbolt University, and there was a long report from a student denouncing him for some critical remarks he made about the government in 1965. The informant's name is Erich Burchert, and there was some personal background about him in the file. In 1965 he was a graduate student in chemical engineering. But listen to this! His contact in the Stasi gave him an assessment of extremely reliable, and noted that he and his wife had recently adopted a young boy whose parents fled to the West."

Gisela gasped. It must be him. "Did it give his name?"

"No. But how many other boys could that have happened to then?"

Gisela's heart was beating fast and questions raced through her mind. "Was there a file for Walter or me? Maybe there's more information about Dieter in it."

"I did find part of a file, mostly about Walter, but nothing about Dieter. It looked like some papers had been pulled out or lost."

"What about this major? Say his name again so I can write it down. Do you know where he is now?"

"The name in the file was Erich Burchert," Claudia said slowly. "The Stasi headquarters was in a shambles when I got there. Many documents were destroyed, and files were scattered all over. I didn't find any listing for him in the Berlin telephone book, but somebody in the Volksarmee must know where he is."

"Thank you so much, Claudia. You don't know how much this means to me now." She went on to explain about the cancer and her treatment. "I don't know how soon I can travel. I'm so excited. I'd like to leave right away."

"I'll try the Defense Ministry and see if they have an address for Burchert. But you know, Gisela, even if they have, I doubt if they will give that information to me."

"Yes. I know. But please try anyway. And check anywhere else you can think of."

Before hanging up, Gisela jotted down the phone number Claudia was using and made arrangements to call her again in two days. Thanking her profusely, she replaced the receiver and knelt by the bed. First she must thank God for answering her prayers. Then she would call Fred.

Claudia's phone call energized Gisela, and she spent the day making more calls and planning another trip to Germany. She left a message that she needed to see Dr. Williams, and got an appointment for early the next morning, before her scheduled chemotherapy.

Dr. Williams listened patiently as Gisela explained why it was so urgent that she go to Germany. "I understand why this is important, Gisela, and I'm pleased at what this news has done for you." She leaned forward in her chair, and her tone became firm. "But it's vital that you complete the remaining sequence of chemotherapy. If you stop now, the cancer will remain and could spread more rapidly in the ensuing weeks. Gisela, if you become sick while you're traveling, you could lose valuable time in getting the right treatment. I can't approve your taking on the stress of such a trip." Her voice softened, and she put a hand on Gisela's arm. "You need to get well so your son can come to know you when you find him."

Discouraged, Gisela started to protest and then remembered that Gail had advised something like what the doctor was saying. "How long do you think it will be before I can travel, doctor?"

"At least two months, I'm afraid. But I'll monitor your progress carefully, and possibly that might be shortened. Isn't there someone else who could help you?"

Gisela thought about her conversation with Gail, and said, "Yes, doctor. I think there might be."

But after her chemotherapy she again felt weak and had difficulty concentrating. As expected, Claudia couldn't get an address or phone number for Erich Burchert from any government office. By checking with a friend who knew somebody working in the Defense Ministry, Claudia did learn that Burchert was a retired general, probably living in or near Berlin.

Two days later Gisela was thinking more clearly, and remembered the doctor's suggestion. When she was trying to come to grips with the threat of cancer, Gail had been comforting and helpful. With both husbands gone on Desert Storm, Gisela had felt even closer to her. Now she needed her help again. She went into the den, sat down at the desk, and dialed the Parker's number. It was mid-morning, but Gail was home.

"Gisela, that's exciting news! It sounds like something solid that could lead to Dieter. But what about your treatment? Have you finished the chemo?"

"Not for a couple of months. That's the problem. The chemo makes me very tired, and my doctor says it would be a mistake to travel until I recover. She wants to be sure that the tumor's gone, and I don't need more treatments." Gisela paused and spoke hesitantly, "Gail, can I ask you and John to do something for me?"

"Of course, Gisela. What is it?"

"On your trip to Germany, would you please go to Berlin and try to find Erich Burchert for me? My friend, Claudia, might be able to come up with an address by the time you are there. You can tell the Burcherts about me, and explain that I won't threaten their relationship with Dieter." Then in a choking voice she added, "I just want to see him again!"

Gail didn't hesitate. "Oh Gisela we'd be glad to help. We were thinking of going to Berlin anyway. Now we have a reason."

"Thank you, Gail." The relief in her voice was perceptible. "I feel better knowing that something is being done to find Dieter. When do you think you would be in Berlin?"

"Let me see. We leave next week, on the tenth of July. Berlin was going to be the last part of the trip, if we had time. I'm sure we can change things around a little to get there earlier. Let me talk to John, and get back to you."

"I don't want to spoil your vacation, Gail. You don't need to change everything just for me."

"Nonsense, Gisela. We want to help. Whenever your name comes up, John asks if there is any news about Dieter. Just give us the latest information from Claudia, and we'll do the rest."

After they finished speaking, Gisela leaned back in the desk chair and closed her eyes. She could feel Dieter's presence. She prayed it wouldn't be long before they were reunited. When she opened her eyes, she felt better than she had in weeks. It didn't matter that tomorrow's chemo would make her sick again and that her hair was falling out. She felt close to Dieter.

Kemal Muhsin entered the Mukhabarat building in the Manseur district of Baghdad; and after passing through the X-ray security scan, made his way to the private office of Brigadier General Naji al Hakim. Since his perilous return from Kuwait, during which enemy jets had twice strafed him, Kemal chaffed at his country's impotence against the foreign invaders. After recuperating from his ordeal of traveling on foot at night with little food, he had been summoned to the headquarters of Iraq's Intelligence Service.

"Sit down, Kemal," Brigadier Hakim said, after Muhsin marched into his office and saluted. After a few pleasantries, Hakim said," I need a man who is familiar with Germany and has contacts with the Red Army Faction. Didn't you have a hand in that bombing of a nightclub in West Berlin a few years ago?"

"Yes sir. I did!" Kemal said proudly. He recalled with relish the explosion that ripped apart the La Belle discotheque in West Berlin, a favorite hangout of American servicemen and their girlfriends. The devastating blast killed two GIs and injured 41. Although Libyan agents trained by the Stasi were the alleged perpetrators, Kemal Muhsin, had helped plan the attack as part of his training. In the aftermath of the indiscriminate attack, western politicians had denounced the perpetrators as cowards.

But Kemal was no coward. He had risked his life many times before and was ready to do so again. What motivated him was intense nationalism, and hatred. Ever since Israeli air force planes destroyed the Osiraq nuclear bomb plant near Baghdad in 1981, an attack that killed his older brother, Muhsin was committed to the use of terror to wreck vengeance against Israel and the Americans who supported them.

"Are you sufficiently recovered to leave in two weeks on an important mission?"

"Yes sir. If I can strike a blow against our enemies, I am eager to go."

"This will indeed be a severe blow against the air force that destroyed so much of our country. The plan has been approved by Saddam himself, and it will let the world know that the war is not over and Iraq is not defeated."

Kemal leaned forward in his chair. "What can I do to help achieve this victory?"

"You are to leave today for our chemical weapons production facility at Al Hakam. There you will train with a scientist who has developed a weapon, which you will employ against a target in Germany. Our embassy has located a safe house for you, and the engineer who will accompany you, in Kaiserslautern. I need you to activate your former contacts to find someone with access to the American air base who can help you."

He slid a manila folder across the desk to Muhsin. "The details are in this folder. Take it into the next office and memorize your instructions. I want the folder back before you leave the building. Any questions?"

"My transportation to Al Hakam?"

"A military vehicle and driver are standing by." Hakim paused, but Kemal had no other questions. "If there is nothing further, may Allah go with you."

When Kemal opened the folder in the adjoining office and began reading, he could hardly contain his excitement. What an ingenious plan, he said to himself. His brother's death will be avenged a hundred times over.

CHAPTER 21

On a late afternoon in July the Parker's rented Mercedes turned off the E8 autobahn, passing the former border crossing point, and headed toward the center of Berlin. It had been a long, but pleasant drive from Fulda. Initially they made good time, cruising at 75 miles per hour, sometimes faster, as John got accustomed to German driving habits again. But soon after crossing into the former East Germany territory frequent bottlenecks for road repair slowed their progress.

"Tell me the name of our hotel again," John said, removing his sunglasses and rubbing his eyes. He wondered if it wouldn't have been easier to take a train. But they would need a car in Berlin, and he had enjoyed their stop for lunch in Eisenach and a quick side trip through Weimar.

Gail reached for a sheet of paper tucked into a Fodor's tour book. "It's the Bristol Hotel Kempinski—supposed to be one of Berlin's classic hotels." She read for a minute and added, "It was heavily damaged during the war and rebuilt in the Fifties. Oh, I forgot to mention, it has a four star rating!" She smiled mischievously. "I warned you it was going to be expensive."

"After living in a tent in the desert, I'm looking forward to some luxury. I don't care what it costs." He thought a minute, and amended his comment. "That is, within reason. Remember, I said we should splurge. We owe it to ourselves."

Gail tossed her head back and laughed. "You know, you're a lot more fun when you're not haggling over prices. I loved the Hotel Maritim in Fulda."

"Yeah. Well it's fun to come back and stay in places like that when you can afford it. Don't forget those early days when we were so short of money at the end of the month, we couldn't afford a movie. And the tickets to the Post Theater were only twenty-five cents."

"Oh, I haven't forgotten, honey. It just makes me appreciate times like this all the more." They had rearranged their itinerary to begin with Germany and end with four days in Paris. John was glad they went to Fulda first, before embarking on the Berlin task. It allowed them a chance to get acclimated to the time change, and a leisurely visit to Downs Barracks. They didn't know any of the Americans, but he made a call on the Regimental Commander, and everyone had been friendly and pleased to welcome them back. Then they spent a day with Kristl and Georg Schlanker, friends whom they had kept in contact with through the years. The Schlankers took them across the former border into parts of Thüringen that had been patrolled by the Grenstruppen. It was a nostalgic start to what she hoped would be a romantic vacation.

The "Kempi" wasn't as large as some of the newer West Berlin hotels, but it lived up to its reputation. Located on Kurfurstendamm in the heart of the city, on its doorstep were some of Berlin's best shops and boutiques. Gail was pleased with the decor of their room, and the baggage porter explained that all rooms were recently renovated.

When the porter departed, John called out from the bathroom, "Hey. Look at this."

Gail ducked her head into the bathroom where John was washing his hands. "Wow! She exclaimed. A marble bathroom with gold-plated fixtures. With this room and the shopping, I think I could stay here a long time."

"With this room and your shopping, we may be washing dishes to pay the bill." John playfully tossed a hand towel at his wife who threw it back forcefully.

"Anyway it was your idea to live it up," she added.

"I know. And I don't regret it. Especially the air-conditioning. I don't remember it ever being this hot when we were stationed here."

"I don't either. It must be ninety degrees or more." Gail moved to the window and looked out. John stepped over and put his arm around her while they savored a view of the bustling city.

John was first to break the spell. "I think I should call Gisela's friend and see what's involved in locating this Burchert fellow. Then maybe we can take a walk and look in some of the shops before dinner."

With some help from the hotel operator he finally made the right connection and a woman's voice answered. He spoke in German. "This is John Parker, Gisela's friend. Are you Claudia Schuman?"

"*Ja, Ja.* I was expecting your call. Are you in Berlin?"

"We just arrived. We are staying at the Hotel Kempinski. Gisela said you were trying to locate this General Burchert. Have you found an address?"

"*Nein.* A friend told me where he might live, but I'm not sure. I don't have a car, and it's quite a distance."

"We have a car. Perhaps we could meet tomorrow, and you can fill us in on what you know. It would also help if you could go with us, and help with directions."

"*Ja, natürlich.* It's about thirty minutes by car from your hotel to where I live. Is ten o'clock all right?" John agreed and she gave him directions to her apartment building.

It took nearly forty-five minutes to find the ugly, six-story building in the Friedrichsfelde residential neighborhood, where Claudia's apartment was on the top floor. Constructed of prefabricated concrete blocks not long after the end of World War II, the building was clean but sorely in need of maintenance. The apartment buzzer was out of order, and the paint in the hallway was drab and peeling.

Gail looked around. "Where's the elevator?"

"It doesn't look like they have one." In a sarcastic tone John added, "Maybe it was part of the communist plan for physical fitness." Starting up the stairway he said, "Come on, we can use the exercise too."

Several minutes later, and breathing hard, they stood in front of Apartment 6B. John rang the bell, and a woman in her mid fifties opened the door quickly. Claudia Schuman was small and thin with pale skin and brownish hair tied in a bun. She wore a lavender blouse and gray skirt. John introduced Gail and himself, and Frau Schuman beckoned them into her living room. The furnishings of the apartment were modest and old fashioned, an impression that seemed to fit Claudia. On a coffee table in front of a bulky sofa was an ashtray with a burning cigarette.

"It's a long climb up the stairs. *Ja.* I should have warned you," she said in German. "When the city was partitioned after the war, the west got the zoo, the parks, and the nice suburbs. We got the State Opera, the government buildings, and some damaged housing. These buildings were put together in a hurry, and not many have elevators." Then in a practiced phrase she asked in English, "May I offer you some coffee or tea?"

"Thank you," Gail said. "Coffee would be nice." Fred indicated coffee also. "I'm glad you speak English. I've forgotten most of my German."

"I know only some words in English," Claudia replied as she went for the coffee. "Your man can say to you what I say *auf Deutsch.*"

As they waited, Gail gestured toward a picture of a young man on an end table. "That must be her son. He's about the same age as Dieter."

"What about her husband?"

"Gisela said they have been divorced a long time."

Claudia brought in the coffee and set it on the table. Gail mentioned the picture, and Claudia said in German, with John translating, "*Ja.* That is Hans. He lives in a small town outside Berlin, and works at the automobile factory." From the other end table she proudly handed Gail another framed photo. "That's his family. I have two grandchildren already, Karin and Michel." Gail passed the photo to John who made a polite comment and returned it to Claudia.

"I feel badly for Gisela," she said, putting the picture back on the table. "She was a good friend and helped me when my husband left. I know life was better in the west, but if they had stayed, she might be playing with Dieter's children now."

Sipping their coffee, they continued chatting in a mix of German and English, getting acquainted. Finally John asked, "Where is it that you think Dieter's parents live?"

"In Wandlitz, about twenty kilometers north of here. I don't know where exactly, but my friend who works at the Defense Ministry said he could be living in the same area with other government big shots."

"Are you familiar with the town?"

"Not really. I've only been there once."

"Hmmm." John thought a minute. "I have an idea. Let's drive around the area and look for someone who we can ask directions from. We can make up some excuse, like we lost a note with their address. If we're lucky someone might help us."

Claudia said, "I don't know. People there are suspicious of strangers—especially if they see West German license plates.

As they stood to leave, John explained his plan in English to Gail who looked dubious. "Isn't there something that would be less conspicuous?"

"Not that I know of. Anyway, we don't have a lot of time, and I can't think of a better idea. Can you?"

"No, but I'll try to come up with one. Just be careful about asking too many people."

It took them almost an hour to find the residential area of Wandlitz where there were a number of spacious homes. As they cruised along the tree-lined streets, they saw an old woman on the sidewalk carrying a shopping bag. John pulled over to the curb, and used his control button to lower Claudia's back window.

"Excuse me, please. Can you tell me where General Burchert lives? We're visiting from out of town, and we lost the note with his address and phone number."

The woman stopped, looking puzzled. "What street does he live on?"

Claudia frowned and said. "I can't remember. It was somewhere in Wandlitz."

"I'm sorry. I can't help you. The name is familiar but I don't know where he lives." She walked away.

They continued driving slowly down another street of single-family homes until they saw a man walking his dog. When Claudia asked for directions to the Burchert residence, he acted wary and said he had no idea.

In the front seat Gail mumbled, "I don't think this is going to work, John."

He turned the corner and drove on for several blocks. Suddenly Claudia said, "Stop up there at the end of the street. I have an idea." John pulled up beside a corner bakery, and Claudia got out. "Wait here. I'll be right back." A few minutes later she came out smiling. Stepping back into the car, she said, "I've got it. Two streets over. Number eighteen. The baker delivers bread in the neighborhood. I thought they would know."

As John pulled up to the curb and parked, Gail asked, "Now what do we do?"

"We go up there to see General and Mrs. Burchert and try to find out where Dieter is," John answered.

"What if they won't talk to us? Then we're stuck. I've been thinking while you drove around." Gail explained her idea and said, "I'll stay in the car. Too many people may frighten them, and I can't understand when you're speaking German."

John and Claudia got out of the car and walked up to the front door. John rang the bell and, hearing footsteps, stepped back. The door was opened by a tall, striking woman in a pink dress. *"Ja?"* she said, taking in the two strangers and the Mercedes parked in front.

"Frau Burchert?" John asked.

"Ja." Her eyes were questioning.

"I am John Parker, and this is Claudia Schuman. We have some important news about Dieter. May we come in?"

"About Dieter?" Inge Burchert stood blocking the doorway. "What kind of news? How do you know Dieter?"

John turned to Claudia who said, "We are friends of Dieter's natural mother. It's about a medical problem that could affect him. Please, can we talk with you?"

Inge looked stunned, but moved aside. Claudia stepped inside quickly as John followed. Inge gestured toward the living room and said, "Wait in there. I will get my husband." Moving down the hallway, she called, "Erich. Come here. I need you."

As they stood in the comfortable and well-decorated living room, Claudia's eyes roamed the furnishings with obvious envy. Observant as ever, John remarked, "Not bad for a classless society, is it?"

"I understand he is an important man, but they have luxuries here that you never saw in East German shops." Then she noticed something. "Look! That must be a picture of Dieter." She walked over to a small desk in the corner. Next to a batch of mail was a picture of a handsome, young man in uniform.

The door opened, and the Burcherts entered the room. John stood facing a grim-faced man. The general was not quite as tall as his wife, but with wide shoulders and a thick chest, he was still an imposing figure. The top of his head was bald, and he walked with a slight limp. He was wearing a crisp white shirt and slacks.

"Who are you? How did you get this address?"

"*Herr, General.* My name is John Parker, and this is Claudia Schuman. I am from America, and Claudia lives in Berlin. We are here because we are friends of Dieter's natural mother who is dying of cancer in America. She asked us to help find Dieter so she might see him before she dies."

Erich Burchert's expressionless face looked at them silently. Finally he sat down in a large leather chair, and motioned for them to sit. "How do I know what you say is true?"

John took his military identification card out of his wallet and handed it to the general. "I was a lieutenant patrolling the border near Fulda when Dieter's family tried to cross. I helped get his mother and sister across the border, and I saw Dieter lying on his father's back crying." He continued to explain what had happened to Gisela, how she had tried to locate Dieter over the years, and that she had no wish to threaten their relationship with him.

"If you doubt us," Claudia said, "here is Gisela's telephone number in the United States. You can call her yourself."

"That is out of the question," Burchert said firmly, passing the ID card back to Parker. "Dieter believes his mother is dead. We have raised him as our son. It is too bad about his mother, but it will do no good for Dieter to contact her. He is going through a difficult time. His army career is finished, and he's bitter and depressed. He looked at his wife, and muttered, "These are difficult times for all of us."

He stopped for a moment, thinking. Abruptly he stood. *Nein.* His mother's cancer is not a threat to Dieter. Turning his life upside down is what would threaten him. Now I want you to leave."

John started to argue, but noticed Claudia shake her head and nod toward the door. Puzzled, John took business cards from his pocket, and handed one to each of the Burcherts. "Very well. But if something should change, here is my card with an office telephone number where someone will always know how I can be reached." He stared at them for several moments. Inge averted her eyes. Then he followed Claudia out of the house.

John caught up with her on the front walk. "What is it? We needed them to tell us where Dieter is. If they thought Dieter could have a medical problem…"

"It doesn't matter," Claudia said. "I know where he is. I'll explain in the car."

They got into the car. "What happened?" Gail asked.

"You should drive on. They're watching us," Claudia said, ignoring Gail.

As the car pulled away, she answered their questions. "When I was looking at the picture of Dieter, I noticed the mail on the desk. There was a letter addressed to Dieter in Leipzig. His address is Number 21 Magdeburger Strasse, Apartment 8."

"*Wunderbar*, Claudia!" John slapped the steering wheel and flashed a broad smile in her direction. In the next block, he pulled over and explained what happened to Gail. Then he addressed Claudia. "We'll drive to Leipzig tomorrow and look for Dieter. Will you go with us? I'll gladly pay for your hotel room. You've been a great help."

Claudia hesitated. "I should go to work, but this is exciting. And I want to help Gisela." She lifted her head resolutely, "I will make an excuse and go with you."

The next morning, the Parkers checked out of their hotel and picked up Claudia. On the way out of the city they drove by some of Berlin's tourist attractions taking advantage of Claudia's willingness to act as a guide. Leipzig is about one hundred miles southwest of Berlin, and it was late afternoon when they found Magdeburger Strasse 21.

Again Gail waited in the car while John and Claudia went to the door of the apartment building. At the entrance John ran his finger down the directory. When he reached number eight, his finger rested on a hand written name, D. Burchert. "That's it!" he said, stepping aside so she could see the name. He pressed the buzzer, but there was no answer. After a minute he put his hand on the stairwell door and pushed. The lock was broken, and he beckoned Claudia to follow him up the stairway.

Apartment eight was on the second floor with three others. John knocked on the door, and rang the doorbell. No one answered and they heard no sounds in the apartment. After a few minutes he said, "I suppose we should find a hotel and then come back." At that moment a young man came out of number six, walking toward the stairway landing. "Excuse me," Claudia said. "Can you tell me where we might find Dieter?"

The man looked at them suspiciously. Then he shrugged and said, "This time of day, he's probably in the *Keller* on the corner." He pushed by them and walked down the stairway.

They returned to the car, and John told Gail what they had learned. "I'm going to drive around the corner and park. Then I'll buy you ladies a drink."

Even in daylight the tavern was dark and smoky. Its patrons were mostly working class people, and it had two rooms. The larger one with the bar had booths along the far wall and tables in the center, several of which were occupied by an assortment of men in rough clothes. Beside the bar a passageway led to a smaller room. Gail saw only one other woman, snuggled close to a young man in one of the booths. John motioned to a nearby table, and they sat down feeling conspicuous.

As they looked around, the bartender came over to their table. "*Was wollen Sie haben?*" he asked. Claudia asked for a glass of Riesling and John ordered another for Gail and a Beck's beer for himself. After the bartender left, John leaned across the table and said, "I don't see anyone that looks like him."

"Neither do I," Claudia added, surveying the room again.

"I'll look in the other room." John got up and walked past the bar.

A minute later he was back. "There's only one young guy in there, passed out at a table, but I don't know…"

The bartender interrupted with their drinks, and John waited for him to leave. "Give me a few minutes to go back in there and be sure. If it's Dieter, I'll signal you to join me."

There were only four booths and a few tables in the room. In a corner booth, a young man, with long, unkempt hair was leaning back against the wall, eyes closed. A large mug of beer, nearly empty, was on the table. The only other patrons, a middle-aged man and woman, were getting up to leave.

John crossed the room with his beer, and slid into the seat across from the disheveled fellow. He sat quietly contemplating what might be the object of their search. Despite John's movements he didn't stir. He was sound asleep, breathing heavily, head cushioned by a light jacket. His face had the stubble of a dark beard, and it was evident that he hadn't bathed in some time. He was about the right age and build, but he certainly didn't look like the confident officer in the Burchert's photo. John hesitated, but realized there was only one way to be sure. He leaned across the booth and shook the man's arm, gently at first, and then harder.

His eyes opened and he pushed John's arm aside. "Go away. Leave me alone," he said, and closed his eyes.

"Dieter. Dieter Burchert. Wake up." He shook him again. "I need to talk to you."

The eyes opened once more, and he squirmed toward a more comfortable position.

"I'm tired. Go away."

"Dieter. I need to talk to you about your mother. Your birth mother."

The body straightened, and his right hand came up to rub his eyes. "Who are you?" His speech was slow but not slurred, as John was expecting. His eyes began to focus. "What about my mother?"

"My name is John Parker. I'm from America and, if you are Dieter Burchert, I know your real mother and sister."

He sat up and looked Parker over. "I'm Dieter Burchert," he said wearily, "but I don't know what you are talking about."

"Your father is General Burchert who lives in Wandlitz?

"*Ja.* So what." Dieter's eyes were suspicious.

"Thank God," He raised his hand, as a gesture for Dieter to stay where he was. "Just a minute, please." John jumped up, rushed to the doorway, and motioned to the ladies. Seeing his excitement, they hurried to join him

"It's him! He said his father was General Burchert."

"At last," said Gail smiling broadly as she walked into the room. Claudia gasped and fumbled for a tissue to catch the tears forming in her eyes. As the three came toward him, Dieter, looking confused, tried to stand up in the cramped booth. John made hurried introductions, and sat down with Gail across from Dieter. Claudia, still dabbing at her eyes, slid in next to Dieter.

"Dieter, I need to tell you about an East German family who tried to flee across the interzonal border to the West in the summer of 1964. At the time I was a lieutenant in the American Army patrolling the border near Geise. As the family reached the last row of barbed wire, a mine exploded. The mother and daughter she was carrying were blown clear, but the father was lying in the wire with a child on his back.

Dieter's eyes were alert and he watched John intently. "My soldiers carried the woman and baby girl across the border, while I checked on the man. As I got closer, I heard the shouts of the East German guards. Then I saw the little boy. He was strapped on his father's back crying. When he saw me, his eyes were begging for help. I tried to go to him, but…" John's voice choked, and he paused to get control of his emotions. "But the Grenztruppen were shooting, and I was under orders not to cross the border." John looked down for a moment. "So I turned back and left him there. I have regretted that ever since."

He lifted his head and fixed his gaze on the man across the table. "Dieter, you were that boy!"

Except for a sharp intake of breath, Dieter said nothing. John continued his story. "Your mother was wounded, but she was frantic to know about you and your father." Looking at Gail he continued, "My wife and I helped her find work and a place to live in Fulda where she hoped to learn what happened to you. Eventually she learned that your father had died and you were placed somewhere for adoption. But she never gave up hope that she would find you. Now she has cancer and is receiving chemotherapy that prevents her from traveling. She sent this letter for you."

There was a pained expression on Dieter's face, but he remained silent as he took the envelope from John. When he opened the letter and rosary beads fell out, a flash of recognition showed in his eyes.

My dearest Dieter,

For many years I have longed for this moment, when you learn about me and what has kept us apart. I wanted to see you myself, to hug you, and to give you the kisses I have so often wished to give. Because I am sick, I must rely on my dear friends, John and Gail Parker, to find you and give you this letter.

I suffered a great loss when your father and I fled from East Germany seeking a better life in the West. Yet through the darkest days, the Lord has been my shepherd, and I knew that someday he would guide me to you. I hope the enclosed rosary beads remind you of the ones you had with you when we were separated.

When I hear that you have been found, I believe it will give me the strength to overcome my illness. With God all things are possible, and I know that your sister, Anna, and I will be reunited with you again. I wait for the call that will bring my rejoicing. I love you.

Your mother,

Gisela Hurwitz Newman

Dieter finished reading and picked up the string of beads. "I've seen this somewhere..." A startled expression appeared on his face. "I used to sleep with this!"

"It's a rosary that your mother uses when she prays," Gail said, with Claudia translating. "When you were little you were fascinated with her rosary, and she gave you one like this."

The rosary was still in his hand as he unconsciously rubbed his ear. "It can't be," he said hoarsely. "They said my mother was dead." He looked into each of their faces, and then dropped his eyes. "I don't know what to believe, anymore."

John cleared his throat and said, "If you doubt us, Gisela said to mention the scar where you were burned." Dieter looked up, surprised. "*Ja,*" Claudia went on. "When you were about two, you bumped into an electric heater in the bathroom and got a bad burn. It left a red mark on your left thigh."

They could see the acknowledgement on Dieter's face. He looked from one to another, and leaned back against the wall, covering his face with his hands. His body began to shake, and tears ran down his cheek. For a long time no one said anything. Then Claudia put her arm around him, and said, "It's all right, Dieter. It's all right."

Finally, Dieter lowered his hands, and straightened up. In a husky voice he said, "Tell me, please about her...and my sister." Gail looked at John, and handed Dieter another envelope. In her fractured German she said, "*Hier sind* pictures, uh-*Bilder*, from Gisela."

Dieter took three pictures from the envelope and examined them like they were something precious. Claudia pointed to the worn, black and white family photo. "That is your mother and father, you and Anna, a few weeks before they left. Except for his glasses, you look like Walter. The same jaw line and dark hair."

"He looks like a scholar, but she is very pretty." Dieter looked bewildered. "And that is my sister, *Ja*?"

"Yes," Gail answered. "And this picture shows her with us a year later in Fulda. There are Gisela and Anna with John and me and our daughter." Dieter looked from the photo to John and Gail, and said slowly, "*Ja*. You are the people in the picture."

John pointed to a color photo. "This is a recent picture of your mother and sister with Fred Newman, the man Gisela married."

"My mother is still pretty." He held the picture closer to the light. "Somehow she seems familiar." After a few moments he said, "And Anna is pretty too. But this man is in uniform. Is he in the American Army?"

"Yes. He was stationed with me in Fulda when he met Gisela. Now he is a colonel. They live in the Southeastern United States, in Georgia." Dieter took the snapshot and held it next to the first photograph of him with his birth family. He took a long look.

"I used to wonder about my mother and father, and I sometimes had strange dreams. I thought I had a sister, but my parents said they didn't know. They made me believe no one in my family was alive." Clenching his fist, he banged the table. "How could they do that?"

"Maybe they were afraid you would grow up questioning the system, if you knew about your real mother and father," Claudia suggested. Dieter looked skeptical.

"You should know, Dieter," John added, "that we went to the Burchert's house yesterday and talked to them. General Burchert said you were going through a difficult time."

Dieter sighed. "*Alles ist kaputt*. What you've told me makes it even clearer. I've wasted my life, and now even the Bundesarmee won't take me."

"I understand," John said sympathetically. He pointed to Dieter's beer mug. "But in life the glass is either half full or half empty. We've brought you the truth. What you do with it, is up to you."

Dieter said nothing, but stared at John thoughtfully. Then he held up the Newman family photo again. "You say my mother has cancer. How bad is it? Will I be able to see her?"

Gail answered and John translated. "She learned that she had breast cancer over a year ago, after returning from a trip to Germany to try to find you. Her doctor thought the initial treatment was successful, but not long ago she had a relapse. I think it is serious, but your mother is a remarkable woman. Finding you is the best medicine I can imagine."

John looked at his watch. "Let's see. It's about eleven in the morning in the states. Why don't we call her with the good news? Do you have a telephone in your room, Dieter?"

"It doesn't work," he said glumly.

"Then please help us find a hotel, and we'll call from there."

Within the hour they were grouped around the telephone in the Parker's comfortable room in the Hotel Mercure, directly across from the Leipzig Opera House. Gail took her address book from her purse and dialed Gisela's number. On the fourth ring Gail hastily began preparing a message, but her thought was interrupted when a soft voice answered.

"Hello, Gisela. This is Gail. Are you feeling all right? Yes, yes. We are in a hotel in Leipzig and I have important news. We found Dieter, and he is here." Gail held up the receiver, and the others could hear Gisela's scream of joy. "We told him about you and Anna, and gave him your letter and pictures." Gail listened a moment and then said, "He looks fine. Just a second." She handed the phone to Dieter. "She wants to speak to you."

Dieter hesitated, looking flustered. Then he took the phone from Gail, and said, "Hello, this is Dieter." There was a long silence, and he sat down on the bed listening. "This is all so new and confusing. I don't know what to say." He paused. "*Ja.* I want to see you too." There was another pause. "I need some time to let this sink in. Let me call you tomorrow." Dieter was again silent several moments before his concluding words, "*Ja. Ja. Auf Wiederhören.*"

He handed the phone back to Gail who asked several questions, and then passed the phone to an eager Claudia. While Claudia filled in the background of their search, Gail said to John, "She's finished with her chemotherapy, and determined to fly over at once. We'll still be in Europe, but maybe it would be better if Dieter flew to the states. I think you should call Fred tomorrow, and see what can be arranged. I'm sure Anna will want to be there too."

It took two days and many phone calls for John to sort out the details. One of the determining factors on where to meet was Anna's already scheduled trip to a conference at Ramstein Air Force Base the following week. Fred's final call to John confirmed that Gisela's doctor would approve her travel to Germany.

Knowing Gail wouldn't miss it for anything, John adjusted their itinerary so they could accompany Dieter to the reunion. Everyone agreed that this plan would also be less awkward for Dieter than his traveling alone to the States, and that Ramstein Air Base would provide a comfortable location with a taste of America.

CHAPTER 22

Gisela settled back into her seat as the Boeing 767 roared into the nighttime sky from the Atlanta runway. She finished her prayer for a safe flight and a joyous reunion as the jet leveled off. Turning to her husband she said, "Now that we're so close to meeting Dieter, I'm worried about the effect this is having on him."

Fred closed the magazine he had started to read, and said, "What do you mean?"

"You know what Gail and John said about his background and the depression he's been going through. I'm afraid he won't be as excited to meet us, as we are to see him. It's been so long, we live in different cultures, you and Anna are American military officers, and…"

Fred held up his hand and interrupted her thought. "Wait a minute, Gisela. Don't talk nonsense. Dieter knew he was adopted, and he grew up with a natural longing to know about his real parents. It might be awkward at first, but he's your flesh and blood." He put his hand on her arm. "Don't worry so much. He'll be fine. Why don't you push your seat back and take a little nap. I'll wake you when they're serving supper."

Gisela sighed. "You're probably right, and I am tired." She depressed the control button, stretched back in her seat, and closed her eyes. But falling asleep was difficult. She couldn't shut off the thoughts of Dieter…as a little boy on their last night together…how he would look, and what he was like as a man.

Across the Atlantic Dieter was also finding sleep difficult. He was still angry about the deception of his parents. It was several days after receiving the astonishing news about his mother and sister before he was composed enough to call the Burcherts. Of course, his news was not a complete surprise to Erich and Inge, but it was obvious that they hoped the Parker's would have given up their search.

"Why did you tell me they were dead?" he asked.

There was silence at first. Finally Inge stammered, "We didn't want you confused about…about where you belonged. Your mother and father were enemies of the state and we were afraid you might develop some romantic notions that would identify with their dissension."

Erich interjected, "*Ja*. Dieter you must understand how threatened we were then. Enemy propaganda and spies were undermining our government. We needed to seal our borders and limit our contacts with western imperialists to survive. We never expected there would be any possibility that your mother would come back into the picture."

"But you lied about my sister too. How could you?"

"Dieter, we thought it was best for you," Inge pleaded. "When children are adopted, records are kept confidential to allow children to feel totally a part of the adoptive family. We wanted only what was best for you." Her voice broke. "We love you."

"Love should be honest," Dieter answered, and hung up.

He hadn't talked to them since. In two days, on August 8th, he would be meeting Claudia and the Parkers in Frankfurt, and they would all travel together by car to Ramstein Air Force Base where he would finally see his mother and sister. Perhaps he should let his parents know about the reunion with Gisela and Anna. Or maybe he should wait until after he saw them.

Helmut Zimmerman, chief custodian at the Ramstein Officers Club, answered his pager and headed toward the first floor office of the club manager. Entering the office, he moved past the counter and walked into the cluttered office of the civilian manager. Katrina Fischer looked up from her desk. "Ah, Helmut. There you are. We have a big job next week. Commanders from the States and from Europe are coming to Ramstein on Friday for a three day conference."

Helmut asked, "A lot of generals' flags then?"

"*Ja.* That's right. We'll need all of them, one star up to four stars. Now I want you to have the main ballroom set up for noon luncheon on Saturday. Round tables of eight for about one hundred forty, so we'll need…hmm…eighteen tables. Plus a head table for ten with a lectern. This is a big deal, so you better figure on some overtime this weekend." Projecting an air of confidence Helmut smiled and said, "*Ja.* No problem." Although he had been in the job only six months, he knew the manager considered him reliable. Two days ago she had said as much in his presence to the club officer.

"One more thing," Katrina added. "Every Air Force General in Europe will be here. Colonel Appleton wants this club to be spotless. I'm counting on your crew to make it so."

Helmut snapped to a position of attention, tossed a mock salute, and smiled again. "No problem, boss. Everything will be in order."

As he returned to the maintenance room in the basement, Helmut was excited, but not about the prospect for overtime pay. A few weeks earlier a former contact from the Red Army Faction put him in touch with a sinister-looking Arab who was trying to recruit a German national with access to the air base. He had jumped at the prospect of making big money with little effort. Now he had what he needed to make the contact. He locked the door, and took a slip of paper with the foreign name and phone number out of his billfold. He dialed quickly, and on the third ring it was answered by a voice with a Middle-Eastern accent.

"This is Helmut. Is Kemal there?"

"*Ja.* Speaking."

"I have the information you wanted, but I can't talk now."

"*Ja, gut.* Can you meet me at the same place in two hours?"

"Make it three hours. I'll be finished with work."

"*Ganz gut.* I'll be waiting."

At 7:55 a.m. Wednesday, August 7th United Flight 65, non-stop from Atlanta, arrived at Frankfurt Main Airport; but it took another hour for the Newmans to reclaim their baggage, clear customs, and pick up a rental car. After some initial confusion with the maze of expressways, interconnecting around Frankfurt, Fred finally got his bearings and headed southwest toward Kaiserslautern.

"There's a lot more traffic than I remember from the last time we were here," Fred commented.

"That's been over three years for you Fred. And we didn't drive this route very often. The autobahn south of Frankfurt is supposed to be the busiest in Germany." Gisela yawned. "What time do you think we'll get to Ramstein?"

"We still have about one hundred twenty miles to cover." Fred looked at his watch. "Figure almost two hours, so it should be around noon." He glanced at Gisela and her fatigue was evident. "Why don't you push your seat back and take a nap. The coffee I had on the plane is working. I feel wide awake."

"Okay, Fred. I think I will. I do feel tired." Although the temperature was warm and the sun was shining, Gisela covered herself with Fred's jacket and snuggled down in the reclined seat. In less than a minute Fred could hear her deep breathing and knew she was sound asleep. He reached across and pulled the jacket up higher on her. I hope this trip is not going to be too great a strain, so soon after her chemotherapy, he thought.

Gisela was still fast asleep when Fred turned west onto Autobahn 6 near Mannheim, traveling in the direction of Saarbrucken and the French border. As he drove through the rolling hills and vineyards of Rheinland-Pfalz, his thoughts turned to Ramstein Air Force Base. Although Fred had served six years in Germany in a variety of army assignments, he had never been to Ramstein. He was surprised to learn from a pamphlet Anna sent him, that Ramstein, including affiliated installations at Landstuhl and Kaiserslautern, was the largest American community outside the United States.

Headquarters, U.S. Air Force, Europe was located there with a full wing of F-16 fighter-bombers as well as large contingents of other NATO air forces. Fred had expected an abundance of visiting officer's quarters. Surprisingly, they were only able to get reservations for themselves and the Parkers at Cannon Guest House for two nights. Because of the influx of senior officers for the conference, they were being bumped from the Cannon on Friday. So they decided to move to a nearby German hotel where they would join Dieter and Claudia for the remaining two nights of their stay.

As they passed the Autobahn exits to Kaiserslautern, Fred slowed down, recalling from the map that Ramstein was just ahead. A few minutes later he spotted the small military road sign and pulled off the expressway onto a busy two-lane road. The movement woke Gisela, and she raised her head.

"Where are we?"

"Almost at Ramstein, dear. How do you feel?"

"Better. But still tired." She stretched and pressed the control lever to raise her seatback. "And a little hungry too."

"Yeah. So am I. I think we should find the officers club and have lunch before they finish serving. Then we can check into the guesthouse and get some more rest. John said it would be early tomorrow afternoon before they get here with Dieter."

In fact it was almost four p.m. on Thursday when the Parker's reached the main entrance to the Air Force Base. It took several minutes at the Visitor Center to get clearance for Dieter and Claudia to go on base, and John took the opportunity to make a telephone call and alert Fred that they had reached Ramstein. The flight from Paris was late, and it had taken longer than John expected to locate Dieter and Claudia. Then they ran into heavy traffic outside Frankfurt, so he knew Gisela must have been pacing the floor.

There had been some awkward moments in their conversation with Dieter on the long drive. But when John mentioned some of his military experiences, Dieter began to perk up and started talking.

John was surprised to learn that Dieter had received extensive nuclear, biological and chemical training, and his knowledge about NBC operations was on a level with U.S. Army experts.

Driving past the security policeman at the gate, John glanced at Dieter next to him. He must be nervous, he thought. Outwardly he seemed calm, and his appearance had certainly improved. His hair was neatly cut, and he had shaved. He was wearing a brown, open-neck sport shirt and beige slacks that, except for some wrinkles from traveling, looked sharp.

Sitting in the back seat next to Claudia, Gail made an obvious effort to ease the tension. "Have you ever been on an American military base, Dieter?" At his perplexed look, John translated.

"Nein," Dieter said, looking intently at the large commissary and Base Exchange complex they were passing. "This is a new experience for me."

As John drove past several blocks of apartment buildings, Dieter commented dryly, "The American military certainly makes it comfortable for their soldiers."

"The apartments are for sergeants and officers with families," Gail explained. "The younger airmen live in barracks."

After a stop to consult the base map he got from the Visitor's Center, John made a right turn and a minute later pulled up in front of the General Cannon Hotel, the temporary lodging facility for senior officers and Defense Department civilians. They got out of the car, unlimbering from the long drive. John looked up and saw Fred Newman bounding down the front steps.

"John! Gail! It's great to see you," Fred said, hugging Gail, and shaking John's hand. "Thank you so much for all you have done!" Before either of the Parkers could make introductions, Fred moved toward Dieter and took his hand. "And you must be Dieter," he said in German, clasping the young man's shoulder with his other arm. "At last we meet. I'm Fred, Gisela's husband."

He's tall, and has the bearing of a soldier, Fred thought. But as good-looking as he is, no one would ever mistake us for father and son.

"She's waiting for you inside," he said. He released his grip on Dieter and introduced himself briefly to Claudia. Then he faced the group.

"Gisela and I are in room seven, and you're going to be across the hall in room eight," he said, looking at John and Gail. After you get checked in, if you don't mind, Claudia and I will wait in your living room until Gisela calls, and then we can all get together in our suite. I think it best if I take Dieter to his mother and leave them alone for a while." When he turned toward Dieter he noticed the young man clenching and releasing his fingers nervously. It struck him that it might help to give Gisela's son a few minutes to get his bearings.

"Dieter, perhaps you would like to use the rest room before you see Gisela?

Dieter quickly nodded his agreement and followed Fred and the others up the steps and into the reception area.

A few minutes later Fred led Dieter down a first floor corridor. Fred used his key to open the door, and motioned for Dieter to go in.

Gisela was sitting on a couch in the small living room, but she got up quickly when the door opened. Dieter moved past Fred who closed the door, leaving mother and son alone. Gisela put a hand to her mouth as she saw her son clearly. It was as if Walter had just walked through the door. Not the Walter she remembered. But a taller, muscular Walter, without glasses, and more handsome.

"*Lieber Gott*," she exclaimed. "You look so much like your father." And then the tears came, and she sank down on the couch sobbing.

Dieter stood awkwardly a minute as a flood of emotion overwhelmed him. He sat next to her and put his arms around her.

"Oh, Dieter. Forgive me," she said between sobs. "Forgive me for leaving you."

Tears were rolling down Dieter's cheeks, and he said in a choked voice, "There is nothing to forgive, *Mutter*. I know you did everything you could to find me. Now we have found each other."

Gisela leaned back against the couch, closed her eyes, and murmured something. "Are you all right?" Dieter asked.

She opened her eyes. "I'm just thanking God again for bringing you to me."

He noticed that she was fingering a gold cross hanging from a chain around her neck.

"Why do you wear that?" he asked.

"It's a religious symbol." She must have sensed that he didn't fully understand because she began telling him how her faith in the teachings of Jesus had kept her hope alive.

Dieter listened intently, hardly noticing that Gisela had taken his free hand in hers and was caressing it. Suddenly she said, "But I've been doing all the talking. Dieter I want to know about you. How has life been for you? Were your adoptive parents good to you? Do you have a serious girl friend? Are you happy?"

So he told her. As he described his loss of identity, his depression, and how recent events made him feel worthless, a sense of calm came over him. It was like a catharsis. The more they talked, the more reassured he became, and the bond between mother and son began to form again.

When Helmut entered the Gasthaus on the northern edge of Kaiserslautern, Kemal Muhsin was already sitting at a corner table, a glass of apfelsaft in front of him. Helmut got a beer from the bar and joined him. After they exchanged greetings, Kemal got right to the point.

"What information do you have for me?"

Helmut explained that many senior officers would be coming to Ramstein Air Base soon for a conference. Before continuing he asked,

"What's it worth to you to know the dates and details of where they are meeting?"

Kemal was silent, his eyes boring into him. Then he reached into a small bag at his feet and pulled out a large manila envelope. "There are ten thousand marks in there. That's for the information. There will be another ten thousand if you can provide some further assistance."

Helmut considered refusing to do anything more, but this hulking man with the pockmarked face didn't appear to be someone to trifle with. Besides he needed money fast to cover his drug debts. He reached for the envelope, trying not to look too eager, and told Kemal about the scheduled conference. Then his eyes narrowed and he asked, "What other assistance do you have in mind?"

"Nothing difficult. I just need you to make a small adjustment to the air conditioning system in the club that will require help from an outside contractor."

Helmut looked dubious. "I don't know. What exactly are you planning to do?"

"Listen. The less you know, the better off you'll be. But I assure you that the risks for you are minimal. If anything goes wrong, no one will ever know that you were involved."

"Hmm. It sounds dicey." Helmut took a sip of beer and his eyes turned to the envelope stuffed with fifty mark notes. Finally he said, "Make it thirty thousand, and you've got a deal."

Surprisingly the Arab didn't haggle. Rather he simply said, "Very well. Now tell me everything." When Helmut had filled in the details, Kemal said, "Meet me in the parking area outside this place tomorrow at the same time. I'll bring another five thousand and explain the plan. You'll get the rest of the money after you disable the air conditioning system."

He leaned closer, fixing Helmut with his eyes, and growled, "Don't make any mistakes that attract the attention of the authorities." With that, he strode out of the Gasthaus, leaving Helmut imagining what would happen to him if he tried to cover himself by contacting the Polizei.

The next afternoon Helmut drove into the Gasthaus parking lot and looked around. At the far edge he saw a green van with a familiar figure in the driver's seat. He pulled up on the other side of the van and parked. He saw no one in the lot when he climbed into the seat next to Kemal. The Arab handed him an envelope, and he thumbed through bills inside, satisfied that what he expected was there. As usual Kemal wasted no time with small talk, and quickly outlined the time sequence and the phone number he was to call. Kemal added one other detail about a chemical spray, and suddenly it became frighteningly clear to him what the Iraqis intended. He fought against an urge to back out; he was in too deep to escape their wrath.

But by the time Helmut arrived at the small apartment he shared with his girlfriend, Monika, he was feeling more confident.

"Come here, Monika, and give me a kiss. I've got something to show you."

A tall blonde in her mid-thirties came out of the bedroom and leaned against a table with her arms folded. She eyed him suspiciously. "What is it?"

Helmut pulled a wad of Deutsche Marks from his pocket and flashed them in front of her. "That deal I told you I was working on. It's beginning to pay off."

Monika's countenance brightened and she crossed the room and threw her arms around him. "That's wonderful, Helmut. Let's go out and celebrate."

Helmut relaxed that evening and had a lot to drink. After his fourth glass of Schnapps, caution left him; and he told Monika about his role in the plan that was unfolding. It was late when they got back from their carousing, and Helmut was so drunk that Monika had to help him into bed where he immediately passed out. He never realized that she spent a sleepless night worrying about the people who might die.

Gisela and Dieter were oblivious to time, and would have continued their dialogue well into the evening if a ring of the phone hadn't interrupted them. Gisela answered and heard Fred's voice. "I'm sorry to interrupt, dear, but all of us want to join you. And we have to get Dieter and Claudia checked into their hotel."

"Of course. I've forgotten about the time. Bring everyone in. I must thank John and Gail, and Claudia too."

The four crossed the hall and crowded into the tiny sitting room. There was much hugging, and more tears flowed in what soon turned into a joyous celebration. Fred opened a bottle of champagne, and they toasted the success of their search. When Gisela mentioned Anna's name, Dieter turned to Fred. "You said my sister is an Air Force officer. What will she be doing when she comes here?"

"She'll be attending a conference with her commander, taking care of administrative details for him. You know, writing notes or calling his base for more information on issues that come up. Then on Saturday she's receiving an award at a luncheon, and we're all invited to attend." Fred looked at his watch. "That reminds me; we should be going. After Dieter and Claudia are settled, we can eat supper together at the hotel."

Just outside the town of Landstuhl, Kemal turned onto a dirt road leading to a stone building with large, wooden doors on one end. Someone, hearing the approaching vehicle, opened the doors from inside, and Kemal drove in. At one time this part of the building may have sheltered cattle, but in recent years it was used for storage. A door at the end led to a kitchen, bath, and two modest rooms, once the living quarters of a small farmer. It had been vacant for some time, so the owner, a lawyer living in Kaiserslautern, was delighted when Kemal had paid for three months rent in advance.

Kemal got out of the van and said, "Ah, Majid. Things are falling in place. How goes it with the devices?"

"They are ready. Come, I'll show you." Majid Abu Jaber was a slight, mustached man of about thirty whose glasses gave him a studious air. The appearance was not deceiving, for Majid had a degree in chemistry and eight years of experience working at the Al Hakam chemical weapons site. He walked over to a cabinet on the other side of the garage, and unlocked it. From a shelf he removed a large canister, the type one might use to spray in a garden for insects.

"As you can see, I have removed the standard trigger mechanism and replaced it with this spring loaded device. We can set this timer for up to thirty minutes delay. When it goes off, it releases the spring, which in turn presses the trigger, activating the aerosol spray."

"Are you sure it will work? Have you tested it?"

"Of course." Majid shot his companion an irritated look. "It worked fine on another can of insect spray. And I tested the device on an identical can filled with the real thing before I left Al Hakam. Believe me, when it gets into the air supply, it will kill almost everyone in the building within fifteen minutes."

Later that evening Dieter decided to call his parents in Berlin. Although Gisela didn't want the evening to end, it was apparent to everybody that she was exhausted. The party broke up before ten o'clock, with the promise to meet the next morning after the Parkers and Newmans moved to the Pfalzerwald Hotel. Dieter climbed the stairs to his room, at peace with himself for the first time since the Leipzig demonstrations began almost two years earlier. Knowing they would still be awake, he dialed the Burchert's phone number.

When his father answered, Dieter said, "Hello, Father. I'm calling to let you know I'm in Ramstein, near Kaiserslautern. I've met my mother, and I just want you to know that I'm not angry with you anymore."

"Dieter. I'm so glad you've called. Let me get your mother—ah, Inge— on the other extension."

In a minute Inge's hesitant voice came on the line. "Oh, Dieter. We've been worried about you. How are you?"

"I'm fine. In fact I feel better than I've felt in years. It was emotional to meet my mother, but I feel like a mystery I have never understood has been solved. I'm calling to let you both know that I love you. I don't approve of the lies you told me, but I know that you care for me, and I will always care for you."

"Dieter, Dieter." Inge was crying and her voice was choked. "We love you too."

Erich blurted, "How long will you be there? When will we see you again?"

"A few more days. My sister Anna arrives tomorrow. Can you imagine? She's a pilot in the American Air Force. Anyway, she's accompanying a colonel to a big conference taking place at Ramstein Air Base this weekend. We're supposed to go to a luncheon Saturday where she is receiving a medal."

Erich said, "Please tell us where you are staying and the telephone number."

Dieter gave him the information and paused, wondering what else to say. Inge broke the awkward silence, "Thank you for calling, Dieter. I think we understand now how much this meeting means to you. Whatever happens, we will always think of you as our son."

"I know, Mother. I'm trying to adjust to the situation of having two families. I'm not sure where I'm going from here, but I'll call again soon. *Auf Wiederhören.*"

It was early afternoon before they heard from Anna. Dieter was sitting in Gail and Fred's room in the Pfalzerwald Hotel, where they were all now staying, when the phone rang. Gisela was resting on the bed but eagerly reached for the phone on the bedside table. From Gisela's sudden animation, Dieter knew his sister was on the line.

"Anna, you're here! And your brother is with me." She paused a moment, struggling to keep her composure. "Just to be able to say that makes me feel wonderful. When can you come to meet him?"

Dieter noticed that Gisela was smiling at him as she listened. Then she continued eagerly, "We can pick you up. Just a moment, I'll put your dad on. I'm too excited to think."

Ten minutes later Fred, Gisela, and Dieter left in the rental car for the short drive to the air base. After passing through the main gate,

Dieter took an interest this time in the aircraft. Approaching the flight operations area, Fred turned onto Fairchild Avenue, and Dieter could see several large runways to his right. A jet fighter was taking off from the nearest one. Then they passed a number of maintenance buildings with airmen clustered around. In the distance, through gaps between buildings, a couple of huge transport planes could be seen. Perhaps, he reflected, he should have trained to be a pilot.

Fred parked in front of a four-story building across from Flight Operations. Dieter and Gisela stayed in the car while Fred went into the building. A couple of minutes later, Fred returned accompanied by a tall, slender woman wearing a flight suit with captain's insignia on her overseas cap. Dieter got out intending to open the front car door for Gisela, but she was already outside and moving quickly toward her daughter.

Despite Air Force protocol, Anna gave her mother a big hug, and then stepped aside, shielding her eyes from the sunlight.

"Anna, this is Dieter." Gisela's voice broke, but she managed to say, "Your brother."

For a second they just stood, looking at each other. Then Anna stepped forward and embraced him.

"Dieter. I used to dream about having a brother. Now I do."

Dieter did his best to answer in English. "I too had dreams. About a sister." Then to Gisela he added, *"Sie ist sehr hübsch. Genau wie dir."*

"She is very pretty. Just like her mother," Fred translated.

"I know what he said, Dad. I speak German too, remember? But I sure don't feel very pretty after traveling for ten hours. My boss gave me a pile of paper work to handle, so I didn't get much sleep."

Fred looked embarrassed. "I'm sorry, Anna. It's been so long since we spoke German to each other, that I forgot."

On the way back to the hotel Anna said to Dieter, "I understand that you were an officer in the East German Army. Are you still in the Army?"

He smiled weakly. *"Nein.* I was ten years in the Volksarmee. A major even. But now there is no place for me."

294

There was an awkward silence until Anna said quickly, "I'm going to be away from the military too. The Air Force is sending me to Princeton to get a masters degree in international relations."

"That's terrific, Anna," Fred grinned. "What happens after that?"

"I'm supposed to go back to the Air Force Academy to teach."

"Where is Princeton?" Gisela asked. "And when do you start?"

"It's in New Jersey, Mom, near New York City. I begin in the fall and after two years, I should be moving on to Colorado Springs."

Dieter didn't say anything. He was thinking about his life in the Volksarmee and what little he had to show for it. It sounded like his sister had a bright future, whereas he didn't seem to fit in anywhere.

CHAPTER 23

Saturday morning after everything was in place for the luncheon, Helmut went out the back door of the club and lit a cigarette. He had been awake much of the night thinking about a discreet way to shut down the air-conditioning so that an outside contractor would need to be called. He leaned against the wall enclosing the garbage cans, smoking, and waited for another employee to go inside. Then making sure he was not observed, he stepped quickly over to the condensing unit and switched off the power.

Helmut went back inside and marched directly to the mechanical room, locking the door behind him. He took a screwdriver from his tool belt, and approached the mechanical equipment that circulated coolant to the outside condensing unit. He loosened one of the electrical wires on the pump motor, leaving it attached, but in a way that it wouldn't make contact. A casual observer would think nothing was wrong. When the pump stopped operating he gave a grunt of satisfaction. The air-handling unit was still circulating air, but it wouldn't be long before that air turned warm. Helmut picked up a mop and bucket and left the room.

About a half hour later his beeper went off. When he called the office, Frau Fisher told him, "The building's getting warm. Please see what's wrong with the air-conditioning."

Helmut retraced his steps to the mechanical room and waited a few minutes. He was just coming out of the room when he saw the

Base Services Officer, Lieutenant Colonel Appleton, hurrying toward him. Without any preamble Appleton asked, "Did you fix the air-conditioning?"

"No sir. It's either the pump or the condensing unit, but I don't see anything wrong."

Appleton moved toward the door and said, "Let me take a look." Helmut's heart sank, but he opened the door, turned on the light, and followed the officer inside. Helmut pointed to the blower fan, which was still circulating air and then to the inoperable pump motor. As Appleton bent over the motor, the ring of his cell phone distracted him. He straightened up and took the phone from his pocket.

"Yes sir. We're all set for the luncheon, but we may have a problem with the air-conditioning. I'm checking on it now. Yes, sir. I'll call you as soon as we have a handle on it."

As he replaced his phone, he looked at his watch. "We don't have any time to waste. Call the company in Landstuhl that services this equipment. Tell them it's an emergency. Let me know if they can't fix it quickly." He opened the door to the hallway. "I'll be in the office working on other alternatives."

When the door closed, Helmut hesitated, his mouth dry. But the image of the bundle of Deutsche Marks coming to him bolstered his resolve. He punched an outside extension on the wall phone and dialed a number he had memorized. On the first ring a voice he recognized as Kemal's answered.

In case anyone was listening on the extension, Helmut simply said, "The air-conditioning at the Ramstein Officers Club is *kaputt*. We need someone to repair it immediately."

Kemal's reply was equally brief. "We have a truck in that vicinity that we can send right away."

Saturday morning Monika Sauer was also involved in a clandestine action. She waited for Helmut to go to work. Then she left the apartment and drove until she found a store with an outside pay telephone. She didn't want this call traced to her. She was so nervous that she had to dial twice before she had the right number.

"*Hauptpolizeiwache Kaiserslautern*," a police receptionist responded.

"Listen carefully," Monika said, knowing that her call was undoubtedly being recorded. "I'm calling to warn you that terrorists are planning some sort of chemical attack against the American Air Base at Ramstein this weekend."

When the policeman demanded to know who was calling, Monika hung up abruptly, and hurried away in her car.

Three minutes later, after personally verifying that the call sounded authentic, the Polizei Desk Sergeant contacted the 86th Security Forces Squadron Duty Officer at Ramstein Air Base and relayed the warning. Captain Lon Michelson snatched a three-ring notebook, marked Emergency Procedures, from a shelf above his desk. While he leafed through the pages, he shouted to his duty sergeant.

"Sergeant Lambert, we just got a warning from the German police about a possible chemical attack against the base. Give me a hand here."

He found the page tabbed, Terrorist Threats, and together the two security policemen frantically began implementing a sequence of actions on the checklist.

"Remember," Kemal cautioned his companion in Arabic. "Let me do the talking. Your accent is too noticeable." Kemal was at the wheel of a green Volkswagen van approaching the main gate of Ramstein Air Base. Next to him Majid grunted his agreement, but was obviously feeling the butterflies of his first mission. His eyes darted back and forth at the security police, making Kemal wonder if his companion had the nerve to play his part in their scheme. They were dressed in dark blue overalls and wearing workmen's caps. On both sides of the van, painted in yellow letters, were the words *Landstuhl Heizungs u.*

Luftungsbau, and in the back were storage bins filled with heating and cooling equipment.

Kemal rolled down the driver's window as he pulled abreast of the guard shack. He handed his identification card to a security policewoman in battle dress uniform and blue beret. Airman First Class Sharon Goodwin looked at it carefully, and handed it back.

"Where's your ID card?" she asked the man in the passenger seat.

Majid looked blank, until Kemal hissed, *"Kennkarte,"* and gestured with his own. Then Majid hastily pulled his card from an inner pocket and handed it over. The cards, required for Germans working on the air base looked authentic. They should Kemal thought. He had obtained them for a considerable sum from one of his underworld contacts.

. Airman Goodwin looked at the card and then at Majid who avoided her eyes. "So you're from Turkey. How long have you been in Germany?" Majid looked around nervously, but said nothing. Kemal said, "He's only been here a few months, and doesn't speak English. But he's a good worker."

Goodwin continued staring at Majid, but by now several cars were waiting in line behind the van. Returning the card, she said, "Okay. Go ahead," waving them through the gate.

Traffic was relatively light for a Saturday morning and only a few more vehicles passed through the main gate when Airman Goodwin's radio crackled with the voice of the duty officer. "This is a ThreatCon Charlie alert for all security posts. The base is now under Threat Condition Charlie for a possible NBC attack."

"What did he say about an NBC attack?" Airman Ron Patterson shouted from the other side of the gatehouse.

"There's a warning about a terrorist attack with chemical weapons."

"Jesus Christ. What do we do now?" Airman Patterson had less than a year in the Air Force and was new to Ramstein. "Are we supposed to get into MOPP (an acronym for gas masks and protective clothing) gear?" He ran into the gatehouse and began frantically rummaging through a footlocker in the corner. "Our gas masks aren't here. What if they attack us?"

"Calm down, Patterson. Most of these warnings are false alarms. Anyway, the sergeant is bringing them. Now just follow the SOP and turn everyone away unless they live on base or are on duty. This probably will turn out to be nothing." Goodwin wanted Patterson to remain calm. Actually she was more worried than she let on. Stopping fanatics with chemical weapons could be a nightmare.

"That was Fred," John said, hanging up the phone. He turned to Gail who was putting on her makeup in their hotel room. "He said there is some sort of security alert on base, and we should leave early to get cleared through the gate."

"I can be ready in ten minutes, but you better call Gisela and the others and see if they're dressed.'

As usual John was up and dressed early. He had been reading the *Stars and Stripes* when Fred called. Because Anna needed to stop by Flight Operations, she and Fred had gone on ahead to the base and would meet them at the luncheon. John made the calls, and a few minutes later walked down to the lobby with his wife.

"You know, last night was pretty special," John said after they sat down on the lobby's sofa. "At first I thought Dieter and Anna were rather stiff with each other, but I was glad to see that change as the evening went on."

"I think that was only natural. They were really two strangers who had just met." Gail smoothed a wrinkle in her skirt and added, "It probably didn't help that Dieter's first impression of Anna was in a uniform. She looked a lot more feminine last night in a skirt and blouse."

"That's for sure. And when we went into the bar the ice really melted. I've never seen Gisela look so happy."

"Yes. She was"…Gail seemed to be searching for the right word… "positively beaming. You wouldn't think she had any health concerns at all. I knew being reunited with Dieter would be the best medicine for her."

"*Guten Morgen.*" They looked up to see the tall figure of Dieter step into the lobby. "You sleep good?"

"Yes. Thank you," Gail answered for both. "I didn't realize until last night that you spoke English."

"Ja. Only a little. I have English in school for three years studied. But not much practice speaking."

John looked at his watch with some concern, but at that moment Gisela and Claudia came down the steps. They were both wearing dresses and chatting gaily. Claudia's outfit was colorful but cut in the severe style of Eastern Europe, whereas Gisela's was both attractive and fashionable. Gisela crossed the room and kissed Dieter. After greeting John and Gail, she said, "I don't mean to embarrass you, Dieter, but I promised myself that when I found you, I would kiss you every day that we were together."

Dieter didn't act embarrassed. He put his arm around his mother and gave her a look of understanding. *"Ich verstehe."*

"We should be going," John said, starting for the door. "I don't know what the problem is, but Fred said it may take some time at the main gate."

Safeguarding the commanders was Major Tom Cassidy's prime concern as he approached Brigadier General Weaver at the rear of the room where the conference was in session. Cassidy, plans officer for the base security forces, was there at the direction of the base commander to brief the USAFE Chief of Staff about stepped-up security measures necessitated by the terrorist threat. Dick Weaver, a fighter pilot with over 100 combat missions in both Vietnam and the Gulf, was no stranger to threats. Yet this warning, delivered a few minutes earlier by a security guard, had him worried. General Weaver stepped outside the room with Cassidy and asked for an update of the situation.

"Sir, we've closed off the streets leading to this building and set up more guard posts outside. A top to bottom search of the headquarters hasn't turned up anything suspicious."

"What are the chances this is a hoax?"

"It's possible, but the German Police don't think so. I have someone meeting now with the Germans to evaluate a tape of the warning. In the meantime we're treating this as authentic. The base commander has shut down all non-essential activities. Access to the base is restricted, and the commissary, BX, bowling alley, and theater are closing. He also wanted me to bring up the question of closing the Officers Club, but we know you have a luncheon scheduled there in about an hour."

"That's right. I've already discussed it with the boss," referring to the Commander of U.S. Air Force, Europe. "General Moore is adamant that it go on. It's a big deal where a number of awards are being presented with all the commanders present. I know it's a risk; but, frankly speaking, the general is putting this in the hoax category. Unless your guys turn up something more specific, I'm afraid the luncheon is a go."

"Very well, sir. I know they only have to walk across the street, but I strongly recommend that the officers leave the building in groups of ten to fifteen. The streets in the area will be blocked to traffic and they'll be surrounded by security, but it would be wise to present as small a target as possible."

"No problem, major. We can live with some delay. I'll see to it."

For a few minutes after notification of ThreatCon Charlie, Airman Goodwin had her hands full screening vehicles and passengers seeking entry to Ramstein Air Base. When she noticed another maintenance van parked at the Visitor's Center, she remembered her doubt about the green van with the two foreign workers.

She yelled to her partner. "Ron, take over for me for a couple of minutes. I need to call Base Operations." While Airman Patterson dealt with the stacked up line of vehicles, she depressed the transmit button on her radio.

"This is Airman Goodwin at Gate One," she said when her call was acknowledged. "Just before we were notified about ThreatCon Charlie, a green VW van entered the base here. Two workmen were in front with valid IDs, but the passenger who's Turkish, acted suspicious. Also the driver had a German name, but he looked like an Arab. He said they were supposed to repair something in one of the buildings on base.

"Roger, Gate One. Did you get the license number of the Van?"

"Negative. It was a German license, with letters LS, but I didn't get the numbers."

"Roger. Good work. We'll get on it. Out, here."

Kemal pulled the van behind the Officers Club and parked it next to the wooden fence around the garbage dumpster, concealing the van partially from the road. Helmut was waiting anxiously by the back door for them.

"Where's my money?" he said, blocking the door.

Kemal reached inside the top of his overalls and fished out a thick manila envelope. "It's all there, fifteen thousand."

Helmut took a quick look, satisfied to see the crisp bundles of Deutsche Marks. Soon he would be free of debt, and free of this place too, he thought. "Come on. They're in a panic to have the air-conditioning back on."

Kemal and Majid each carried a large toolbox and followed Helmut into the building and downstairs to the mechanical room. Helmut showed them what he had done, and Majid asked, "Where is the blower fan located?"

Helmut moved around the furnace, and pointed to the near end of the main supply duct. Kemal took him aside while Majid ran his hands along the ventilation shaft.

"Call your superiors and tell them that we have found the problem and the air-conditioning will be functioning within ten minutes. Then you should leave. We'll need another five minutes to complete our job, and then we go also."

Helmut dialed the office number and relayed the message to a very relieved Lt. Colonel Appleton. Kemal gestured for him to fix the connection to the pump motor. When he finished, he noticed Majid was cutting into a section of metal ductwork near the fan. He was relieved when Kemal told him to leave and to turn on the condensing unit on his way out of the building.

"I'm sorry, sir, only duty personnel are being allowed to go on base now." The security policewoman was courteous, but firm. Nevertheless, in case someone ignored her instructions, fifty yards inside the air base two SP cars were parked in blocking positions.

"What's going on?" John asked. "We have invitations to the commanders luncheon at the Officer's Club."

"All I can tell you, sir, is that we're under ThreatCon Charlie. You'll have to get clearance to get on base at the Visitor's Center, over there."

John made a U-turn and drove past the line of waiting vehicles to the building where they had gotten their original visitors permits. It took nearly thirty minutes of verifying identification cards and phone calls to base headquarters before they were given special passes necessary for access to the base under the new security conditions. When they were finally waved through the gate, John noted the time.

"It's almost twelve," he muttered to Gail. "I'm afraid we're going to be late." They were stopped again at a check point two blocks from the club, but after the SP verified their ID cards and passes, John let the women get out. He and Dieter were directed to a parking area several blocks behind the club.

"Can't you hurry," Kemal hissed to his partner. "If we don't get out of here soon, someone might find us." Majid was standing on a stepladder, his head and arms inside the air duct. "I'm almost finished," was his muffled response. Two minutes later he shimmied out of the hole, bent the sheet metal back in place, and covered the opening with duct tape.

"The timer is set for thirty minutes," Majid said as he descended the ladder. "Then the aerosol will discharge the gas. We should be far away by the time they figure out what happened."

"Praise Allah. Now follow me, and walk normally." Kemal unlocked the door, and the two men went up the back stairway, carrying their toolboxes.

John and Dieter trotted along the street toward the Officers Club. Having to park far away was definitely going to make them late, which John hated. As they drew closer he decided to take a short cut through the back door of the club. Bounding up the back stairs, he was almost knocked down by the taller of two dark-skinned men in work clothes coming out the door. He grabbed a railing and regained his balance. The big man said, "Pardon," and stepped aside. Dieter hesitated momentarily and then followed John through the door that the other man held open. As they hurried along the hallway, Dieter said, "That man you bumped into. I've seen him somewhere before."

"Where? You mean in East Germany?"

Dieter glanced over his shoulder, but the men were gone. "I don't know. Maybe he just looks like someone I've met."

When they reached the entrance to the main dining room, John was relieved to see that the luncheon had not started. An SP stopped them and checked their identification against a list of names on a clipboard, before allowing them to enter the ballroom. Officers in dress uniforms were still arriving, while in the dining room people stood around tables talking with one another. A head table was set at one end of the room with the flags of general officers displayed behind it. Looking across the room, John saw Fred waving at him, and moved in that direction.

"A good thing you called to warn us about the delay in getting on base," John said when they reached the table designated for Anna's family and guests. "For a while I thought we were never going to make it. What's the reason for all the extra security?"

"Anna told me there was some sort of warning about a possible terrorist attack," Fred said.

Anna was standing next to Fred. She leaned over and added, "Apparently someone called the Kaiserslautern police and they passed on the information."

John glanced at Gail chatting across the circular table with Claudia and Gisela. She acknowledged his arrival with a nod and continued her conversation. On his side of the table Dieter appeared puzzled by what Anna and Fred were talking about. Finally he asked in German, "What are you saying about terrorists?"

Between them, John and Fred explained in German what they knew about the situation. John noticed Anna listening to his comments with a bemused expression, so he asked, "Do you think this ThreatCon is exaggerated?"

"I don't think it's anything to get alarmed about. One of the pilots told me they get these warnings every few months. The extra security is just a precaution."

Dieter wasn't so sure. He was about to ask Anna for more details when her attention was distracted by a voice behind them.

"Is this seat vacant, Anna?" Dieter turned to see a boyish looking full colonel approaching the table.

"Yes, sir. I was saving it for you. Mom and Dad, this is Colonel Harrington, commander of the 45th Airlift Wing and my boss." Anna continued with introductions around the table. When she finished, Colonel Harrington said, "You folks should be mighty proud of Anna. She landed a C 141 with an engine out during Desert Storm, and everyone walked away safely. She's a fine officer and I think it's great you could be here when she receives the Air Medal."

Anna blushed, and mumbled something about it being a team effort of the crew. "We are proud of Anna, Colonel," Fred spoke for the group. "Award or not, she has always done well." Gesturing toward Dieter, Fred continued, "And we're also proud of her brother, Dieter.

I don't know how much Anna has told you about this reunion, but Dieter was a major in the East German Army."

"Yes. Anna told me about him. We're pleased to have you here on this occasion, Dieter." Then addressing Gisela directly, he added, "I'm very happy for you, Ma'am, and your family."

Dieter's response was drowned out by an announcement. "Ladies and Gentlemen, the luncheon will begin momentarily. Will you please stand for the invocation by Chaplain Jones?" The crowd became quiet as the Base Chaplain, a lieutenant colonel with two rows of service ribbons, approached the microphone.

"Our Heavenly Father, we ask your blessing on those assembled here today. We pray that our work and planning at this conference be acceptable in your eyes, and we ask that our efforts will serve to make the world more peaceful. Help our weapons and training be a deterrent and not an instrument of war. Now we thank you for the food that we are about to receive, and for the many blessings you have bestowed upon us. Amen."

Dieter leaned across Gisela and asked Anna in German, "Why was that man saying a prayer?"

"We normally have a prayer at events like these." Anna thought a moment and added, "All of our wings have a chaplain assigned."

"You mean that man is a pastor? But why does he wear a uniform?"

"Because in our Armed Forces chaplains are officers." Dieter still was confused, and Anna added, "They provide religious services and counseling to service men and women and their families."

Gisela put a hand on her son's arm. "Dieter, when I was depressed thinking that I would never see you again, it was an Army Chaplain who helped me."

Dieter responded, "What a contrast with the Volksarmee! Instead of chaplains we had political officers spying on us!" Then he sat back in his chair thinking about his military assignments. The mention of terrorists troubled him and he remembered a Stasi officer boasting about training some Red Army Faction members who set off a bomb at this base several years earlier. Something else was nagging him. That man who bumped into John didn't fit in this place.

307

His thoughts were interrupted when John chided Colonel Harrington, "Don't Air Force clubs have air conditioning?"

Harrington was mopping his forehead with a handkerchief, and chuckled. "Yes, but I heard they were having trouble with the air-conditioning. Someone said it was just repaired. It must take awhile to get the temperature back to normal."

Then it hit him! He knew where he had seen that workman before—in General Steiner's office. *Zum Teufel!* He's a terrorist! Suddenly he dropped his fork. "It must be," he muttered. He stood and moved quickly around the table to where John was sitting. He whispered a quick explanation.

John immediately stood up and said, "Excuse us. We need to check something." Without further explanation, he and Dieter rushed out of the room. As he was leaving Dieter looked at his watch. It was 12:15!

"Is something wrong?" Fred asked Gisela.

"I don't know. Dieter said something I didn't understand, and suddenly got up."

Outside the dining room John spotted an SP Captain talking with a woman wearing a club nametag. He grabbed the officer's arm, and said excitedly, "Captain, I'm Colonel Parker. When I came in through the back door, I bumped into a workman who we now believe is a terrorist. He may have placed a bomb or something in the building."

Katrina Fischer gasped. "We had two men here this morning working on the air-conditioning,"

"Holy Shit." The captain, whose BDU nametape said Slade, reached for his radio and shouted into the microphone, "Base Op, this is Slade. Send a Disaster Prep team to the Officers Club immediately. Someone might have put something in the air-conditioning system. I'm going to evacuate the club and check out the mechanical room, but I need some NBC assistance. Over."

Slade ended the transmission and yelled to the security guard. "Hit the fire alarm, and get everyone out of the building." Moving toward the staircase, he asked Frau Fisher, "Where's the mechanical room?"

"In the basement. At the end of the stairs go toward the back of the building."

John kept pace with Captain Slade. "Captain, this man is a German chemical weapons expert. We can help."

Slade glanced at Dieter and saw no reason to refuse the offer. "Fine. Come on."

The three men scrambled down the stairway, turned left and ran down a hallway that made another turn toward the back of the building. Halfway down the hallway they slid to a stop at a door marked, "Mechanical Room." Slade jerked the door open and hit the light switch. For a moment they stood panting, and surveyed the room. Dieter walked over to the compressor and examined it while John and Captain Slade looked around frantically. John was the first to spot tape on the air supply duct.

"Up there," he pointed. "Isn't that duct tape covering something?"

"Let me see." Slade grabbed a stepladder and positioned it under the main air-ventilating shaft. In seconds he tore the tape free, exposing two vertical cuts connecting to a horizontal cut in the sheet metal. "This doesn't look right to me." Gingerly he pried up the sheet metal with his bare hands. Taking a flashlight from his belt he looked inside.

"There's a big spray can in there, with some wires attached to it. We'd better have your expert take a look before we touch it. I'll report what we've found and see where that NBC team is."

Captain Slade clambered down the ladder and pulled the radio from his belt. Dieter took the flashlight from Slade and replaced him on top of the ladder. He leaned in and took a good look. Pulling his head back out of the hole he asked, "*Wieviel Uhr ist es?*"

John's watch read 1227. "*Sieben und Zwanzig minuten nach Zwölf*"

"*Ach, du lieber. Zu wenig Zeit.*" Dieter laid the flashlight on the bottom of the shaft and leaned in again.

"Wha'd he say," Slade asked.

"That there's too little time." Climbing up the ladder behind Dieter, John shouted, "*Lass mich helfen.*" But there was no room to help, and Dieter was inching his way backward, holding the container with both hands. When he reached the near side of the shaft, he left the aerosol can in the shaft and rotated it so he could work on the device attached to its top. He said to John in German, "The triggering mechanism is depressed, and the only thing holding it back from firing is this disk attached to a timer."

John watched Dieter use the thumb of his left hand, to hold the disk in place while he tore the timer loose. Keeping his hand and thumb in position on top of the can and his right hand on the bottom, he removed it from the air duct and gingerly followed John down the ladder.

"Gas," he said in English. "*Zwei minuten und....*" Dieter rolled his eyes.

"My God!" Captain Slade exclaimed. "The fan would have sprayed it through the whole building! There could have been hundreds of casualties."

"Nice work, Dieter..." John intended to say more, but just then two men in MOPP gear with gas masks strapped on their hips burst through the door. The leader took in the scene in front of him and addressed Captain Slade. "Sir, I'm Master Sergeant Ferguson, Base NBC detachment. What have you got there?"

"Some kind of chemical weapon that was put in the main air supply duct. It would have gone off, if this man hadn't disabled it." Turning to Dieter, he said, "Better let them take it now."

Dieter handed the canister to Sergeant Ferguson keeping the plastic disk in place with his thumb. He pointed to the danger of the depressed trigger mechanism, and Ferguson's companion hastily wrapped electrical tape around the disk to temporarily secure the device.

"Get your mask on, Charlie. We ain't takin any chances with this baby. Then you hold it while I get masked. We'll get it out of the building, Captain, and take it from here."

"Make sure you get plenty of photographs before its destroyed," Slade cautioned.

"Now," he said, turning to John. "What did those workmen look like?"

"They both have dark complexions and were wearing blue overalls. One guy is big, about six-two and built like a football player. His face is pockmarked and he has a bushy mustache. The other guy is small with a thin mustache and wears glasses."

"What type of vehicle were they using?"

"I don't know. I was in a hurry, and didn't see what they were driving."

"Okay, let me get that out." Captain Slade depressed the transmit button and radioed descriptions on the Security Police network. Then he relaxed and clasped Dieter's shoulder.

"Thanks, pal. You saved our butts." He hesitated and looked at John. "How did he come to be here?" he asked Parker.

"That's a long story, but I'll give you the short version while we walk upstairs."

An hour later John and Dieter were seated again in the dining room as the interrupted luncheon drew to a close. By now everyone in the audience knew that a terrorist threat had been thwarted. But the Chief of Staff, concerned about causing undue alarm, did not reveal how close a thing it was when he explained the reason for evacuating the building. The awards portion of the luncheon was nearly over, and Anna was standing by the head table with Colonel Harrington, her wing commander. A major was reading the citation to her award.

"…Captain Anna Newman's outstanding performance of duty during a crisis situation in a theater of war reflects the utmost credit upon herself and the United States Air Force."

Then General Moore stepped in front of her, and pinned the Air Medal to her uniform blouse. As he shook Anna's hand, the audience applauded while a photographer snapped several pictures for later public information releases. Gisela and Fred were beaming with pride, and Dieter applauded enthusiastically. Anna and Colonel Harrington returned to their table, and Anna handed the written citation to her stepfather who admired it before passing it around the table. General Moore moved to the podium for the expected closing remarks.

"Ladies and Gentlemen. It is indeed a pleasure to have these bright young officers with us today for recognition of their outstanding achievements. We have completed the presentation to those individuals listed in your programs, but there are two more persons present whom I wish to recognize. Both are here to witness the award just made to Captain Newman. One is Colonel Parker, a longtime friend of the Newmans, and the other is Captain Newman's brother, Dieter, with whom she and her family have only in the last few days been reunited. That is a remarkable story, but even more remarkable is the role Dieter Burchert played today in preventing a tragedy."

Heads turned and a buzz of excitement swept through the room. General Moore continued. "You already know that an attempt was made today by terrorists to attack us at this conference. Some of the details will have to remain classified, but I can tell you that it was defeated by the alert actions of Colonel Parker and Dieter Burchert. Gentlemen, will you please come forward?"

John stood first and beckoned Dieter to follow him. Again there was a murmur of conversation as the two made their way to the speaker's table. An aide handed General Moore two sheets of paper.

General Moore turned and faced the two men. "Gentlemen, these certificates are tokens of our deep gratitude for your quick thinking and bravery. I will be forwarding my report and recommendation for more appropriate decorations for each of you to the appropriate officials in the United States and Germany."

The room erupted with applause, and everyone stood as General Moore presented the certificates to Dieter and John. As he thanked the general, John added, "Sir, it would help if your letter included a recommendation that Dieter be integrated into the new German Army."

General Moore smiled and said, "Of course. Be happy to do that."

Dieter didn't understand much of what General Moore said as he shook Dieter's hand and gave him the certificate. He was a bit overwhelmed by the applause of the crowd of uniformed Americans and the flashbulbs of the photographer. Later, after the photographer took more pictures of him with his family, and also with the Parkers, John told him about the request he made to the general.

Dieter thought about that as they finally left the club, and he viewed the activity of a military base. So much had changed in his life in these past weeks. So many of his beliefs were challenged and found wanting. Even if the German government changed their opinion of his Stasi connections, did he really wish to remain in Germany and follow a military career? He didn't know.

Seated in the back of the car next to his mother, Dieter looked at Anna in the front seat beside the only father she had known. He wondered where he belonged. Could he really be a part of this family? Gisela was still bubbling with excitement over the events at the luncheon, and was speaking rapidly in English with Fred and Anna. As if sensing his exclusion, Gisela switched to German, and took his arm in hers.

"Oh, Dieter. I am so proud of you and Anna. If only Walter..." She checked herself, looking at Fred and Anna in the front seat, then at Dieter. She took a deep breath, and Dieter realized she was making an effort to put the past behind her and focus on her present family. After a moment she said, "Dieter, I want you to do something for me, please."

"*Ja.* Of course."

"Before Anna leaves tomorrow, I would like to have you come to church with us to give thanks to God for reuniting us."

Dieter thought, Why not? There was something about his mother's faith that intrigued him. Aloud he said, "Yes. I'll go with you."

EPILOGUE

JULY 1998

Early in the afternoon of a warm summer day, John Parker stood looking at flowering meadows and green patches of woodland stretching before him into the Ulster Valley. It was a lovely pastoral scene that, except for the close proximity of two stark watchtowers, wouldn't cause anyone to consider it memorable. Yet this peaceful setting was where the front line troops of the forces of democracy and communism faced off during the long years of the Cold War. In those days an observer standing where he was, would have seen the metal fence of the Iron Curtain, with all its fortifications, running from one horizon to the other.

John was on top of a thirty-foot tower at the former US Observation Point Alpha, between the towns of Rasdorf and Geise. About 300 meters to his right front was the East German guard tower, and close by was a two-lane track along which Grenztruppen vehicles had patrolled. Further to his right, a section of that Iron Curtain remained as it was in 1989, an eight foot grid of interconnecting, open triangles of sharpened steel, much more formidable than the barbed wire fences of his day. Gail was below the tower, reading an inscription on a memorial stone erected by the Germans. Her knees were troubling her, and she had turned down John's suggestion to climb the steep steps of the observation tower.

They had arrived the previous day for a reunion of veterans of the Armored Cavalry Regiment (first designated the 14th, then re-flagged as the 11th), which patrolled this area of the border for almost a half century. Standing next to him was Sam Erwin, the Howitzer Battery Commander for one of the years John was in the regiment. Sam was peering through binoculars and talking about places where his artillery concentrations would have fallen if the Russians had attacked. But John wasn't paying attention. His mind was flooded with emotions; some that had haunted him for 34 years.

He focused on a spot about 150 meters in front of him on a line with the remaining section of fence. It must have been there, he thought. That's where he saw a man killed, and where he left a little boy to be separated from his mother. He looked across the field at the East German tower, and felt some of the old anger return. In ten years a high school student wouldn't have any idea of what the communists did to their own people. It was incredible that in such a short time the pace of reunification had removed nearly all vestiges of the wall that had separated families and neighbors from one another.

If some Germans with a sense of history hadn't had the foresight to preserve Point Alpha, with its towers, fortifications, and museum, there would be little evidence of the Cold War tensions that reverberated along this border. As John took a last look, and turned to climb down, he wondered whether young people would ever understand what his generation had experienced here.

The day began with a visit to the only American armored cavalry unit left in Germany, the lst Squadron, 4th Cavalry, located forty miles south in Schweinfurt. The older veterans were impressed with improvements in equipment, such as night vision goggles, long-range radios, and global position locators. However the ladies were more pleased with the hospitality of the Squadron Commander's wife who invited them to her home for coffee and gave them a glimpse of family life in the modern army. On the bus ride back, Gail commented about the lengthy deployments to Bosnia and Macedonia that these families were experiencing. She pointed out that it was difficult enough for young military wives without being left to fend for themselves in a foreign country. John had to agree, knowing that drastic cuts in the military after the Gulf War had resulted in a shortage of deployable units.

Later in the afternoon, after returning to the Hotel Maritim, John and Gail walked through the modern section of the hotel to where it connected with the Baroque rooms of the ornate structure known as the Orangery. They passed through the dining room with its stucco walls and magnificent ceiling mural, and came out on a spacious open-air patio. In front of them on the terrace were several umbrella tables moved together, and sitting around the tables was a group of casually dressed Americans laughing and sipping drinks.

"Hey, John," bellowed a man's voice from the far end. "Pull up some chairs, and join us." It was Charley Collins, John's former company commander.

George Baker scrambled to his feet and wrestled a heavy metal chair for Gail over to a place next to his wife. The chairs weren't designed for easy movement, and John noticed an imperious waiter frowning at the rearrangement of patio furniture by the festive Americans.

Tough luck, *Herr Ober*, John thought. There were plenty of open tables on the porch. In our day a waiter would have fallen all over himself trying to help. Some things have certainly changed. John dragged another chair to a spot between George and Al Damon and sat down.

As if reading his mind, Al said, "We were just talking about all the changes since we left." Al and his wife Jenny were one of the older returning couples. They had joined the Regiment on their first assignment in 1948, and had lived in a requisitioned German house only a few blocks from where they now sat.

Pete Austin leaned across the table. "I was telling Al how much I would have liked one of those Humvees for patrolling in the winter. Remember how cold it used to get up around the *Wasserkuppe?*"

"I sure do," John said. "I used to get so damned cold in those open jeeps without heaters. My hands and feet were numb half the winter. And if we'd had a real alert with bullets flying, a Humvee would've been a lot safer than a jeep."

"Speaking of alerts," Pete said. "Did anyone else here make it to that crazy Saturday afternoon alert? It was one of those readiness exercises in the spring of '65 or '66, I think."

"I remember that one," Charley Collins said. "Most of the troops were in town, or gone on a pass. I could barely scrape up enough people to get the vehicles out of the motor pool. If the Russians had attacked that day, our tank commanders would have been loading each round themselves, and scrambling to the TC position to fire it."

John ordered a round of drinks, and the stories continued.

"Hey, Pete," Charley Collins laughed. "How about that time at Wildflecken when you took your first platoon test?"

"Oh, yeah," Pete grinned, thinking about his initiation to the bantam-size training area. "I had just joined the company and couldn't find any of the landmarks on my map. Everybody else knew the place like they knew their own serial number. I was always scrambling to keep from being lost."

"When I came by you were on top of a tank trying to read an azimuth with a compass," Collins laughed.

"Not one of my smarter moves," Pete admitted, "considering all the steel around, but, hey, I was a brand-new second lieutenant."

John listened to the talk swirling around the table, noticing that for the most part it consisted of pleasant recollections of experiences shared with people who became as close as family, at a time when everyone was far away from parents and relatives. Memories of homesickness and hardships were repressed and forgotten.

"Does anyone know if Fred and Gisela Newman will be here?" Jean Austin asked.

"They're supposed to arrive today," Gail answered. "They've been in Munich for a few days, and they're driving up this afternoon."

"I heard she finally found her son. Whatever happened to him?"

"That's quite a story." Everyone looked at Gail and conversation dropped around the table. "After the Berlin Wall came down, Gisela went to East Germany, but she ran into a dead end when she couldn't get his adopted name from the authorities. Then she went through a couple of treatments for cancer that kept her from traveling. To make a long story short, John and I were involved in finding him, but he was in sad shape. At one time he was a dedicated communist, but when we met him he'd lost interest in everything. He was out of work and depressed."

Everyone looked expectantly, waiting for her to continue. But Gail smiled and said, "Anyway, things worked out for him, and Gisela wants to show him off. So I promised I would let her tell you about him when they get here."

There were some groans and more questions from the group, but Gail waved them off. "That's all I can say. I promised Gisela."

"There is one other thing," John interjected. "Fred and Gisela have invited all of us to a memorial service for Dieter and Anna's father Wednesday morning in St. Michael's Church. You remember he was killed trying to cross the border with them in '64. It would mean a lot to Gisela for as many of us to attend as possible."

John didn't feel old as he took his seat the following day among the others assembled in front of the regimental headquarters building. Originally built for Hitler's Wehrmacht, it had become the center of operations for the three squadrons stationed in Bad Hersfeld, Fulda, and Bad Kissingen. As he looked over the audience of Germans and Americans forming a semi-circle in front of the podium, he noticed that nearly everyone was over fifty. Now the buildings stood vacant and ghosts of Cold War troopers stood guard around the empty military post.

Already seated next to him, Gail chatted with their German friend, Trudi Schlanker. His wife's blonde hair shown in the sunlight, and her smiling face reminded him of the bride who had accompanied him here thirty-five years ago. Following a request by their former regimental commander, he wore four rows of miniature medals on the lapel of his blue single-breasted suit.

Jean Austin leaned back from the row in front of them and asked Gail, "Did the Newmans get in yet?"

"Yes. They arrived last night. They were delayed, and it was late by the time they got to the hotel."

"How's Gisela doing?"

"She seems fine. There's been no recurrence of the cancer, and she looks great."

John interrupted to say, "Here they come now." He stood and beckoned to a middle-aged couple and a young woman making their way through the crowd from a line of cars parked along the edge of the parade ground. As Gisela came closer, her appearance bore out Gail's comment. She looked radiant. Wearing a yellow linen dress, Gisela's face conveyed a message of serenity. She was tanned, her figure fuller than it had been during those frightful days of chemotherapy, and her eyes sparkled as she greeted old friends.

Reaching their row, she said, "Hello everyone. How wonderful to see you again." Jean Austin leaned over a chair to hug Gisela, while her husband stood and exchanged greetings with Fred Newman. Behind the Parkers a woman cried out, "Hi, Gisela. Remember me—Marina Roberts!" Turning, Gisela waved toward Marina and then pulled the young woman forward. "This is my daughter, Anna. She's a major in the Air Force, married to another officer. And I have two lovely grandchildren."

"Oh, Gisela. She looks just like you," Jean Austin said. "But where's Dieter?"

"He'll be with us tomorrow." Gisela smiled and started to say something when the First Armored Division Band struck up *Gary Owen*, and the ceremony began. A color guard from the First Infantry Division, carrying both the 11th and 14th Armored Cavalry Regimental Colors, marched to a central position behind the row of speakers.

John was pleased to see the regimental flag with the familiar motto, *Suivez Moi* (Follow Me), again being carried next to the American flag. He admired the sharp appearance and military bearing of the six soldiers who made up the color guard. Except for their M-16 rifles and Kevlar helmets, the soldiers looked the same as those he had inspected for guard mount on the same parade ground many years before. He felt sorry for the color guard, standing stiffly at attention. It was already hot. The weight and constriction of helmet, rifle, and dress uniform would make this a sweating ordeal for the young soldiers, like some he remembered.

Werner Rupp, a former civil affairs representative for American commanders, walked to the podium. Nodding to the bandmaster, he asked the audience to rise for the playing of the American and German national anthems. Rupp introduced Fulda's Lord Mayor, Dr. Wolfgang Hamberger. As the mayor walked to the podium, John glanced to his left at Gail who was absorbed in the ceremony. Without meaning to, his mind drifted to memories of their first home in Fulda. He wished that he had been more supportive. He realized now that she had often been frustrated and lonely with him away and her parents unable to visit when Susie and Matthew were babies.

Even while daydreaming John was conscious of many friends from long ago around him. Their comradeship had lasted over the years, although he hadn't seen some of them since that assignment in Fulda. He thought about Susie, Matthew, and Paul—all on their own now with their own careers and families. There were six grandchildren, and a seventh on the way with Susie expecting her third in October. Now that he was retired from the Army Reserve and taking more time off from business, life was turning out well for them. Still, looking at the soldiers in the band and the color guard, he felt a sense of nostalgia for his time in the army.

The mayor's voice jarred him back to reality. Doctor Hamberger was welcoming the American veterans and their families, and he thanked them for traveling so far to commemorate their service at this "outpost of freedom". John knew that this was no time for regrets. He was proud of the contribution he and Gail had made to the peace the world now enjoyed. And he was glad that they had the leisure to visit children and grandchildren. The future would bring more reunions, and opportunities to renew friendships with old comrades. He reached over and took Gail's hand. At her surprised look, he simply smiled and gave it a squeeze.

Speaking first in English, then in German, Doctor Hamberger was an impressive orator for any audience. With obvious sincerity, and little need for notes, the Lord Mayor traced the history of American involvement with his city. "You came as victors, but instead of treating us as vanquished enemies, you treated us as human beings, and that has made all the difference. While your government helped us establish democracy, you defended our fragile country from the communist threat across the nearby border."

As the Lord Mayor continued to express his appreciation for American defense of the West German border, John felt a sense of closure. Although his mind had registered it earlier, this was the first time he knew in his heart that the Cold War was over. He looked at the others around him, a few hundred Germans and Americans representing thousands who were in the front lines of this struggle. Except for Korea and Vietnam, Cold War casualties were negligible, but countless lives were forever changed by the sacrifices demanded by competing ideologies.

How would future generations regard this period that had consumed so much of their lives? Certainly Susie, Matt, and Paul, had some understanding of what their parents experienced. But those born after the Cold War would have no idea except for what they might learn from history books. Still, isn't that the way it has always been? Life moves on.

John looked up. Mayor Hamberger had concluded his speech and a German minister was giving a benediction. He closed his eyes and realized that their mission had been accomplished.

Wednesday morning Hotel Maritim's lobby was jammed with Americans. It was the last day of the reunion, and some were checking out early to catch their mid-day return flights. But many were dressed up, men in coats and ties, and women in dresses and pants suits. At 10:45 Gisela, and Fred stepped off the elevator, followed by Anna. Gisela wore a two-piece navy silk dress, complimented by a silver pin centered with a cluster of pearls. Anna was also wearing a blue dress and looked like a younger version of Gisela. For a moment they stood still, looking across the lobby at their friends.

Gail walked over to them and gestured to those who were lounging about, and said, "We've been waiting to go with you to the Memorial Service."

Gisela's eyes began to water as she looked around at her friends. "Thank You," was all she could say. Fred stepped toward the group and cleared his throat. "We want to thank you for joining us for the memorial service. It's just across the street in St. Michael's, but we should get started."

He took Gisela's arm and walked to the door with Anna on the other side of her mother. The Roberts and Bakers were waiting outside by the hotel driveway. They fell in beside Fred and Gisela as the group strolled up the driveway to *Paulustor*, a remnant of the baroque wall that encircled the ancient part of the city, and crossed the cobble-stoned road. Walking next to Gisela and Anna, Joan Baker asked, "Gisela, where is Dieter?"

"Oh, he's meeting us at the church." Ann looked at her questioningly, but Gisela simply smiled without further explanation.

As they reached a balustered wall on the far side of the street, a two-towered circular building of simple beauty and dignity was in full view. Built in Carolingian times about 820, it is thought to be the oldest church still standing in Germany. Originally St. Michael's served as a burial chapel for monks, and was modeled on the rotunda in the Church of the Holy Sepulcher in Jerusalem.

A few more friends, both German and Americans, were waiting on the steps outside the entrance. They filed in through a door in the bell tower and followed Gisela down a semi-circular staircase to a crypt in the lower level. This was the oldest and most venerable part of the church, and the visitors passed by the sarcophagi of the builder, Fulda's fourth abbot, Eigil, before entering a circular sanctuary with a brick altar. Those who had never visited St. Michael's were awed by their surroundings and soberly moved toward the chairs that lined the walls. A missal and order of the service were on each seat.

Gisela, Fred and Anna took seats closest to the altar with Gail and John beside them. Joan Baker nudged Gail and whispered, "I don't see anyone who could be Dieter."

Gail put a finger to her lips and said, "I'm sure he'll be here any minute."

After a few moments of silence that seemed longer, a silver haired priest entered by a side door, knelt in front of the altar, and made a sign of the cross before rising. He began a prayer in Latin, and, taking their cue from Gisela and Anna, everyone stood. When he finished the prayer, the priest turned and said, "Dominus Vobiscum," meaning "The Lord is with you." Those familiar with Catholic Liturgy responded, "Et cum Spiritu Tuo—And with thy Spirit." The priest took a Lectionary from the altar, and surprised many by speaking in scholarly English, "A reading from the Book of Wisdom." Then he read painstakingly,

"The souls of the just are in the hand of God,
   and no torment shall touch them.
They seemed, in the view of the foolish, to be dead;
   and their passing away was thought an affliction
   and their going forth from us, utter destruction.
But they are in peace."

By now most of the audience had found their place in the order of worship and took part in the Responsive Psalm that followed. Then the priest concluded his part with a reading from the Gospel of John, and took a seat near the altar.

A younger priest entered from the same door, and repeated the initial ritual before standing to face the audience. Even in his vestments his dark hair and handsome features were noticeable. He reached into his pocket and removed a pair of glasses, which he put on to peruse some notes that came from another pocket. Then he looked up and cleared his throat.

"We are gathered here to commemorate the life of Walter Hurwitz, a brave man who died nearby 34 years ago seeking freedom for himself and his family." His voice was loud, somewhat husky, and his accent was more colloquial than the older priest.

"Walter Hurwitz, the son of a Jewish father and a Catholic mother, miraculously survived the Holocaust and moved to Berlin where he met a young woman," he paused and gestured toward Gisela, "who would become his wife."

"He was passionate about freedom, this man who survived one form of tyranny only to find himself under a new form: a Godless society dedicated to central control of individual thought and expression. Like many fathers, Walter yearned for a better life for himself, his wife and his children. He wanted his family to live where they were free to express ideas openly, and where they could choose those who would govern them. He wanted to live in freedom where neighbors didn't spy on each other.

"Unfortunately the path to those dreams was cut off, and the only opportunity to reach them in those days was through great personal risk. His wife, Gisela, shared his dreams, so together they faced the danger of escape across the border. As we look back, the tragedy is that Walter died in the pursuit of his dream; while his family was broken apart, mother and daughter in the west, a son lost in the east.

"But for the undying faith in God of this woman," he paused again looking directly at Gisela, who was wiping away tears, "this might have been the end of Walter's dream. Yet Walter's spirit bolstered her determination to find their son and bring him the promise of freedom." He stopped again, visibly struggling with his emotions, before saying in a hushed voice, "I know because I am that son."

A gasp came from the small congregation, and people looked at one another, many reaching for tissues. Tears could now be seen also in the eyes of the priest, this man who was Gisela's lost son. He struggled to compose himself and looked solemnly around the sanctuary before continuing.

"So we are here today, at a site which honors many who were martyred for their faith, to celebrate the life of Walter Hurwitz who died for his. In the words of the one we call Christ, *'Whosoever believeth in me shall not die, but have everlasting life.'*

"God bless the soul of my father. We lift him up to thee. In the name of the Father, Son, and Holy Spirit, Amen."

Dieter made the sign of the cross and spoke a benediction. Then he stepped forward and put one arm around Gisela and the other around Anna. After a few moments of closeness with his family, Gisela led him around the sanctuary, introducing him to her friends. Dieter thanked each person for the support and assistance they had given his mother and sister. Finally they completed the circle and came to John and Gail. Gisela thanked them again for finding Dieter for her.

John looked first at her and then at Dieter. He said, "I still feel guilty that I didn't rescue you when your parents tried to cross."

Dieter held his arm and looked him in the eye. "But you did rescue me—you and Gail. You came back and found me. If it weren't for you, I may never have found my mother and sister—and the path God has chosen for me to follow. Be at peace with yourself; I am!"

THE END

Printed in the United States
31669LVS00004B/1-42